*What Is What Was*

# *What Is What Was*

RICHARD STERN

THE UNIVERSITY OF CHICAGO PRESS :: CHICAGO AND LONDON

RICHARD STERN is the Helen A. Regenstein Emeritus
Professor of English and of the Humanities at the University
of Chicago.

The University of Chicago Press, Chicago 60637
The University of Chicago Press, Ltd., London
© 2002 by Richard G. Stern
All rights reserved. Published 2002
Printed in the United States of America
11 10 09 08 07 06 05 04 03 02     1 2 3 4 5

ISBN: 0-226-77325-6 (cloth)
ISBN: 0-226-77326-4 (paper)

Library of Congress Cataloging-in-Publication Data

Stern, Richard G., 1928–
        What is what was / Richard Stern.
            p.    cm.
        ISBN 0-226-77325-6 (alk. paper) — ISBN 0-226-77326-4
(pbk. : alk. paper)
        I.  Title.

    PS3569.T39 W48    2002
    813'.54—dc21                                        2002019125

# Contents

# *Preface*

This is the fifth book of a sort that I call an "orderly miscellany." It gathers pieces written for different reasons, assignments, occasions (the death of friends, a burst of anger or amusement at a scene, or an—often public—event) and links them in ways which couldn't have been anticipated when they were written. Linkage is the aesthetic pleasure of the miscellany-maker and may qualify him as "orderly." In earlier miscellanies, the commentary, opinions, reviews, and reportage were studded here and there with short poems, playlets, or parodies. This miscellany includes four poems (one by Alane Rollings) and some fiction related to the essays surrounding it.

Some pieces here are autobiographical or contain autobiographical fragments. I've used these miscellanies (and the memoir *Sistermony*) as substitutes for the full-fledged autobiography which many elderly men, especially men of letters, feel almost obliged to write (see "Over the Hill" and "An Old Writer Looks at Himself."). As I hope the end of my road is not immediately up ahead, I resist looking back to spot its curves of deficiency or accomplishment. (Let what's been be; what comes come.)

Most of the pieces here were written after 1993, when I published *One Person and Another*, a miscellany less miscellaneous than its predecessors since every piece had to do with writers and writing. Nonetheless, some pieces here, such as the account of the 1992 Wimbledon tennis tournament and several of the memorial eulogies, date from before that year.

As for the book's title, I haven't adequately, let alone fully, dealt with what it promises: the transformation of felt experience into words and—related to this—the partial formation of the original experience by earlier words. The discrepancy between the truth of what one's been, known, and felt and the historical, biographical, fictional, or even cosmological (see the essay "Dark Energy, Dark Matter, and the Waves of Genesis") reconstruction of it done years or even minutes later by oneself or someone else is a motif here. When the discrepancy is large, the reaction to it may be olympian indifference, anger, outrage, laughter, or litigation. Some gap is always there; from it issues the rumble under biography, history, and reporting which can never be completely silenced.

## OTHERS SEEN THROUGH ME

*This section consists of seven partial portraits and one fictional portrait. The fictional portrait isn't partial, because all that exists of the central character has been put down. That all would of course be a totally inadequate biography. We know next to nothing of how, where, and with whom she grew up, very little of her own thoughts and feelings. She exists as part of the narrator's largely retrospective anger, contempt, and resentment. The "real life" portraits are partial because the only parts of the real people portrayed in them are those which bounce off the small chip of the writer's own remembrance of them. Their effect on his life is here more important than their own lives. Nonetheless, the weight of their lives is felt as part of their impact on him.*

# With Auden

🐟🐟 SEPTEMBER 1947. NEW YORK CITY.
I have a new B.A. degree from Chapel Hill and a mother who doesn't
like to see it going to waste. Six dawns a week, she rouses me with anti-
inspirations; my comebacks are unspoken: "You won't find a job on your
back." *Michelangelo did the Sistine on his.* "You know who catches the
worm." *Who's fishing?* "Jobs go to go-getters." *I don't want to go anywhere but Paris.* She has never held a paying job. I am her nonpaying one,
and know there'll be no peace 'til I am out the door.

I walk or bus downtown; subways are for go-getters. For four wartime years, I rode them every school day, rousing the threats and curses
of women whose silk stockings the loose struts of my book bag ripped
while my nose was buried in *The Ring and the Book* and the *Dialogues of
Hylas and Philonius.*

Up and down Fifth, Madison, Park, and Lexington, I walk in and out
of buildings whose tenants' names I study on lobby directories. Now and
then, I elevator up to advertising agencies and publishers, fill out job
forms, and, if a personnel officer is bored, have an interview. I talk about
my honors B.A. in English, my job experience in shoe and jewelry stores
(sweeping and polishing, wrapping, running an addressograph), on Wall
Street (a bonded messenger—attesting to my trustworthiness), on Vermont farms (haying, weeding, milking, to show I'm competent in pas-
toral as well as urban life). I've published poems, stories, and essays in
the *Carolina Magazine,* reported and written editorials for the *Daily Tar
Heel,* am, in short, accomplished, experienced, worldly wise, hard-working,
and willing to improve their operations. "A quick learner," for, I manage
to get out, five thousand dollars a year.

This figure has been supplied by my Chapel Hill girlfriend, Jo B.
With the $2,300 a year she is making back in her hometown, pre-Disney

Orlando, Florida, it would enable us to live the way she wants to live. She and I exchange daily multi-page letters, and until my mother's chilly intervention, telephone each other twice a week. Now, terrified by Mother's voice, Jo never calls, and only when my father remembers that I'm still his dependent and slips me a few dollars (which I change into quarters to call from a pay phone in the Hotel Bolivar around the corner) do I. Jo has the ring I won in a game of Casino from my Great Uncle Herman. Its tiny diamond sits in the navel of a gold nude. Jo is saving for a more neutral setting; the ring stands for an engagement of which my parents know zilch.

A cousin gets me an interview with the editor of *Coronet Magazine*, Larry Spivak, not yet the founder-host of *Meet the Press*. In his tiny office, tiny Spivak, a suspicious-looking fellow in shirtsleeves, eyes me over spectacles which straddle his beak. "Understand you want to be a writer."

"I am one."

"Are you? Well, now you can go out in the world and get yourself some experience. Nothing's more important for a writer." I disagree but say nothing. "Get a job in a coal mine. A cannery."

"I could do research there, or anywhere else you send me."

A breeze of annoyance furrows his brow, but he simply changes gear and asks what sort of salary I had in mind. Assessing the office and the brow, I lower Jo's figure a thousand dollars.

Another breeze. "There's no one in this city or any I know that'd pay you half that. Get experience, write a hundred stories, then we'll see." Eyes lowered to deskwork, he holds his hand in the air. "So long."

I shake it, say "Thank you," and wish him a short, painful life.

That evening, my father is sympathetic, my mother puzzled and suspicious. "There may be no jobs in publishing or advertising. You'd better think about business." *Chez nous*, business is a sacred word and concept. Mother's brothers left school in their teens to go into it. First employed by their uncle, Gustave Veit, the founder-president of York Manufacturing, they went on to work on their own and, like him, succeeded. Business is our family *Tao*.

A year ago, Momma sat daily at Uncle Gus's deathbed. She fetched, fed, and consoled the old man but would not give him what he daily begged for, poison. "His last smile was for your Phi Beta key." How she wishes Uncle Gus were here to guide me now. Failing that, she calls Bert, her oldest brother, an ex-cotton goods salesman, now living off annuities. Bert makes calls, the last to tell her that I have an appointment with important men at *Consolidated Retail Stores;* he hopes that I "won't be a wiseacre and ask for five thousand simoleons a year."

彡〜〜

On Seventh Avenue, I dodge racks of suits and go up four stories in a service elevator to a smoke-clouded office where two rawsteak-colored faces behind cigars give me the once over. One face tops a small, the other a huge body. "Boit Veit's nephew?" This from Big Beef.

"Yes."

"Good."

Small Beef: "We gotta store in Evansville. Bon Marche. Ed Schneiderman—your uncle knows his dad—'s the manager. He needs help dere."

Big Beef: "Toity-five a week, trainin' you couldn't buy. He wants you should start Monday."

Small Beef: "You gotta question? Ok, good luck to youse."

彡〜〜

I've never been west of Newark. My mother, relieved, even proud, is also apprehensive. Frantically, she packs and repacks my bags, shedding advice: Don't be impatient, don't lose your temper, get plenty of sleep, drink milk.

2.

The second plane ride of my life. (The first was from LaGuardia to Raleigh, my last year at Chapel Hill.) I arrive in Evansville at dusk, am met by Schneiderman, a short, dark, pleasant-looking-and-acting man in his late thirties who, after carrying my bags to the hotel room he's reserved for me, drives me to his home for a meal his nervous, black-eyed wife has cooked. "Tomorrow, Joannie'll drive you around till you find a room. Then come on down to the store and start learning the ropes."

The meal in the white leathery house is the kind I know from home; I feel a little better; Ed and Joannie are sympathetic and kind.

Only not my kind. Nor is Evansville my kind of town, this my kind of life. In the hotel room, on what is probably the loneliest, most unhappy night I'd spent since, age six, I was sent away to summer camp, I take out of my bag the one link I have to the life I want, the *Collected Poems of W. H. Auden*. It's the only book I've brought with me. I read it that night, as I will read it every single night of the six weeks I spend in Evansville, and as I've read few books since, with almost desperate need.

3.

I see the book now, the black-on-white cover, the Random House logo, the generous spacing of the poems on the page. I still know several hundred lines I never tried to memorize: "To throw away the key and walk away / Not abrupt exile, the neighbors asking why . . ."; "Our hunting fathers / Told the story / Of the sadness of the creatures / Pitied the limits and the lack / Set in their finished features / Saw in the lion's intolerant look, Behind the quarry's dying glare / Love raging . . ."; "Lay your sleeping head my love / Human on my faithless arm"; "A shilling life will give you all the facts / How father beat him, how he ran away / What were the struggles of his youth? What acts made him the greatest figure of his day"; "Consider this, and in our time, As the hawk sees it, or the helmeted airman"; "That day, far other than that day / They gave the prizes to the ruined boys"; "Sir, no man's enemy, forgiving all but will / His negative inversion, be prodigal / Send to us power and light, a sovereign touch / Curing the intolerable neural itch"; "Doom is dark and deeper than any sea dingle / Upon what man it fall"; "Let me tell you a story / About Miss Edith Gee / She lived at Cleveland Terrace / At Number 83."

The sound of these poems was deeper than any instruction, but I was endlessly instructed by them. From Miss Gee's story, I "learned" that cancer originated in suppressed desire; from "Freud," I learned about the historical component of illness; from "Spain," the stakes of the past and the future in the Spanish Civil War. I learned that old masters like Brueghel were never wrong and that suffering and great events like the fall of Icarus take place when nobody is watching. Everywhere, I learned about the viciousness of the old guard, the hunting fathers and the befurred tourists constellated at reserved tables in snowy resorts while the devil's agents spread rumors and disasters around the ports and in the eyes of stoats. I imbibe the meters of chic brilliance, the semantics of assonance, the rhythms of civility and passion. Auden was a world every bit as intricate as Evansville, more intact, more concentrated, more insistent, and more, a novel individual, one who made no promises, only poured out delight. Underneath the poems, his voice said that there wasn't any class but intelligence, no requirement but sensibility. The poems were gifts, they were yours and you were part of others who read them. With them you weren't lonely. The mind that made them was your friend.

4.

At Bon Marche, I learned other things. A three-story, not unhandsome brick building, it stood on Main Street (although I don't remember if this was the street's name) near other stores, including the town's fanciest, De Jong's. The street looked like those in Andy Hardy movies. There was an iconic charm about it, and about my actually being on it.

There was less charm in the work. The first day, Edgar gave me a book on retail merchandising, as boring a tome as I'd ever read. The matter therein was fleshed out in the counters, the cash registers, the saleswomen, the sweaters, dresses, stockings, shoes, bras, panties, coats, and accessories displayed in the glass cases or mounted on racks. At six every evening (and a few Sunday mornings), Edgar and I went over the day's receipts, matched them against the orders, then discussed returns, slow movers, new orders, seasonal fashions. We hauled merchandise from desired to undesired spots and packed up the least desirable items for return.

During the week, I worked in different parts of the store, Packaging (I wrapped dresses, suits, and shoes), Advertising, where "Cele," the charmingly goofy copy writer, showed me what to stress in newspaper and radio ads, Windows, where Kolya, a—now that I think of it— Yeltsin-looking window-dresser, showed me the display tricks of his art, and Sales, where saleswomen, young and old, instructed me in the ins and outs of their specialties. Tying my tie and putting a jacket over my sleeveless yellow sweater, I floor-walked up and down the aisles, greeting and joking, although I don't believe that I could have radiated much confidence or delight. One day, the homunculus who was president of the hundred Consolidated Retail Stores appeared on the floor, fingered the yellow sweater, and told me, "Sonny, never wear this garment here again." The word "preppy" did not then exist, but what it stood for was, I'm sure, the loathsome suggestion of the sleeveless yellow sweater.

Sale days were a revelation. From the faces bunched behind the glass and then from the almost abstractly insane drive past me toward the garments whose price reductions Cele had featured in her ads, I understood what a mob could do, what revolution might be like, what Goebbels and

Hitler had manipulated, what the class Auden hated built their fortresses against.

5.

No, my days at the store weren't good ones. Nor was home life much better. I had a room in the rickety bungalow of Ev and Ginny Metcalfe on Walnut Street. I was the only boarder. Ginny was generous, maternal, hungry for talk. An enormous woman with bristles of iron-gray hair, she told me about her surgeries. "The doctors mapped out my back." (The back was the size of the Western Front.) Slapping at it, "They cut here and here and here." Ev, a laconic, kindly man, drove a taxi at night and slept much of the day. He'd owned a bar in Chicago. Ginny said that there'd been trouble up there, he'd had to leave. I'd read "The Killers" and was as alert as Nick Adams had been to those who might come down from Chicago looking for Ev. No one at all came near the house the six weeks I lived there.

Ginny and I were closest at breakfast, which she cooked for me until calls to Jo left me without the fifty cents a day she charged for it. I read the Evansville paper while she put perfectly fried eggs and bacon on the plate beside a rack of toast, dishes of fresh butter, and strawberry jam. There was orange juice with bits of fruit meat in it and wonderful coffee with fresh cream and sugar. (I weighed a hundred pounds less than I do now, and anyway, back then, people I knew didn't diet.) I read Ginny the newspaper's Poem of the Day, rhymed quatrains, often by Edgar Guest. She told me that she'd reread and meditate about them for hours. If Auden was my link to high life, these poems were Ginny's to hers. Although the structure of their sentiment went deeply against my grain, I was grateful that these poems existed to enrich her life. The few seconds it took to read them to her every morning were special for both of us.

My rent was fifteen dollars a week. If it hadn't been for the calls to Jo, I could have made it on the thirty-five-dollar weekly salary. (There were no tax withdrawals that I recall, although I know that Beardsley Ruml had invented the Pay-As-You-Go system during World War II. If there were, I don't remember what they were. I did know that every single quarter counted for me.)

Despite the unprincely salary, in Evansville I seemed to be regarded as a person of standing. When I opened a bank account, I was treated with a respect I'd never before encountered. Then too, some of the salesgirls seemed interested in me, and I played to the interest. There were miscalculations: one evening, one girl with whom I flirted introduced me to a husband. Since I hadn't noticed her ring finger, I was amazed. Another girl, whom I persuaded to stay late one evening to help with inventory chores, made it clear at a certain difficult point that her erotic geography was also circumscribed by that finger.

I had no money to take girls to a movie, let alone dinner, so I had no other dates. On Jo's urging, I wrote my parents to send on the war bonds—about two hundred dollars' worth—into which for several years most of my pre-Evansville earnings and birthday money had gone. Grumbling and suspicious, my mother sent them on. They paid for my getaway to Orlando.

6.

It was Auden's father-in-law, Thomas Mann, who got me fired. In the Evansville Public Library, I read *The Magic Mountain* every working day after my fifteen-minute, sixty-cent lunch in the drugstore, and again, at night, after my dollar-thirty meat loaf, mashed potatoes, and string beans in a diner gloomier and emptier than Edward Hopper's. I lost myself in the snowy Alpine clinic among the uproarious arguments of Settembrini and Naptha, the speculations of the great doctor, Hofrat Behrens, the sex-boggling lisp of Claudia Chuchat, the ups and downs of the fever charts. It was so wonderful I could hardly bear to stop reading, and every day I was later getting back to work. The week after Thanksgiving, Edgar called me into his office and told me that it was clear that the retail life should not be mine, I would be happier doing something connected with writing. He understood, he himself had read the obscene parts of *Ulysses*. He would write to explain all this to Uncle Bert, he wished me well, and if there was anything he or Joannie could do for me, let him know. I'd just finished *The Magic Mountain*. Like Hans Castorp going back into the world, it was time for me to leave.

7. ⁂ WINTER 1965. CHICAGO.

In his room at the Quadrangle Club, I find Auden rummaging and fuming. "I thought this was a club. They tell me they don't serve liquor before 5:00 P.M." I tell him about the Baptist roots of the institution. Meanwhile, he's found a bottle of gin in his bag and two glasses in the bathroom. He drops into the other armchair, drapes stockinged feet over the arm, and talks in crowded, nasal, amiable oxcamese of his peripatetic life. "Only way I can live. A tour every two years. In a month, I'll have my sixtieth birthday alone in an Oregon motel room."

I'd seen hundreds of pictures but had never laid eyes on the living man. In the flesh, the famous face looked as if it had survived an awful siege. A pox that strikes only the rarest sinner had pitted, trenched, puffed, bewarted, and empurpled the white faceflab. The lips too were loose, large, unintegrated. It took minutes to get used to this bizarre topography. Meanwhile, talk, drink, amiability. The man was immediately direct, decent, unposed, and, if not exactly warm, eager for talk.

We talked of Skelton. He wanted to meet my friend Arthur Heiserman, whose *Skelton and Satire* he admired. Then Anglo-Saxon: he condemned Pound for getting the accent wrong in "Seafarer," Yeats, Brecht, and Claudel, three poets who were bad men, all mistreaters of women. He mused over his old friend MacNeice, who "caught a cold and died," over his Austrian house, "the first I ever owned," over what poets can and can't alter from life: "If Joan rimes better than Mary, call the girl Joan, but you can't change Nos to Yesses. . . . It's hard to be a religious poet in English. Nothing rhymes with God."

I start to tell him what the first *Collected Poems* had meant to me eighteen years earlier, but it's clear that such stories were familiar and without intellectual or, in this case, emotional interest for him.

At the reading, I sit in the front row next to the political scientist Hans Morgenthau, whose English was good but not good enough to understand Auden's. I myself miss a third of what I hear. The meters, however, are clear, and since he reads from his translation of Icelandic sagas, this goes a long way.

Afterwards, there's a small party at the Heisermans'. Despite the zero degree cold, Erich Heller, an Auden friend, has come down from Northwestern. He talks of his trip to the Greek monastery where the only females around were insects. He'd befriended a monk who took him aside to beg a favor: would Heller, for God's sake, please send him from America a carton of Milky Ways. In the slippers he carried everywhere, Auden listened, gabbed, laughed, drank. It looked as if he could go on for hours. Heller left, my wife and I followed. Our car is stuck in the ice ridges. Out comes Auden in slippers, a great scarf round his neck. The image of his pushing at the car is the most memorable of these days, although matched by one the next day.

At noon, he came into the Quadrangle Club and sat alone. I left my companions to sit with him. We talked about his time in Spain. "I just wanted to drive a car, but they didn't need me, and I came home. During the Strike of '26 I'd driven Tawney's car. Driving was what it was all about. I liked driving cars." His name? "From Odin, surely." (I remembered an early picture of him, an Icelandicly blonde boy with untroubled skin and flabless face.) Would there ever be a plaque on his St. Marks Place house? "There should be," he said. "Trotsky lived and edited *Pravda* there." He was off in an hour, and I had a class. I got up and shook his hand. He said, "Thank you so much for sitting with me."

The "Thank you" I owed him was so deep, I nearly broke down.

8. ⋙ SEPTEMBER 1973. VIENNA.

I give a talk to the Vienna PEN. My host, the fiction writer Peter von Tramin, works in a bank but apparently has time to read and keep up with world literature. On the way out, I notice that Auden is giving a reading here in a couple of weeks. "I wish I could stay for it." Peter says that he'll let me know how it turns out.

Back in Chicago, I learn how it turns out. After the reading, Auden went back to his hotel, had a heart attack, and died.

9.

For the past fifteen or so years, I have ended a course in the great modernist writers of the twentieth century with the poem that's said to be the last Auden wrote, days or weeks before his death in the Vienna hotel room. It's called "Archaeology." One thread of the course is that the twentieth century was the archaeologizing, anthropologizing century, not only digging up the remains of cultures in the Schliemann tradition but seeing in what would once have been called primitive, strange, or alien societies complexities of organization and intelligence equivalent to our own. Auden has subtilised and expanded this notion, turning words, à la Rilke, from one grammatical function to another and ending with the note that surfaces again and again in his poems.

The coda of the poem reads:

> From Archaeology
> one moral, at least, may be drawn,
> to wit, that all

our school text-books lie.
What they call history
is nothing to vaunt of,

being made, as it is,
by the criminal in us.
goodness is timeless.

# Remembering Pound

In the fall of 1962, I was a Fulbright Visiting Professor at the University of Venice, then called the Istituto Universitario di Venezia because the Minister of Education, a Padovan, wanted no competition for his venerable alma mater.

I didn't think there'd be much competition in the English and American literature faculty. The young assistant, Sergio Perosa, was first-rate, but he spent most of his time teaching in Trieste. The main lectures were in the care of the only full professor, a distinguished-looking gentleman with a distinguished name, Benvenuto Cellini.

Professor Cellini had a pointed silver beard, large blue eyes, a bald head, and the flexible politics which had advanced his academic career though the fascist, wartime, and postwar years. He had odd ideas about what students of American literature should study. Thus, for his single course of lectures that year, he was going to enlighten them about the novels of Henry Wadsworth Longfellow. I had never before met anyone who'd read, or even heard of, these works and was not surprised when Professor Cellini informed me, two weeks before the first lecture, that he was having difficulty locating books for the students and was, therefore, changing the lecture subject to the plays of Eugene O'Neill.

On the two days a week the professor granted Venice—for of course, like all good Italian professors, he lived in Rome and commuted by first-class train to his provincial assignment—he cordially summoned me to accompany him to lunch. We walked grandly by the Venetian citizenry, the professor acknowledging their salutes with inclinations of the silver beard.

It turned out that I was the Professor's other beard, that is, the front for his luncheon trysts with the Professoressa d'Arabo, a charming, cross-eyed scholar—scholaressa?—of a certain age who roared at Professor

Cellini's witticisms and—although this was harder to assess—ogled him lustfully.

I soon felt that I had skimmed the cream of these enchanting encounters and took to wandering around the city by myself. One day, in a small gallery, I met a young American sculptress, Joan FitzGerald, who'd come to Venice from Oak Park a couple of years earlier because there was a foundry here which cast her bronzes well and cheaply. It was Joan who'd spotted a remarkable-looking old man eating at Cici's Restaurant with a white-haired companion. A sculptress knew that such a head belonged to someone who counted. Cici, a genial, slow-witted host—he'd once served the poodle of a guest a plateful of meat on which he'd thoughtfully placed a knife and fork—was persuaded to get the remarkable old man to sign a menu. A day or two later, Joan told me that the signature read "Ezra Pound."

Short of telling me that Dante was taking tickets at the Fenice, Joan could not have surprised me more. Running into one of the pillars of modern literature was like discovering that the graffiti on your fence had been done by Picasso.

Even though, back then, I had read very little, understood less, and disliked a great deal of what I had read of the *Cantos,* I loved many of Pound's short poems and admired much of his literary prose. I knew a bit about his place in literary history and more about his scandalous attachment—as I saw it—to fascism and anti-Semitism, although I had not yet read the wild and pathetic—if not tragic—broadcasts from Italy transcribed by American enlisted men during the war years. (I'd read only the snippets quoted in the newspapers during the controversy about his receiving the Bollingen Prize.)

I wrote Hugh Kenner about Pound's presence. Hugh suggested that I ask him for the letters Louis Zukofsky had written him; Zuk—as Hugh called him—was thinking of publishing their correspondence. I remember wishing that there'd been another, less Semitic bridge to the old fellow; I didn't want to stir up any Protocols-of-Zion conspiracy ideas in what I believed might be his lunatic head.

Anyway, mission in hand, I set off, accompanied by my five-year-old son, Andrew. I rang doorbells asking if there were, by chance, an old American who called himself Pound there.

I was guided to a little brick house on Calle Querini. The bell brought the white head of Olga Rudge to a third-story window. *"Chi desidera?"* she asked.

*"Sto cercando un vecchio chi se chiama Pound,"* said I.

Then, in English, "What do you want with him?"

"I'm an admirer of his. And my friend Hugh Kenner suggested that I look him up and ask him a few things."

"I'll be right down."

Miss Rudge brought Andrew and me upstairs past a great Chinese wicker chair and a pot-bellied black stove. Pound, in an old sweater, was sitting up in bed by a pile of books among which I discerned three or four new American novels. I remember thinking, "So even now, this old fellow is keeping up with what's going on." It was one of the first signs that I was not meeting a loony.

We shook hands. I told him my name and what I was doing in Italy.

He said very little but had a sweet, amiable look which was also somewhat sly, as if he were on to something. He seemed both knowing and innocent, as if, after all he'd seen and been through, he was not going to get upset about whatever swam into his ken. I was relieved: the man was not foaming at the mouth at this Jewish presence.

Olga Rudge—whom I never called Olga, as she didn't call me anything but Mr. Stern until our last talk twenty-five or so years later—and I made conversation. It turned out that we were both reading Aldo Palazzeschi's stories and novels. Ezra looked on benignly, apparently delighted that Olga was having literary conversation. Occasionally, there was some domestic exchange between them. "It bores you, doesn't it, Ezra?" "No," he said. "You take care of everything, Olga." His speech was slightly burred, as if from Dublin or Glasgow; the full round "O" of "Olga" was touching. I felt there was love in it. In fact, in this narrow gondolier's house—Miss Rudge told me that her father had bought it for her, sight unseen, a year or two before the crash of 1929—I felt not November chill but the warmth of long-tested affection.

The old fellow did tense a minute when Olga asked if she could give one of his new birthday cookies to Andrew. He finally nodded okay. She chided him about his sweet tooth. "Remember how much you liked the Gluttony episode of *The Seven Deadly Sins?*" He blushed but smiled. It was the *esprit de la casa,* clearly crucial for his esprit.

Pound and I did talk a bit that first afternoon. I asked him if he were working. He tossed his leonine head toward a pencil and notebook. "A line a month."

It was made clear that he'd not recovered from a prostate operation; he was also suffering from infected teeth—there'd be much dental work that year—and the bitter cold of what was already one of Venice's coldest winters. There was also, apparently, preparation for what was coming, although it did not come for ten years: besides the novels, he was reading the *Paradiso*.

Andrew and I did not stay long. Pound shook hands goodbye with an especially sweet smile—perhaps delighted to be rid of us—but Miss Rudge invited me—"and your wife too"—for coffee next week. "Or any time. A day's notice is all that's wanted."

So began my almost-weekly visits to Calle Querini. Sometimes Pound opened the door himself. Social formulas were not taken for granted. "How are you today, Mr. Pound?"

"Senile."

Senile, he wasn't. We talked about Frost and Eliot, a bit about his work too, although he was usually dismissive of it. When I congratulated him on getting a prize from *Poetry* magazine, he said that it was a rare event: not only didn't he get prizes, nobody he recommended got them.

There was something heartrending about his situation. Miss Rudge said that scholars came from all over to see him, whereas he didn't have the money to visit Greece and Egypt, countries he'd always wanted to see. I decided to do something about raising money for that, but someone or something beat me to it, for either that year or the next, he did get to Greece.

Now and then, I ran into him and Miss Rudge walking arm in arm around the city, mostly in the almost empty and besnowed piazza or in the early afternoon after lunch, on the Zattere, the sunny fondamenta along the Giudecca Canal. When it got warmer, we sometimes had ice cream together at one of the cafés there.

He was a good walker, swinging along in his black cape, a beautiful cane punctuating his progress. His greeting was warm. For all the combative fierceness that others found in him from time to time, I was mostly aware of that other Pound whom, I believe, always existed, first in the credulous boy other boys sent on prank missions, then in the man who encouraged all sorts of writers and artists and who treasured the *popolo minuti* and downtrodden. That's the other side of the despairing, maddened polemicist who made some of the largest mistakes a political human can make and who'd paid dearly for them.

Pound's insights into books and people were never banal. He seemed to weigh every word, literary or social.

"Norman Pearson asks to be remembered," said the visiting John Hollander.*

Responded Pound, "He's in no danger of being forgotten."

Miss Rudge too was a wit and epigrammatist. One day her daughter Mary was at the house. She'd just returned from the United States, had seen Robert Frost a few days before his death, and visited Yale (where she was to work for many years). She reported to her parents that the New Haven campus was so gothic that "even the swimming pool was housed in a 'cathedral.'"

*"La cathédrale engloutie,"* said Miss Rudge.

Also present that day and others was Gianfranco Ivancich, brother of the Adriana whom Hemingway loved and celebrated in *Across the River and into the Trees.* Gianfranco and Pound were equally brilliant masters of what Isaac Babel calls "the genre of silence." They could sit for a long time without saying anything, unembarrassed by it. I couldn't and neither, I think, could Miss Rudge. She, Mary, and I supplied the chatter. Once Mary asked what was meant by the expression "throwing the baby out with the bathwater." I pointed to her father as the proper authority on language. Said Mary, "Oh, I'll never learn then." When I later read her *Discretions,* the brilliant memoir which so distressed her parents, I understood more about the domestic strain I felt that afternoon.

Hemingway's death the year before had been a grievous thing for Pound. I'm not sure that he accepted it as a suicide. "I always thought Hem was Catholic," he said to me once.

Although there were occasional recollections of "Hem" or Henry James—"so stout he couldn't squeeze through a door"—most of his small talk was about whatever came up. Occasionally, it was fiercer. So, of an English publisher living nearby: "He's a fool and a charlatan." Returning from my first trip to Rimini, I told him my impressions of Sigismundo Malatesta's Tempio: "It reeks of egomania." Said Pound, "I wanted to show the other side of the record." It was a quiet defense of the *Cantos'* depiction of Sigismundo, at least an explanation of his method. He hoped there was nothing historically wrong in there. "Wrong" was a very serious word for Pound.

* One day after revising this piece, I received a letter from Hollander enclosing his recently reissued 1976 book *Reflections on Espionage,* on page 37 of which is a poetic version of this encounter. In the new introduction, he says that I accompanied him to Pound's house. I believe that I only suggested he call there.

Memory, though, was the central worry of that year.* My one emotional session with him turned on it. Joan had come back from America, and we went over for tea. There was mention of Peggy Guggenheim, who lived a two-minute walk away. I was going there for supper. (The woman had fastened onto my wife.) I repeated something she'd told me about Pound in his Paris days. Pound frowned, fretted a while, then said I was testing his memory; he was relieved to know for sure that what I said was fiction. (One of my novels was on his table.) The words froze the room. The two women talked a bit above them, then went downstairs. I told myself, "Well, he's shown his hand at last. I guess the stuff I've heard about him is so." I debated leaving him with a nod but went over to the bed, held out my hand and said that he was probably right, most social talk was a mix of persiflage and fiction, I was sorry to inflict it on him. He held my hand tightly, then drew me down to the bed. My face was within a foot of his. The blue eyes were charged with—what? appeal? reaching out? "No," he said, in his almost-Scotch burred English. "Wrong. Wrong, wrong. I've always been wrong. Eighty-seven percent wrong. I never recognize benevolence."

It was something, but I managed to say that maybe he had been wrong, but that those who delighted to tell him he was weren't in the same league when it came to verity.

"You don't know what it's like," he said, "to get off on the wrong path . . . not to remember."

I tried something comforting. "You've been on the bull's eye plenty in your time."

"No," he said, "I've only left scattered notes. Haven't made anything clear."

I'd been reading him and mentioned things that were not only clear but radiant.

It was no time for mollification. He quoted something from Dante about imperfection, and there was more, some of which I didn't follow. The old man was touching bottom, holding on meanwhile to something human on the surface. After I don't know how much time, minutes perhaps, I withdrew—though I thought afterwards that I should have stayed with him until he came all the way back. I touched his hand for goodbye.

---

* Much of what follows is adopted from my "A Memory or Two of Pound" in *One Person and Another: On Writers and Writing* (Dallas: Baskerville, 1993).

For a while, I didn't see him. The emotion of that scene was so strong, I thought that, like a flooded carburetor, it had to leak away before we started up again. The next time I came, my wife was with me. Pound was in bed but spruced up, throwing the blanket over his feet, sitting up straight. He talked about his version of the *Women of Trachis* ("not much Sophocles there"), of walks in France and Venice.

By the time we left Venice in the spring of '63, Joan had made a wonderful bronze of his head.* He loved it, as he did the very different one she made later and sold to the National Portrait Gallery in Washington, D.C.

I'd occasionally send him a card—never answered but supposedly welcomed. A card which Miss Rudge said that he especially appreciated was a Rossellini Madonna and Child sent at Easter "as a bit of spiritual Esperanto from a skeptical Jew to a skeptical Confucian."

We never talked directly about Jews. His anti-Semitism had been—I think—a wicked rhetorical habit, part populism, part the casual snobbery of upper-middle-class Europe and America, part the notions of such intellectuals as Ernst Renan, for whom Semitic monotheism and morality were the jailers of scientific progress and enlightenment.† During his worst days, it was reinforced by the slime fury dredged up by the Nazis. It was attached to his historically flawed notions of usury and, now and then, to that nineteenth-century orthodoxy which had a Hebraic cast. Miss Rudge spoke deliberately of his Jewish friends, and I noted the dedication of *Guide to Kulchur* (to Bunting and Zukofsky). I doubt that he had ever prejudged a human being or a work on racial grounds.‡

When I saw him again in the fall of '65, he was much cheerier. More of the world had forgiven him, he was honored here and there. We took a marvelous gondola ride to his favorite places. (Offering the one cushioned seat to Miss. Rudge, he heard her quote him: "They will come no more, / The old men with beautiful manners.") We exchanged stories

---

* I gave the bust to the University of Chicago in 1998.

† See Renan's 1883 attack on Islam (printed in the *Journal des Debats)* and answered there and elsewhere by Islamic intellectuals and others ultimately responsible for the birth of serious Islamic studies. (I owe my small knowledge of this controversy to a talk given on February 6, 2001, by my colleague, Professor Heidi Schissler.)

‡ In *The Genealogy of Demons*, Robert Casillo levels a much more severe and better-documented indictment.

about Hyde Park Corner speakers. (I'd just come from there with a handful.) He remembered an atheist in about 1906 describing hell: "the walls a mile thick and a mild 'igh, and wot hi wants to know is 'ow they get in." Miss Rudge wondered what presents they should carry to Paris. "I believe lace and handkerchiefs are still considered indispensable."

That summer I'd brought over a copy of the novel *Stitch*, which centered on the encounters of a romantic Chicago advertising man with Nina, author of the first woman's epic, and with Thaddeus Stitch, an old sculptor who'd carved a history of cultural highs on an island in the Venetian lagoon. Stitch was largely drawn from Pound's history and my encounters with him. Miss Rudge read the book but decided not to let Pound read it. When I saw her years after his death, the book was, apparently, still fresh in her mind, but I neglected to ask her if he'd read it. Of the only book of mine I knew he'd read *(In Any Case)*, he'd offered an opinion—to Joan—so different from anyone else's that I would have relished, if not treasured, any response to *Stitch*. Still, were I Olga Rudge, I would not have let him read another complexly distorted portrait, however estimable it was. He might well have found it profoundly *wrong*.

His last years were, I was told, mellow ones. He walked, drank Scotch, received visitors, went to operas and concerts. He was generally in good spirits, as he was—Joan told me—the night he died. His last birthday party had the usual cookies, candies, neighboring children, and friends. Shortly after it, he was in some discomfort and Miss Rudge got him to the seedy municipal hospital near the great sculpture of Colleoni by San Zanipolo. She and Joan talked with him for hours. He was restless, saw no reason to be there. Joan went back to Calle Querini for his pajamas and to call Mary, just in case. Pound dozed off and died. One blue eye remained open; his coffin was shut on it. That night, he was taken to St. George's, where he remained between four lit tapers. To the brief service—conducted by a priest from St. George's and another from San Vio—came not only friends and family but *contadini* from Rapallo. The coffin went in the black funeral gondola to San Michele, where it lies close to Stravinsky's in one of the few uncrowded sections of the cemetery island. The stone—carved by Joan FitzGerald—reads only "Ezra Pound."

᠁

This miniature portrait relies on a few hours, say, twenty-five or thirty, passed in Pound's presence. Even these few supply much more than could be put down here. Some other details are recorded in my journals; still others surface now and then in my head. Are they significant? Only if one makes them so.*

I have elsewhere† written of my dilemma writing about the genial, touching man I encountered while knowing that he had once allied himself to those who would have had me killed for being born my parents' son. The contrast between such vileness and the courteous, warm, sometimes sardonic, sometimes despairing, bewildered, and troubled man I saw back in Venice resembles that faced by many who know only the courteous and gentle side of people who've done—or approved of doing—monstrous things.

Perhaps everyone who's willing to look hard at himself can see furies and desires he usually suppresses. Is one crucial job of poets and philosophers the expression of such suppression? I think so, and I sometimes wonder why Pound or Heidegger never dealt with it. Did they sense that their own interior was too hot for them to—verbally—handle?

Pound had thought a lot about the lives of poets and the roles they played. I wonder if he distinguished between his own human and poetic selves? At times, his distortion of one or the other made him seem mad. Did he really believe that he could persuade senators and generals to alter national and military policies? Had isolation from so much of the American world made him lose his sense of proportion, or was there always a touch of insensitivity or megalomania there?‡ In the wonderful interview Pound did with Donald Hall for the *Paris Review*, he speaks of the distortions induced by his isolation. I don't think he ever acknowledged, let alone confessed to, distortions wrought by his character, although the "Pull down thy vanity" section of the *Pisan Cantos* comes pretty close.

How would Pound have behaved had he lived in a totalitarian state, and not as its honored guest? I hope that he would have spoken out

---

* Robert Casillo thought that one detail—Pound's reading not only the *Paradiso* but a book on microorganisms—was significant enough to begin *The Genealogy of Demons* by citing it.

† *A Sistermony* (New York: Donald I. Fine, 1995).

‡ Samuel Beckett remembered his annoyance at Pound's egocentricity back in the '30s, though I think he was touched by seeing the silent old man who, passing through Paris a year or two before his death, had, to use Beckett's verb, *summoned* him. Beckett heeded the summons, a matter, perhaps, of literary noblesse oblige.

bravely, even with foolish bravery. Well, we'll never know. Thirty-odd years after I was warmed by the old firebrand's embers, I haven't resolved my contradictory feelings about him, or myself.

Olga Rudge died in the Tirol, weeks shy of her 101st birthday, and was buried near her beloved Ezra on the Isola de San Michele. On April 1, 1996, her daughter Mary de Rachewilts wrote me that her mother had "come around full circle—total innocence." On the commemorative card that accompanied the letter appear the lines of tribute to her from her beloved Ezra.

> That her acts
>
>      Olga's acts
>          of beauty
>       be remembered.
>
>     Her name was Courage
>     & is written Olga

# Ralph Ellison

I met Ralph in 1957. He came out to Chicago for a week to talk to my class about his work and theirs. We spent thirty or forty hours together, jocular ones, serious ones, and became friends. I was the junior by fifteen years and scarcely any publication. Ralph didn't lean on me with years or accomplishment; he had the gift of equality.

Millions of literate people around the world know Ralph's face, the powerful brow, the fine full lips, the mustache of two small crescents, the deep cheek lines. Fewer, but still many, know his rich baritone and all-out laugh.

He was an elegant man. I see him in a double-breasted blue blazer, charcoal slacks, and fine shoes. Shoes, he taught me, were exceptionally important for blacks. I introduced him to the delightful black economist Abe Harris, who, within sixty seconds, asked Ralph where he'd bought his shoes.

The elegance was not superficial but part of a profound self-esteem and construction. It involved Ralph's being simultaneously worldly and parochial, a citizen of world literature and of streets and corners only he knew and wrote about. Ralph was conscious of being—and wanting to be—a complete man, flower to root. (He may have paid too high a price for the wish, or for realizing it.)

Ralph knew many things, what they were and how to do them. He knew music, symphonic and jazz. He'd studied composition, he played the trumpet. He knew electronics. When, that first week, we recorded an interview in the apartment of the composer Easley Blackwood, Ralph helped Easley adjust the equipment. He knew guns, dogs, mechanics, cities, and of course he knew books and writers. His sophistication was as much a part of him as his color, his humor, his good teeth.

That first week, Ralph showed me a Chicago that had been hidden from me in the two years since I'd come. It was a discovery for him, too, an incidental gift of his wife, Fanny, who'd come from Chicago, indeed had been famous here as a great belle. Ralph took me to imposing wood-paneled mansions owned by worldly and Chicago-knowing black men. One fine-looking youngish man, wearing not coat and tie but a confident cashmere sweater, had taken over championship boxing from New York's Mike Jacobs and run it until that slick wheel of fortune made its inevitable turn and put him in prison.

Closer to home, Ralph found out more about our cleaning woman in ten minutes than I'd known in two years. I hadn't even gauged her age correctly. When he spoke to a couple of hundred students in the Ida Noyes lounge, he alerted me that he was going to say three or four things to which only black students would respond. He told me to watch the eight or ten in the audience when he winked at me. I watched, he winked, they lit up and laughed when no one else did.

One evening, my wife's New England parents showed up in Chicago. There was a wine tasting and dance at the Quadrangle Club, and I remember my father-in-law's proud delight as he danced with Fanny, perhaps the only time in his life he'd danced with a black woman (and, I suspect, so charmingly intelligent a beauty). An intelligent if parochial man who'd been turned upside-down by this Jewish son-in-law, he soon gauged the intelligence and grace of the Ellisons. It was a great moment for him, and I thanked Ralph for giving him this second postgraduate course in life and manners.

There were easier, richer meetings. One day I brought Ralph over to Nathan and Charlotte Scott's house. Nathan had written a marvelous piece about Richard Wright which I showed Ralph. It was the bridge to their lifelong friendship. (Nathan, an Episcopal priest, as well as a theologian and literary critic, would preside, thirty-five years later, at Ralph's funeral service.)

Ralph showed me a lot that I'd missed in books I prided myself on knowing as well as anyone. He flipped the pages of James's *Ambassadors* and pointed out twenty-odd sentences underwritten by the diction and sentiments of slavery, emancipation, and blackness. It would be twenty-five years before critics made careers out of what Ralph spelled out for me that afternoon.

2.

Ralph liked Chicago, and Chicago liked Ralph. He wanted a job here, and I thought that giving a set of powerful lectures would secure an invitation. There was a distinguished university lectureship, the Alexander White Lectures, and Ralph was invited to give them. To my surprise, he arrived without anything on paper. His model was jazz: inspiration would arrive as needed, and, therefore, the lectures would be more powerful, fresh, and true.

They weren't. Ralph said good things, but he stumbled, repeated himself, went off on tangents, and then the tangents of tangents. After the first one, I hinted it might be easier to put something down on paper. He wouldn't; he thought the lecture had gone well.

There was no chance of an appointment after that. Ralph was surprised and hurt, and when, a year later, his old friend, housemate, and rival, Saul Bellow, was appointed to Chicago's Committee on Social Thought, he was, I think, hurt and angry.

3.

During Ralph's longish stay as the White Lecturer, I noticed another self-subversive element in him. I already knew that this confident, warm, and charming man was pocked with insecurity, anger, and bitterness and that he countered these feelings with booze. He came to the house four or five evenings a week and we drank martinis. He didn't get drunk, only easy and weary. Then he stuttered, fumbled for words, and occasionally turned sarcastic, angry. His vulnerability made me even fonder of him.

Ralph was not one to talk—at least to me—about weakness, uncertainty, or difficulties. Even half-boffo, he was on top, or wanted to be—which didn't mean dominance, although we had small struggles which could get sharp. We'd walk up and down the side streets of Black and Jew, few holds barred; cleansing and revitalizing sessions.

Sober, he was generous to my work. If he ran into someone who liked it, he let me know. At a Loop literary party for him, he brought over a young woman who'd told him she'd just read a book that meant a lot to her. "Here's the author," beamed Proud Papa Ralph, delighting reader, author, and himself.

At least in spurts, Ralph was fatherly, which meant interesting children as well as caring for them. He was especially fond of our four-year-old, Andrew. He talked to him about staying home alone at that age with his little brother while their mother went off to work as a maid in Oklahoma City houses.

The Christmas Eve he spent with us, he interpreted the diagrams that came with complicated toys, telling me which nut should turn on which bolt and, when I botched an assembly, doing it himself. He never made me feel sorry that he didn't have his own children. Not at all. He made the best of whatever came along, children or their absence. So taking care of his baby brother in Oklahoma City had developed his self-confidence, and his mother's menial job was honorable work which opened up her world and his. She brought home magazines—*Life,* the *Saturday Evening Post*—which laid the foundation of his world-hunger and ambition.

4.

Ralph's ambivalence about the opportunities and penalties of being black was part of his originality. It wasn't easy to handle this ambivalence in art or life, especially because Ralph didn't want to deny himself any experience that rose from it. All, he felt, would deepen his life and art. Yet this credo, this hunger, led to accepting so many invitations that life sometimes seemed to leave no room for art. Was it his self-made trap? Perhaps, but we won't know until the two thousand pages he left behind are assembled into a book.* Who thinks now of the decades in which Proust was regarded as a brilliant wastrel?

I doubt, though, that Proust suffered as I think Ralph did from the four decades that followed the publication of *Invisible Man.* Decades ago, people began hounding him about the second novel. I saw him only occasionally during these years and rarely spoke of it, but it was in the air, an invisible presence, a tremor in his heartiness. The fire which burned the manuscript and his summer home seemed almost as much symbolic as real, the expression of something penelopian which destroyed as it built. (What writer in the age of carbons, let alone Xeroxes and discs, keeps only a single copy of the work of his life?) After some post-fire years of desperate surrender, Ralph started up again and produced the two thousand pages.

One Friday, a few years ago, I was at Bellow's when Ralph called him to say the book was finished, he was turning it over to his editor on Monday. How many other times was *the book* finished?

If it turns out there is no real book, only groupings of scenes and stories, some of them surely wonderful, there will still have been Ralph, the very visible man, complex, brilliant, ironic, generous, a bravely secret sufferer, a powerful charmer, the shaper of a richer answer to the Amer-

---

* An apparently inadequate version, *Juneteenth,* was published in 2000. I have not read it.

ican dilemma than anyone else has offered, the writer of one of the very good novels and some of the best essays of the century. That should be enough for anyone.

But there are—still?—the two thousand pages, which may change almost everything.

# Studs: WFMT, April 7, 1995

### 1.

A lawyer who never practiced, an actor whose parts were few, a television pioneer *(Studs' Place)* who'd opened territory then closed to him, Studs Terkel found a sort of tenure on WMFT, Chicago's leading classical music station, where he interviewed authors, painters, actors, musicians, and before long, all sorts of people who were colorful either before or after Studs interviewed and edited them.

I hauled myself over to Studs's studio when my first novel was published in 1960. I remember nothing about the interview, but I must have enjoyed it because I went back three or four times to do others. In March 1995, we arranged to do an interview, an edited version of which appears below. I had a funereal twinge—I have them more and more these days—telling me that this would be the last show Studs and I would do together. My next book was years away, and who knows how long either of us would be around?* It was, I think, this twinge which made me think it might be a good idea to see how one of Studs's interviews would look on paper, not as a part of one of his marvelously edited books, but alone, another blade of grass in the lawn of Studs's forty-plus years' radio work.

### 2.

These past few years, the studio has been in one of the buildings rising over the Chicago River blocks west of Lake Michigan. Studs has not been all that happy here. He misses the fellowship of the WFMT announcers and of the editors and writers who worked on what had been the station's magazine, *Chicago.* Still, comfortable as a muffin, Studs makes a den

---

* Six years later, we're still here. Studs at eighty-nine, is still Studs, and I'm doing all right the morning I write this.

wherever he is. *Rumpled* is a word made for him. Short, compact, rounder than he was a decade ago, gray-tufted, large-nosed and -mouthed, he's a grand laugher. His sentences, or rather—as my friend David Malament pointed out—his noun phrases float around untethered by verbs. You may think he's a bumbler; he's not. He knows what he's after. He has studied and underlined the book of the day as a conductor does a score. Spontaneous and ready to bend to the interviewee's spontaneity, still, one way or another, Studs's version of the book, the artist, the subject, or the celebration is going to get to the audience which, over years, he has created for it. This includes whatever posterity will listen to the thousands of tapes which in thin white boxes fill the metal racks outside the recording studio.

3.

This Friday, April 7, I'm early. In the anteroom I talk with Steve Rios, a young man who interviews alumni for a university publication relations office in Florida. Studs is his idol. Twenty minutes before recording time, Studs shuffles in. We shake hands and talk with the familiarity of those who don't need to establish anything but the continuity of good feeling. He shakes hands with Rios and asks him if he wants to sit in the control room during the taping. Rios lights up: this is more than he expected. He goes to sit with the engineer, a shy, attractive young black girl. "Her first day on the job," Studs says proudly. A couple of my students have worked for Studs; when they talk about it, they smile. He is a wonderful employer and colleague. Today he wears a light blue herring-bone jacket, slightly too big for him, and an open sport shirt. The only time I've seen him in a tie is at a funeral, and then the tie was down an inch from the unbuttoned top button of his shirt. Studs is eminently unbuttoned.

He inserts a small cylinder in his ear. "I've got no hearing at all in the other ear." In the studio, we sit at a hexagonal table in front of two microphones. He says, "We start with *Für Elise.*" If for no other reason, I know that Studs has read the book, because in it, I mention that *Für Elise* is the only piece my sister Ruth ever learned to play with assurance. Studs listens with pleasure to Alfred Brendel's performance of the beautiful little piece and slides from it into a couple of sentences from the book. The interview proceeds from that. I've omitted some of the float—my phrases were more untethered than Studs's were—but I think one gets a bit of what one doesn't get in Studs's books—since the editing there is pointed to bring out the books' themes. Here you can see some of the

Studs whom we Chicagoans know, as he coaxes and shapes the day's subject.

4.

STUDS TERKEL (*after reading from* A Sistermony): You and your sister made it a point never to show your emotions too much.

RICHARD STERN: In the family, we tried for impassivity. The more you felt, the less you showed. Showing was excessive, low-class.

STUDS: Of course, the *Titanic*, how brave the first-class passengers were. When you see a shot of the steerage passengers clawing at each other. . . .

STERN: Right. To die third-class versus dying first-class.

STUDS: So it seems both of you held in.

STERN: After our parents died within six months of each other, we let go a bit. We were it now. That amazing thing about a brother or sister you suddenly find out: that he or she is the only witness to ten million events, which, as you're growing up, don't mean anything, but are now sacred. There she is, your collaborator, your witness, your sister, precious for that alone.

STUDS: So you call the book *A Sistermony*. Of course, we know of patrimony, matrimony, acrimony, but sistermony?

STERN: I thought, "Why isn't there a word for what a sister gives you?" There are so few words for the relationship between sister and brother. "Fraternal," but no "sororal."

STUDS: There is "sorority."

STERN: "Sorority" and "fraternity," yes. Still, this relationship is impoverished in English and the languages I know anything about. I called up a Greek scholar, the late Arthur Adkins, and asked him about the "-mony" suffix. Patrimony is what you get from a father, but matrimony isn't what you get from a mother. Then there is acrimony and testimony and ceremony. All different. Adkins said, "In Greek you know the meaning of every suffix, but Latin came along with its sledge-hammer accents, and everything was derailed."

S T U D S: The center of the book is your sister's illness at home and in the hospital. It takes over.

S T E R N: The mobilization of dying. And the questioning: What is a life? What is your life? Ruth was a person who, as she said, never wanted to do or be anything. Lack of ambition was her slogan, but she was a presence, and not just a presence. She was an active person, a good citizen. She believed and read and kept up with things; she cared and she did.

S T U D S: In the book, her husband and child and your children become dramatis personae.

S T E R N: Even my grandchildren.

S T U D S: The death of a person who is not celebrated . . .

S T E R N: Right.

S T U D S: At the same time, something else: the Soviet Union was dying. There were two things going on, the specific and the general.

S T E R N: Ruth died on the twenty-first of August, the day the coup failed, the beginning of the end of the Soviet Union. Yet the headlines in my being had to do with Ruth. And there were other events. How much do you include? I finally stripped the book down to brothers and sisters. Several friends died during these weeks, but I stuck with Howard Nemerov because he had a very intricate relationship with his sister, Diane Arbus.

S T U D S: She's Daisy Singer in *Hard Times* . . .

S T E R N: What do you know! I tell about going down with him to see her pictures at the Museum of Contemporary Art. He looks at those fantastic, solitary freaks and says, "I gotta get out of here. They're our relatives."

S T U D S: Come back to your sister then. Married. A kid. What did she do?

S T E R N: She worked. She was a good worker. Her best job was with Simon and Schuster. She became personnel manager and supervisor of contracts. She loved literature, and it was grand for her to be around writers.

S T U D S: When you took Ruth to her last movie, *Thelma and Louise*, you said she didn't like it.

S T E R N: It was new territory, and Ruth lived in the old territory. She was not there to take vengeance on the insults of a lifetime. She couldn't or didn't want to follow the almost satiric intrepidity, boldness, and, finally, suicidal drive of the two women. She herself had lived in a corset. It suppressed or distorted what occasionally showed in a hysteria hooked to laughter. She and I laughed more than occasions called for. And then we were close.

S T U D S: The withheld something came forth in the laughter. Was that with you, too?

S T E R N: I suppose so, though I had another outlet, writing stories in which you could reveal anything without saying "That's me." *A Sistermony* is the first book in which I showed myself without that sort of protection.

S T U D S: Now the hospital visits, and you do a good deal with that. She was in great pain, and it was terminal. Did she know that?

S T E R N: She knew something, but I saw the very moment in which she realizes that this is it. What happened is that her husband and I go to see her doctor, a great doctor, Thomas Caputo, and he tells us that there is no hope. In the corridor, Ralph, my brother-in-law, says, "God damn it to hell. This is the first time that he's said anything like this. I don't know what to do." I say, "Let's go upstairs and see her before the psychiatrist comes."

*(Reads.)*

> In his shorts, sportshirt, long socks and shoes, Ralph looked as if he was going to the country instead of his wife's death bed. His still boyish face, though gray, was smashed by anger, puzzlement, fear. (I myself was throbbing to Caputo's sentence of death.)

We walked down the ugly corridor to Ruth's room. She had a transparent, plastic cone over her nose, a tube in her side. Since I'd seen her, a few weeks ago, she'd diminished tremendously. She was El Greco gaunt, her mostly black hair short, sparse, her nose huge in the reduced face, her arms stick-thin. Turning her head, she saw us and smiled, her black eyes shining. She took off the nose cone. "How wonderful to see you, darling. I'm so glad you came." She held out her arms. We hugged and kissed. "Hi Ralphie darling." They kissed. "I'm feeling a little better. I had my fix." Her morphine. "I was reading." *The Times* and a book, Sue Miller's *Family Pictures,* were on the bed. "But I can't concentrate."

Ralph told her that the psychiatrist was coming. On that cue, a very tall man with light hair standing straight up on a long, stunned, bespectacled face stood at the door. "I'm Dr. French. Is this a good time to come in and talk?"

"Please come in," said Ruth.

Dr. French wore a black suit and dark blue tie. "Do you mind if I sit down? I have a bad back." I got out of the blue vinyl armchair by the bed and motioned him to it. "Do you mind if I put these in?" He took out two hearing-aid cylinders and inserted them in his ears. (I wondered if he was going to insert his pacemaker.) He looked at Ruth solemnly and said, "I've been asked to talk to you about your situation. I'm a psychiatrist with a Ph.D., but I also have an M.D. I've studied your records, and I know your medical situation. As you know, it's not a good one. I want to talk with you about it, see if you have any questions I can answer, any problems I can help you deal with."

Ruth said she appreciated that and said that Ralph would like to talk to him also, it had been such a strain on him.

"Yes," said Dr. French. "It's very difficult for everybody. The immediate problem is this: the doctors have to hear from you whether or not, when a catastrophic event occurs—and that may come any time—you wish to be resuscitated. That is, whether you wish to be kept alive on a machine."

As this load of bricks fell on Ruth's head, I watched her eyes widen with terror. "Oh my God," she said. "I'm going to die."

s t u d s: Well now this guy must be a new kind of man on the planet; he has no feeling at all. . . .

s t e r n: No.

S T U D S: I think Dr. Caputo said it was Ruth's will which kept her going; and this guy just destroyed her will.

S T E R N: Yes, a person who's to help people into the hereafter. It was astonishing.

S T U D S: He just . . . there was no feeling at all.

S T E R N: No. The amazing thing is that when he left, I said to Ruth, "Boy he's not exactly Sigmund Freud." And she said, "Yes, but he's gorgeous." On the lip of death, this moron brought her a bit of life. She was a flirtatious girl. I loved it. She'd turned the situation upside-down.

S T U D S: At the dying moment, she had a sense of humor, and this kept her going.

S T E R N: She said, "I knew I vuzzent in duh best a healt', but dis . . ." She was very funny. I'd always known that, but I never knew it more than when she was . . .

S T U D S: So you're making discoveries about your sister that you hadn't known or were aware of during her life as she was dying, but did you make these discoveries about yourself as well?

S T E R N: I've not been an introspective person. I don't know whether I purposely moved away from that and tried to concentrate on other people, but that's what I did, that's what I do. I think that you and I both concentrate on other people.

S T U D S: I hide a great deal of myself.

S T E R N: Right.

S T U D S: I say, "It's none of your business."

S T E R N: Right, you who get more out of other people's business than anybody in America.

S T U D S: But back to the subject of her suffering, even though this insensitive oaf, this guy said, "Do you want to be resuscitated?" Come to the subject, and it's a big one, of course, of suicide. Dying with dignity. The Hemlock Society. Did that ever come up?

S T E R N: What occurred to me is that my position was somewhat different from theirs. If the agony is not unbearable, dying itself is an extremely important part of life. Dying, Ruth existed in a powerful way. There's no way I can ask her her feelings now, but I think she would say what most of us would say—"The hell with it; I don't want that. I don't need that"—but for me and her son and her husband and most of the people she touched, it was a marvelous time. Terrible and marvelous. Dying was a sort of sculptor that cut away lots of excess, lots of attitudes and pretensions, and somehow, much of the essential person was revealed.

S T U D S: You said that Ruth and her husband had living wills. What does that mean?

S T E R N: They had signed a piece of paper saying that they didn't want to be kept alive by artificial means. It's a help to the law, though as Dr. Caputo tells her, "We want to hear from your lips that you don't want to be Code," that is, kept alive by machines. In the pope's new encyclical, he goes along with that. Anyway, she does get the words out, "No, I don't want to be Code."

S T U D S: Her death, though, came about naturally . . .

S T E R N: Internally, yes, but, with morphine and so on. I don't know the extent of her suffering.

S T U D S: What's also revealing, and most whimsical too, is when someone feels something traumatic and deep, the next thing you know there's a philosophical discussion between well, here, between the cab driver and you. How does that go? Page eighty. You ought to read it.

S T E R N: When I leave the hospital—it's actually the last time I saw Ruth, and I'm full of . . .

s t u d s: Bottom of seventy-nine.

s t e r n: Is that in the elevator where the woman is saying, "Children are the hardest to deal with" *(Reads.)* "I walk past the botched Brancusi to the driveway." It's a horrible marble sculpture in the lobby.

*(Reads.)*

> There were no cabs, just ambulances and wheelchairs. Up on the FDR Drive a cab was discharging someone at the Helmsley Towers. I ran and caught it at the light. The driver said, "I saw you but thought you'd wait for the next cab. Thanks. Hard to get a fare, summer noontime." Was I from out of town? What was I doing in New York? I told him. He expressed his sympathy, then told me about his mother's twelve-year cancer, her death, and his making up at her grave with his "hard-head Puerto-Rican brother." "He fights with everyone, can't settle down. Me, I'm married thirty-five years." We got on the Triboro. "This bridge cost me a job."
>     "How so?"
>     "I was working for a supermarket, got engaged and borrowed the van to show her the Triboro. Who rolls up at the toll but my boss. Out of millions. He waves at me. When I get back, I apologize and he fires me."
>     "Son of a bitch," I did not say. The half-thought was aimed more at the driver than the boss. He thought I was paying for his life story, to divert me from my own. (I was taking it in, would remember it and, in the airport, wrote it down.) But I wanted to sink into one fact: out of Ruth's room, I was out of her life. Back there, Ralph was sitting by her bed, holding on to his papers for dear life, holding on while Ruth was in free fall, with no way out but morphine. Morphine was her papers, her cabbie, her plane.

s t u d s: And the more you think about it, it's quite moving. This guy, in a way, is trying to assuage your pain. In his own way. His own too. So you see, very often strangers will talk to one another when there's a deeply felt something.

s t e r n: Look at you. You've touched all these trees, and each one—it's like a medieval tale—opens up, telling you its story. . . .

s t u d s: Each one is so damn different. Anyway, throughout, you have the events going on in the world. The end of the Soviet Union, memories, the deaths of FDR, your father. I remember FDR's. Walking north on Michigan, suddenly I see people crying. Someone tells me, and I start bawling against the lamppost.

S T E R N: Ruth and I used to be waked up by our father to hear his fireside chats. Even if we didn't understand them, there was the voice we grew up with.

S T U D S: And now we come to something else, the American way of death, the funeral.

S T E R N: Yes, the farce of commercial death, the industry of death, the funeral "home," the limousines . . .

S T U D S: And the cost.

S T E R N: Yes, the unbelievable cost.

S T U D S: You say, "How can poor people afford to die?" So it became almost a comic ritual.

S T E R N: Made more comical by the fact that this famous funeral home screwed up. The limousine for which you pay a fortune didn't show up. Why? Because it had taken Ira Gershwin's widow Leonore to the same cemetery where Ruth was to be buried. We saw her coffin lying abandoned by the Gershwin sarcophagus. The limousine caught up with us on the way back, and we had this amazingly festive, uproarious return trip, Ralph remembering when he'd met Ruth and what had led to his marriage, while Roger, its product, sat there wide-eyed, laughing. This minutes after we'd thrown flowers on her coffin.

S T U D S: You talk about incongruous laughter, but, amazingly enough, it fits.

*(Break.)*

S T U D S: So we resume with Richard Stern. So many years he's taught at the University of Chicago. I asked about a couple of his mentors, especially Norman Maclean, who became celebrated for his writings in the last years of his life. But back to "love withheld," and you were speaking of it as a tribute, at the services, and then you realized how close you were without your knowing it. You knew more about Ezra Pound than you knew about your sister. I think you have a sequence on that somewhere. Do you want to pick up on that?

S T E R N: The day after the funeral I meet my oldest son, and we walked in New York—I grew up in New York—on this nostalgic tour, and then we sat down in a Broadway deli and had a cup of coffee. I told Christopher that I didn't know Ruth meant so much to me, and before I knew it, I was crying. He leaned over and patted me. Which I rather liked. So I let myself go, congratulating myself on this emotional richness of mine.

But the emphasis is on the surprise, the astonishing post-mortem dreams. The body, the mind, is throwing up dreams about Ruth. Which I then try to interpret. But you know, these attachments are so much deeper than we know, and they ambush us. How little we know . . .

S T U D S: "I was puzzled," writes Richard Stern in his memoir.

*(Reads.)*

I was puzzled about why I'd been blind to my own sister most of her life. No wonder that historians debate the character and achievement of far more active and complex people. Revisionism. Almost any thoughtful person revises himself. Which doesn't mean that every day you don't have to put down the judicial foot. The law punishes deeds, not character; yet the deepest relationships are formed by character, not deeds. Frigid personalities often do good deeds.

And daily life goes on. You want to eat at a restaurant that I. B. Singer used to frequent, the famous "Dairy." Because we've got to talk about I. B. Singer. Even if there is no basis. We've got to.

S T E R N: He's one of the threads that hold the book together.

S T U D S: Singer eats at this famous "Dairy" that you didn't find too hot. . . .

S T E R N: Terrible.

S T U D S: Great company. Lousy food.

S T E R N: I go in and see Sam, the waiter who served him every day for forty years, and we shake hands. The day after Singer won the Nobel Prize, Sam said, "Mr. Singer, are you going to give me a bigger tip now?" Singer said, "I'd like to, Sam, but my heart von't let me." Mine isn't the only baffled heart in *Sistermony*.

S T U D S: I asked him once, "Mr. Singer, you believe in witches, don't you?" "And vorlocks, too." You have this juxtaposition here of events and people you know all going on at the same time, many at the University of Chicago. You mention Norman Maclean, who finally came out with *A River Runs Through It*, a memoir of his father and his brother. Perhaps a word about . . .

S T E R N: I was the first person he'd hired to work with him on a committee he'd started and into which he poured much of his energy and intelligence. A letter would come in from a kid in Kansas, and Norman would spend hours writing and rewriting a four-page answer. You can imagine a seventeen-year-old getting such a letter from the university to which he'd applied. We never lost an applicant we wanted. I watched this man, low man on the Chicago scholarly totem pole, retire and then write and publish this beautiful memoir. When I knew him first, he was writing about Custer.

S T U D S: Who was an idiot, really.

S T E R N: . . . an idiot, whose picture was in every saloon and schoolroom in America. To a lesser degree, that happened to Norman, and it was very complicated for him—a mixture of astonishing ego gratification and skeptical disbelief. Then he spent the last dozen years writing the second book, *Young Men and Fire*, which is, in part, a tribute to discovering the truth, to scholarship. Norman became a greater scholar than those who'd humiliated him.

S T U D S: So we come back to you again, your influences, your memoir. In some ways, it's about diminishing distance, isn't it?

S T E R N: I hadn't thought of it that way, but okay, it is. Death setting life's tempo. I didn't feel my own death until I hit sixty.

S T U D S: Let's hit that. We're at our last break and then we'll resume for the last round, or the last laugh, with Richard Stern.

*(Break.)*

S T U D S: And so resuming, we're talking about your sister, her dying days, her death and all that goes along with it, the funeral, the service, but most, your own feelings about her. She had a little journal too, didn't she?

S T E R N: Well, she wrote very good letters, and luckily I found one or two. They surprised me. I thought, "Hey, this person had some gift." Because she was my sister, I'd made her into a page-turner, that is, somebody who wasn't going to play the score, but then, too late, I saw she had her own score, her own gift.

S T U D S: The old Wobblies would call someone a "Jimmy Higgins," the one who did all the mimeographing, all the handing out of leaflets on the streets. Without Jimmy Higgins there'd be no movement.

S T E R N: You and I have spent a lot of our lives making these Jimmy Higginses count for something, giving voice to people who claim they can't or won't sing on their own, absolutely valuable and unique people who will never be duplicated.

S T U D S: Jude the Obscure.

S T E R N: The obscure who count.

S T U D S: Wife of so-and-so, sister of, mother of. That's it.

S T E R N: That was it.

S T U D S: So discovering Ruth, you also discovered yourself. That would be safe to say, wouldn't it?

S T E R N: Why not? At least discovery through her.

S T U D S: Well, as we're talking, we'll close the way we began. A memory of your sister. *Für Elise.* That's the ticket. Very good indeed. Thank you very much.

S T E R N: Thank you, Studs.

Yes, thank you, Studs.

# A Very Few Memories of Don Justice

A pleasant red-haired man
Noticing my red hair
Predicted a great career,
But for the asking mine,
Though whether of sword or pen,
Confessed he could not tell,
So cloudy was the ball.
Now, how could a person
Know that words from a stranger's mouth
Would seem the simple truth
To a boy of seven or eight?

This stanza will not be found in Donald Justice's as-yet uncollected *Collected Poems*. My somewhat unreliable head may be its only residence, although in its perfectly correct, if discarded, form it will be found in one of the hundreds of wonderful letters from Don which I have saved over what is more than a half-century.* Helped—I think—by noting that the poem "The Summer Anniversaries" is dated 1955 in the "Uncollected Poems" section of the *Selected Poems*, I'd guess that this stanza—which may once have belonged to it—came my way that year or the year before. Was it Don or I who said of it, "Too Yeatsian"? Probably Don, although over the years when we criticized each other's poems and stories, no criticism, however harsh, was out of bounds.

How many other slightly damaged beauties exist only in the letters

---

* For students or fanciers of fine epistolary prose, the letters are found in the collection of my papers in the Regenstein Library of the University of Chicago.

and memories of Don and his friends? Collect these discards, and they would make a decent reputation for a lesser poet.

Not that I can be objective about Don's poems. They are part of my life, my sensibility, our long friendship.

⁂

Back in October 1944, I was sixteen, a freshman at the University of North Carolina in Chapel Hill. In the library, I'd just, an hour before, come upon a wonderful book, the enormous anthology *Modern British and American Poetry* edited by Louis Untermeyer. I'd become a poetry reader four years earlier, when Pocket Books issued its first book, the *Pocket Book of Verse*, edited by M. E. Speare (shorn of the magic "Shake," but sacred nonetheless to me). In Speare's marvelous little zoo were the English poets up to, I'd guess, the Yeats of "The Lake Isle of Innisfree." I knew nothing of poems written after that until that hour in the library.

I felt someone looking over my shoulder at the book. "Good." A soft voice, hardly southern. A long-faced fellow with horn-rimmed eyeglasses, tall, thin. "Like it?" Surprise and pleasure, inflected with the slightest patronage. He was nineteen, worldly, from Miami, on his way to New York. In Miami, he'd studied composing with Carl Ruggles (of whom, like much, I hadn't heard). We must have exchanged addresses, because I think the first of his letters came that fall from New York. Months—or was it a year?—later, Don came back to Chapel Hill to do graduate work. I'd formed a literary group, a few students, a few instructors, who met once a week to discuss a book, *Madame Bovary*, *Crime and Punishment*, *Walden*. Each meeting was led by someone. I think Don's book was *Walden*.

I was starting to write poetry. Don introduced me to the rigors of composition. He was generous, too; had to be. Any half-decent turn of phrase or meter fired the generosity. When I finally wrote one fair line, "The sun makes shadows of us all," the generosity was like a confirmation. Early in '46, I wrote my first real story. (I'd written a few sketches in high school.) Don was also generous about that, and I found my vocation.

We worked for the *Carolina Review*, and wrote for it the only joint piece we ever finished, a movie review of *The Big Sleep*. By then, we were part of a group, including Edgar Bowers and Don's fellow graduate student, Jean Ross, who became his wife in the summer of 1946. For a wedding present, I sent them the just-issued tome of one of our masters, Yvor Winters, *In Defense of Reason*. We also read the *Kenyon* and *Sewanee Reviews*, and, occasionally, the *Partisan*. I think the *Southern Review* had stopped publishing, but we knew its back issues.

Jean had a foot in the door of new writing: her sister Eleanor was married to Peter Taylor, who taught at Greensboro. Peter's roommate at Kenyon had been Robert Lowell, and when we went over to a writers' conference at Greensboro, we met him and Red Warren, whose *All the King's Men* was our favorite new novel.

In 1947, Don and Jean were in Miami, and I in New York and then in Evansville, Indiana, where I spent a miserable two months working in a department store. A girl to whom I'd given a ring lived in Orlando, Florida. I went down there, was discouraged by her mother, and took a beautiful bus ride to Miami to stay with Don and Jean in the garage apartment adjacent to his parents' house. The two most memorable events of a lovely week were meeting Norma Troetschel (who died in 1992), a woman I loved, and, with Don, picking the winning round of, I think, the Walcott-Marciano fight and collecting $15, which paid for that and several nights' beer.

When Don and Jean went out to join Edgar Bowers in Stanford the next year, I went to Harvard, and the year after that to France, on a Fulbright. There were many wonderful letters from the Justices, including those that, in 1952, made me decide to go to the Iowa Writers' Workshop for my doctorate.

It was brutally hot when I arrived in Iowa City in June 1952. I stayed with the Justices under a bookshelf of the Baconian landlord's works on the "true authorship" of Shakespeare's plays. Don and I wrote couplets, which began

> Two Iowan Baudelaires,
> Sweating out tetrameters.

After rough weeks—I'd been away from taking classes for three years, my wife was expecting our second child, Iowa City looked grim and ugly after Paris and Heidelberg, and money was very tight—I began to love Iowa. The Army–Joe McCarthy hearings were on. We watched them, raging at the savage carelessness of McCarthy and his minions and cheering every thrust and parry of the Army's lawyer, Joseph Welch. Every afternoon, after classes and teaching, we played fiercely competitive croquet near the banks of the Iowa River, Don and I against Don Peterson and Tom Rogers. Don Justice was a maniacal gamesman, willing to risk fracturing his foot to get better purchase on a ball he'd club into the shrubbery.

Games, poetry, and stories dominated our lives. There are certain Rilke poems which have a garbage aroma for me, because Dee Snodgrass and I discussed them while we emptied pails onto the communal garbage dump.

In 1954, after graduation, I got a job at Connecticut College (then "For Women") in New London. In April 1955, Don wrote that he'd been offered a job by Walter Blair of the English Department and Norman Maclean of the Committee on General Studies in the Humanities at the University of Chicago, but that Chicago, both city and university, scared him. He turned down the appointment and took a job at the University of Missouri. Oddly, the Chicago job was offered to me; I accepted and have stayed almost half a century.

Almost every Christmas the Justices came up from Missouri or down from St. Paul or, mostly, east from Iowa City. Christmas offered new fields for our gamesmanship, the kids' new toys. One year, we raced jack-in-the-boxes hour after hour. Another year, we played tiddlywinks for most of the night. Norman Maclean, who came by every Christmas morning with a bottle of his favorite Louis Martini white wine, laughed his head off at the two maniacs keeping the kids away from their new toys. (When the kids were older—say, five—Don competed with them.) Our competition died with Pounce, a game of double patience. (Patience!) I retreated from competitive frenzy saving myself an ulcer.

Don and I had our ups and downs. There'd be some dumb slight or imputation which would rupture relations for a week or a month. Once we decided to write a play together. We laid it out, scene by scene, and began writing. There was only one comfortable chair in the house. One of us had it one day, the other the next. One day we argued about whose turn it was; that finished our collaborative life.*

﹏

---

* I finished the play. It was called *The Gamesman's Island* and is included in *Teeth, Dying and Other Matters*.

For twenty years, we exchanged fewer letters and saw less of each other. To some degree, our tastes diverged, and we worked different sides of the street, but our old friendship is very strong.* Don's beautiful poems remain one of my life's resources and standards. I'm proud that a rather mysterious one is dedicated to me. The poem was written, as I recall, in a bad time, when Don was teaching out in San Francisco and not in good shape. It appears in the volume *Night Light*.

POEM FOR A SURVIVOR
FOR RGS

Holding this poem
Close, like a mirror,
I breathe upon it.

I watch for some sign.
There is a faint mist
Spreading across it.

It takes hold. It clings
To the lean hollows
As the sun rises,

This sun that is going
To burn the mist off.

I give you the chamois
To clear the surface.

I give you this sun.

The gift of the chamois and the sun stand in my mind for much that Don has given me of clarity and the light behind it.

* We now email each other frequently.

# The Venetian Sculptress

AUGUST 1986. VENICE.
Four of us are eating dinner at Raffaele's Restaurant on a *fondamenta* alongside which gondoliers stroke tourists toward the Grand Canal. Some of the boats cluster around a gondolier tenor whose howls pitch the caramel bravura of this strange city. The sculptress, Joan FitzGerald, and I sit with old friends, Gianfranco Ivancic, whose family came to Venice from Dalmatia in the seventeenth century, and his new wife, Beatrice, a widow from the Friuli, where Gianfranco has the country place from which he's come for a couple of Venetian days. Beatrice tells Joan about a Hemingway exhibit Gianfranco has mounted in Madrid, Pamplona, Murcia, and Estremadura; Gianfranco tells me about the Venice of his parents and grandparents. "Harry's Bar was the first place girls of good family could go by themselves, their first club." Otherwise, they'd sit with their families in the first six rows of Florian's. "Sit in the seventh row, you were already out of it."

I met Gianfranco twenty-five years ago in the little house on Calle Querini which Olga Rudge's father bought for her in 1927. (See above.) I came in one day and found him sitting in silence with the house's second occupant, Ezra Pound. Silence made neither of these gentlemen uneasy. Prompted into civil chatter, they did well, but silence was a medium in which they were at ease. After an hour of it, I went back with Gianfranco to his *palazzo* near Santa Maria Formosa. We drank whiskey in the study, and he read me a children's story Hemingway had written for the children of his sister, Adriana. ("'Pass me a bite of Hindu trader,' said the lion" is the only line I remember.) Hemingway had used some of his May–December love for Adriana in one of his weakest books. His death was still a fresh wound for Gianfranco, who'd gone to Ketcham for the funeral, and now talked of that "dangerous summer" when he drove

Hemingway and others to the *mano a mano* fights of the great bullfighter brothers-in-law, Dominguez and Ordonez.

In 1986, Gianfranco was recovering from a worse wound: three years earlier, Adriana had hanged herself and—Joan told me—if it had not been for Beatrice, Gianfranco might not have survived.

He was saying, "My aunt remembers girls coming to parties in their own gondolas. Those were days when the land gave us ninety percent. Now it gives us ten." His uncle had fought duels, once for dancing the tango too closely with a friend's wife. "He told me how he met D'Annunzio." Gianfranco's long face looked amused. "He was climbing vines to a bedroom on the Lido when down them came another body which crashed into the weeds below. D'Annunzio."

Gondolas tricked out with lanterns went by, the gondoliers' straw hats on a level with our table: "San-ta Luci-i-a, San-ta Luci-i-a." (That this was Neapolitan didn't ruffle the tourists.) "Even that can't kill Venice." A windless night under a three-quarter moon. Gianfranco's love for his home town is so deep it occurred to me that there might be a gene for it. He flipped an empty pack of Marlboros over his proprietary shoulder into the canal. "I stay in the country more and more. But yesterday, out on my balcony—you know, it's the last turn before the Bridge of Sighs—a gondolier pointed his clients to the house and said, 'This was the palace of Marco Polo.' No one cares about the truth. I'm not surprised about this Statue of Liberty thing." The Venetian entrepreneur-painter Ludovico De Luigi had proposed that Venice put up a fifty-foot cardboard copy of the Statue of Liberty in the Bacino. The Comune had the sense to turn him down. "Venice may no longer be the Serenissima," said the Superintendent of Belle Arti, "but it is still unique." Gianfranco said, "For me, there's only one real Venetian left—Joan." He didn't look across the table at the small, blue-eyed, merry-faced woman talking with his wife. "She's the only one who still knows things, the only one who feels things. When I want to know what's really happening here, I come to Joan."

The next day, I went across the canal to visit the ninety-three-year-old Olga Rudge. It was too hot to walk down to the Accademia, cross the bridge, and walk back toward the Salute. I took the *traghetto* over from Santa Maria del Giglio. Three gondoliers were lounging in the shade by the wooden pier. The youngest was asleep, the oldest smoking and dreaming. The third, a fair-haired, middle-aged man, was taking a picture of a seven-year-old boy. After a few minutes, I asked him if the *traghetto* was functioning. He looked familiar—but many in this small town look that way to me. He said it was but didn't move. I waited in the sun, then heard someone call from inside the café, "Memo."

"Memo," I said, remembering. "Good to see you. I'm Joan's friend."

"Ah, yes. Good to see you," and he was up, as was the young gondolier, and, in two seconds, we were in the gondola. The young gondolier was introduced as one son, the little boy as another.

"How was China?" I asked. Joan had told me that Memo had gone there for a "Venice in Shanghai" week.

"Beautiful," said Memo. "And Pierluigi sold the Chinese lots of refrigerators." But he wanted to say something more important to me. "*La Joan,*" he said, "*è un' artista seria.*"

True Venetian, serious artist.

Joan FitzGerald grew up in River Forest and in Hemingway's own Oak Park. She went to parochial schools, barely surviving the nun-teachers, who were terrified by—and punitive of—such intellectual curiosity and energy as hers. Her parents gave her a sense of decorum, self-respect, and independence, but, as a teenager, she left the way of life they thought best for a good Catholic girl. She'd read, seen, and felt her way to art, her chief guide, Michelangelo. Through him, she discovered vocation and comportment. For a while, she studied sculpture at the Art Institute with an obscure, marvelous teacher named Nellie Bar. Meanwhile, she worked at all sorts of jobs—"I sold everything that could be sold in the stores of Chicago except myself"—and saved enough to get to Europe, saw some of what she'd read about, and dodged those anxious to convert a beautiful young girl into an *object*. For a few years, she shuttled between Europe and America, working odd jobs while she learned and practiced her art. "It was expensive in every way to be a sculptor in America." In 1960, she settled in Venice. "There was a good foundry here then, one I could afford." And in Venice she stayed.

A good foundry is crucial to her. FitzGerald's favorite medium is bronze, and, unlike most sculptors, she sees her work through every stage from conception to emergence. When the Venice foundry closed down (like so many small family enterprises), she went to one in Rome. When that one shut down, she found one in Verona. Finding a good one is the bane of her existence. A year earlier, miscalculations at the foundry ruined what she considered the finest work of her life, a life-size Polish rider (inspired by Rembrandt's painting in the Frick and by her feeling for the heroes of Solidarity).

For everything but the actual casting, FitzGerald is her own foundry. Unlike, say, Picasso, who, one Tuesday, selects one of the night's forty-six dreams, sketches a design, and turns the idea over to a foundry for "realization," FitzGerald conceives, sketches, makes clay and wax models, then goes into the foundry alongside the workers to figure out where to place the tubes through which the hot metal pours.

Unlike sculptors whose life work may be thirty or forty pieces of sculpture, Joan FitzGerald has made more than three hundred pieces, most in bronze, a few in alabaster, some in silver; she has also made hundreds of brilliant drawings, some tapestry, some mosaic, some paintings. She works with the world's stuff to make a world of bronze figures rationalized—FitzGeraldized—into golden arcs and triangles which express and intensify the agonized intelligence of a Lincoln, the fatigued gallantry of Marco Polo, the gorgeous muteness of desert-bleached skulls. Her work is the relationship between her special geometry and the inorganic solids which say, "I am here to stay."

⤜⤛

Maybe Joan FitzGerald is more of a Chicagoan than she knows. Maybe the work ethic of old ethnic neighborhoods entered her artistic soul and enabled her not only to create remarkable work but also to recognize the fine work of others. Her famously beautiful apartment and her studio on the Giudecca are themselves works of artistic brilliance: they contain not only her work but magnificent work of often little-known fellow artists. So she has a mysterious granite figure and a marble nude made by Giulio Porcinai, a peasant genius who taught stone-cutting in the country near Grassino and who died a few years ago in obscurity. Of his great nude, FitzGerald says, "It will be in the Louvre someday. Nobody since Michelangelo could cut stone like this." Then there are lithographs and paintings by Ubaldo Bosello, another self-taught man of genius who works in isolation in his native Padova and who, like FitzGerald herself, talks wonderfully about Faulkner, Kafka, Bach, and Chaplin as well as Giotto, Carpaccio, and Cézanne, the artists who instructed and deepened his art.

FitzGerald has created her society as well as her sculpture. Her friends—and many of her patrons—range from the distinguished, famous, and rich to obscure artists and the *popolo minuti* of Venice. For Ezra Pound, she was like a daughter. She made two heads of him, one of which was the stellar attraction of a twentieth-century exhibit at the National Portrait Gallery in Washington, D.C. For Robert Penn Warren and his family and for T. S. Matthews—the man who, as much as Henry Luce, made *Time* magazine what it is—she was a dear companion. When Bernard Malamud wanted to find his way around Venice, I sent him to Joan; he owed some of his *Pictures of Fidelman* to her. Her generosity, loyalty, and purity of heart are rare on this earth. She is, indeed, sought after so much that part of her life consists in devising forms of concealment. The Giudecca studio is her chief protection. Venice has long been another. In this most beautiful and intricate city, one can be center-stage one minute and invisible the next. To sell sculpture here, one must be more or less on stage; to make it, one has to hide.

No one mistakes Chicago for Venice, but the two cities, one fifteen times more populous than the other, have much in common. Both are built on swampland, which necessitates the use of piles and caissons for their buildings; both depend for much of their glory on bodies of water; both are commercial towns filled with fascinating characters on both sides of the law. (In the past few years, more Venetian than Chicago public and commercial men have served time for fraud and defalcation.) Characters in both towns are not content to make deals; they must be celebrated for them. The *bella figura* counts as much in Chicago's comedy as in Venice's. Both towns are great stages which, like the stages of Japanese Noh plays, reveal their theatrical machinery along with the dramatic action. Finally, though, both cities contain, more or less hidden away, artists who bring them more glory than do their politicians, millionaires, and criminals put together. In both towns, Joan FitzGerald is one of the finest of them.

# Ray West and the Iowa Writers' Workshop

I.

Ray was acting head of the workshop in my two Iowa City years. Paul Engle, who'd corresponded with me about coming, was off—at Harvard, at the Harriman estate in New York, in Europe. When, Zeus-like, he did show up in Iowa City, gift-bringing (*Life* would be doing a story on the workshop, Random House would publish an anthology of workshop writers, he would be editing the O. Henry Prize short stories—these gifts were delivered, others weren't), the metabolism rate changed. Everything went faster, the publication world was closer, your internal telephone answered to long distance, you were part of Now.

Ray's world was different. *Now* was the slow labor of art, the scrupulous assessments required for a good issue of the *Western Review*. *Now* was the fragile extension of a long *Then*, a rare addition to a longer *To Be*. Ray loved the possibilities in your stories, loved to help make them what they could be. Paul also loved your stories but saw them as part of the mosaic his vision and brilliant administrative gift brought into being, the best new American poems and stories coming out of the Midwestern heartland where he'd been born and raised.

Ray saw this as well, and it was undoubtedly part of the reason he'd joined Paul in Iowa City despite the clash of their personalities, temperaments, and ambitions. Paul was galvanic. Even sitting barefoot on a porch eating a hot dog, he was aware that the moment was part of other moments, an interval between accomplishments, a potential picture in *Life* or the *Chicago Tribune*. Though not himself at ease, Ray offered it. He wasn't in a hurry. His laughs were slow, as if surprised at themselves. Paul's were explosions.

If you look quickly, Paul should have looked like Ray, Ray Paul. Ray's look was almost bohemian, thick, wavy, swept black hair—graying a bit in 1952—and, like a way station for it, a rich mustache. His eyes were large, brown, eyeglassed. He was slender, 5'7", he walked on the balls of his feet. Paul had thin, straight, light brown hair parted in the middle and, if you looked quickly, bland features; but the nose and chin were sharp, the small eyes alert, rapid. A probing, nervously good-humored face; but the humor was his own, not yours. Ray's face was longer, darker, easier, the small, good teeth under the rich mustache ready for smiles, but these were shared, they took off from what you said more than what he was thinking about it. You relaxed with Ray, were on your toes with Paul.

2.

Ray had single-handedly kept a good literary quarterly going in different places under different names. (The best known before *Western Review* was *The Rocky Mountain Review*.) Paul wanted it as an outlet for the workshop writers' work. Ray wanted to keep it as it was, a place for the best poems and stories submitted from all over. He had published some of the world's best writers in it. Although delighted to discover and publish new writers, he did not want to rush them into its pages. When they did make it there, they'd be printed beside Pound and Tate and would know that they really counted. Everything Ray knew was that this took time.

Like many of the young writers recruited—with his extraordinary enthusiasm and generosity—by Paul, I came to Iowa City unsure of the place and my reason for being in it. My dear old friends from Chapel Hill, Don and Jean Justice, had somewhat prepared me, and had prepared Paul for me, but the first hot days staying in their apartment under the landlord's collection of Baconiana on a street of frightened-looking frame houses were difficult for me and so for them.

I sat in on Joseph Baker's intelligent classes on Victorian literature and thought I was too old at twenty-four to go back to school. I'd been working for three years in Europe. My wife was pregnant, and we had a one-year-old son. Although the job Paul got me at his alma mater, Coe College, would, with a tuition scholarship and such goodies as cheap student housing and the Engle family cradle, enable us to make it through the doctorate without borrowing (I'd saved three thousand dollars working for the occupation army in Germany), I didn't think my spiritual bank account would hold up.

One day I went down the hill to the workshop office and met Ray. He didn't offer the boosting welcome Paul did, he just quietly made you know that this was a place where literature counted and that this was what you were about, it was where you should be.

3.

I'd never experienced anything like the workshop. There were about twenty-five of us in the large group. Ray presided; Verlin Cassill and Mike (Hansford) Martin were the two assistants. There were good students in the class, many as old as or older than I. Some were intellectual wild men and women; the instructors had to deal with some very far-out criticism. (Verlin supplied some of that, although he was usually wise and helpful. It was a special summer for him, too. He met the pretty twin swimmers, one of whom became his wife.) Of one of my stories, a bald, Ghengis-mustached North Carolinian said, "A Harvard instructor wouldn't let peach juice roll down his chin into his shirt." Ray dealt with such criticism patiently, good-naturedly, firmly. He kept after the heart of the stories, then placed them in the tradition, a Hemingway- or Anderson-like story. One story of mine bounced off Goethe's *Werther.* Ray saw that and liked it. He wanted us to feel that we were part of something larger. He didn't parade his learning, but it was clear how deeply a part of him it was. When he praised a story, you felt that literature itself was approving. Mostly, though, there was much to improve. One could always improve a story.

In the group sessions, Ray wanted everyone to speak, and he would easily alter his opinion after a speaker—student or instructor, it was democratic—convinced him that he'd missed the point. I sometimes thought that he purposely misread something in order to give us confidence in our judgments. Some of us needed no boosting here.

In our one-to-one sessions, sitting three feet from him in the small workshop office with the plywood walls and pictures of James and Whitman tacked up beside covers of recent *Western Reviews,* Ray leaned over the pages of the story he'd marked up and, in his rich, quiet voice, spelled out what he thought about it. Even when I disagreed, I respected his opinion. His was not a competing ego; he was a teacher who didn't seem to be riddled with doubt. He wasn't competing with you, he wasn't posing, there was never any question that his experience and sensitivity made him a judge whose opinion counted.

Working with—rather than for—him on the *Western Review* was a wonderful experience. Herb Wilner, Don Justice, Don Petersen, Mike Martin, David Jenkins, Bill Dickey (the *Review*'s remarkably efficient and agreeable secretary), and several others read the submitted essays, poems, and stories, wrote comments, debated merits and demerits, and then went over everything with Ray. It was a lesson in the conversion of individual talent into not exactly tradition but into—how awesome it seemed—publication. When my own workshop story, "The Sorrows of Captain Schreiber," was accepted and printed in the *Review*, I didn't feel the favoritism but the seriousness of the process. Your work was in a magazine which Ray had made count. He would not have lowered his standards for anyone. So I believed, and believe now.

I didn't socialize with Ray. I don't know who did, perhaps Herb Wilner, whose slow humor and strength (a bit more tormented than Ray's) were akin to his. (Later they would teach together at San Francisco State.) Indeed, I knew very little about him. We were so busy with course work, writing, teaching, studying for doctoral exams, watching the Army-McCarthy hearings at the Union, playing bridge, poker, charades and, every decent afternoon at four, croquet by the river, shopping, and taking kids to the doctor, that there wasn't time to socialize with quiet people like Ray. And I suppose we thought that he, like us, was writing.

What about this writing? Full of my own and that of my friends, I didn't think much about it, but one day, our subgroup of five or six prose writers listened while Ray read us a chapter of a novel on which he was working. I thought it very good and loved hearing him read it. It meant an enormous amount to him and thus to us. As far as I know, it was never published. Perhaps it was never finished, but I think it was offered and rejected a few times and Ray, thinking he hadn't brought off something that was as good as he wanted it to be, withdrew it. I have no idea now what it was about except that it was Western, Mormon, Utah, and said more about Ray than anything else. (Did he tell us that there was a section about his proselyting year in Germany? Maybe so.)

The differences between him and Paul overflowed into a break-up a couple of years after I left Iowa City in 1954. Ray asked me to do what I could to preserve the threatened *Western Review*. I had a heated epistolary exchange about it with President Vergil Hancher (an Oxford friend of Paul's), but Ray lost the battle and moved to San Francisco State.

I saw him out there in 1964. I drove to his lovely cedar house in Marin County. He'd put on weight and looked sleek as a seal; happy, too. He seemed much older, the thick upswept hair sugar-white. He, his charming wife, Lou, and I had sandwiches around their swimming pool. He said swimming was very important to him now. It was far from Utah, far from Iowa City. The magazine deadlines were over, even the world of letters seemed remote. He was fifty-eight.

Yesterday, knowing I was to write this, I took out his book of essays, *The Writer in the Room,* and read through his learned, thoughtful, confident but unpretentious accounts of Emerson, Whitman, James, Twain, Crane, Faulkner, Katherine Anne Porter, Pound, and Hemingway. I hadn't put into words back then what I think I sensed and now feel strongly: that Ray was an American literary conscience whose teaching, editing, and writing articulated a writer's obligations. A Henry James sentence he quotes in one of the essays suggests what may be the core of Ray's code and vocation, the essence of the tenacity, kindness, and gentleness which makes him a permanent part of so many grateful students, collaborators, and writers: "It appears to me that no one can ever have made a seriously artistic attempt without becoming conscious of an immense increase—a kind of revelation—of freedom."

*The following fictional portrait is part of a larger work. It's been tailored for the miscellany not just by being placed after nonfictional portraits but by killing off the protagonist before her fictional time.*

## My Ex, the Moral Philosopher

1.

My room in the Hotel St. Louis was so small it felt like an overcoat; when I went out, I felt I should check to see that I wasn't wearing it. But the little hotel squatted in the Marais, one block from the Seine, three from the Place des Vosges, four from Place Bastille, and you took its *petit dejeuner* in a bluish-yellow cave which preserved the stony mystery of a fifteenth-century storeroom. Bliss. I was usually the earliest, sometimes the only breakfaster. I'd taken my constitutional—two blocks to Rue Charles V for today's *Figaro* and yesterday's *Le Monde*—and anticipated the warm, soft-flaked croissants buttered and jammed not from the plastic tomblets served in many so-denominated three-star hotels but from unpackaged slabs of *bon beurre* and rosy gobs of jam which still, forty-eight years after my first Paris breakfast, sing the joy of life to me.

Two years to the week before I read of Rowena's absurd death in the *Times,* I was in the cave hoisting a second coffee-soaked croissant to my mouth when I saw her picture in *Figaro,* not as I'd known her thirty years ago but as the fox-sharp, worn, and trenched ex-not-quite-beauty she apparently was now.

2.

I'd been married to Rowena for two hundred and eighty-seven days: my lawyer counted them when he arranged the settlement I'd resisted and didn't stop resenting until a year or so after her fourth post-Dortmund marriage. Née Hardy, Rowena had kept the Jewish name of her first quickie husband, Herschel Plotnik. Affixed to her blonde, bold, WASP-pure self, Rowena, as I saw it, got academic and public points for sticking to it. My thought was that she thought that if she dropped Plotnik and resumed Hardy she'd be accused of a Heideggerian betrayal. One of her early papers denounced that peasant genius's "debased morality," a high—or low—light of which was his dropping the dedication of *Being and Time* to his Jewish patron, Husserl. (The only humorous note in Rowena's oeuvre was her—unacknowledged—citation of her teacher Abendschlimmer's characterization of this ignobility as "being on time.")

The *Figaro* article dealt with the lecture series Rowna was giving at the *Collège de France*. It described her as "the distinguished, prolific, ubiquitous and beautiful moral philosopher, feminist critic and classical humanist."

My two hundred and eighty-seven marital and fifty or sixty courting days hadn't prepared me for Rowena's academic celebrity. When we met in New York, she was an instructor in comparative literature at Columbia, thrilled that her dissertation, *Eros Betrayed*, had been accepted for publication by the Ohio State University Press. Back then, her self-confidence was flecked, if not with modesty, at least with touches of self-doubt. There was very little sign of that condescending arrogance for which she'd become known. (Abendschlimmer used to talk of the "R. H. Plotnik Foundation for Indulgence and Condescension." "Did you get your Plotnik? Yes? How much was it?" "I got a faceful.") Back then, we were both working hard, I to get free of the newspaper so I could write my own pieces and books, she for tenure and intellectual glory. When she wasn't hidden in a pile of books, she was at the typewriter, clacking away. Minutes after amorous sessions, I could hear what I called "the post-coital clack."

3.

I'd met her—no, run into her. Still not right. She ran into me. It was in Central Park, where she jogged around the reservoir every morning between clacking sessions. (And jogged 'til the last hour of her life.) Having Rowena run into you was, I learned, a well-known hazard of New York jogging. She was near-sighted and wouldn't wear glasses or contacts. The world had to come to or dodge her. By temperament and training, she expected others to give way, but sometimes *the others* were inanimate, which meant she ran into trees. If the others were animate but inhuman, there was also trouble: dogs and squirrels were kicked and, occasionally, revenged themselves by nipping Rowena's ankles or muscular legs. (The year before she ran into me, she'd had an encounter with a

Doberman which brought her to Mount Sinai Emergency for abdominal rabies shots.) In addition to myopia and social *je m'en foutisme,* the jogging Rowena was "listening" to the piece of music she'd decided to play in her head that morning. When oak tree or Doberman struck, she'd been lost in some internal *allegro maestoso.* When I was married to her, she was going through the thirty-two Beethoven piano sonatas. The sonata du jour would be on the hi-fi as she pulled on her leotards and clipped a comb in her hair. Jogging, the interior pianist took over.

Anyway, she ran into much of me, knocked me not quite down, suggested that I look where I was going, then, noticing, I now think, my wedding ring, made the "peace offering"—were we already at war?—of coffee. What struck me about her that first morning—other than her knees and fists—was the density of her blue eyes, a fusion of puzzlement and absorption. (I didn't know about the myopia.) This vulpine Atalanta was hungering for your soul. In the Madison Deli, she poured out her history and plans. "I'm an aristocrat who's spent decades squeezing blue blood out of my veins." (I didn't then recognize the Chekhovian adaptation: the great Russian had squeezed serfdom out of his.) "If my dissertation makes the splash Professor Abendschlimmer believes it will, I'll have a choice of tenure tracks around the country." Much more about the academic territory ahead, then, "For me, philosophy isn't a technical Sahara. I want to alter things." "You want to be a public intellectual." "A stupid redundancy," she said.

So much for my contribution. I suppose she found out what I did, but my memory is that I said very little. It did turn out that we had common friends including Elinor Patchell, my wife's sister. I was treated to thumbnail sketches of their inadequacies and the improvements Rowena had tried to install in them. (Of little Elinor she said that she'd spent hours steering her to German and French sources which "the poor twit should have learned as a freshman.") I listened to all this as if it were coming from the burning bush.

A week later, more or less deliberately, I jogged alongside her in the park. More coffee, more sketches, more revelations. (She'd just sold her jewelry and given the money to Amnesty International.)

A week or two later, the four of us, Jean, Elinor, Rowena and I, were invited to a dinner at Professor Abendschlimmer's. (Had a rowenian flea been put in his ear?) When Jean and I got home, I mentioned the dense blue look. Jean said, "She may look densely at you, she didn't even see

Elly or me, didn't ask us one question about our doings, and when Elly said something, she smiled at her as if she were the house cat. Then you sat on the couch with her, and boom, she opened up, mouth, blouse, thighs, didn't you notice?"

"No."

Of course I'd noticed. There was this large, lean, twenty-five-year-old with this cascade of gold-streaked hair falling about her ears and neck, chest bobbing in counterpoint to Dietrichian proclamations, blue eyes drenching me with God knows what invitation. It was like hiking hours in a forest, then, suddenly, seeing what you'd come to see:" Dr. Livingston!" (Or, in this case, "Mr. Kurtz!")

4.

A couple of days into the 287-day marriage, I discovered what a scholar of make-up Rowena was, how much time, study, and application went into her *I-don't-have-time-to-make-myself-appealing, take-me-as-I-am* look.

Before that, adultery weighed on—and, I guess, sweetened—our sessions. Adultery complicated Rowena's moral position, deepened her as a thinker and person, drove her to subtler descriptions of moral life. "Pleasure and pain are different sides of the sculpture. Sensual pleasure, moral pain. Jean's pain is mine. Even when she doesn't understand it, I understand—and suffer—for her."

Suffering Lover was a Rowenian role. "Living the serious life isn't easy. I hate lying, even to let somebody down easily." (This sentence was the prelude to her revelation that "travel sickness"—her reason for never going out of town with me—was the Princeton philosopher she was banging and blowing. Speaking of which: "Not blow *job*," she early corrected. "If it's *work*, don't do it.")

Even in those first weeks, my head ached from the mixture of passion and pedagogy. I headed home to Jean and little Billy, soggy with guilt. When Jean caught on and took off, there was no philosophic baggage to carry, just—just!—outrage, anger, pain, and exhaustion. Unpretty, but preferable to Rowena's highwire vocabulary. That vocabulary! I remember the verbal contortions after she decided that her dismissal of feminism—"the clichés of ugly women masked by Ms. Steinem's meringue"—was a foolish mistake and that if she didn't get on its express train to celebrity and prestige, she'd spend years on suburban locals.

5.

*Figaro* gave the title of her lecture series in English: *Love's Intelligence* (*par l'auteur de* Eros Trahi) and listed the four lectures in English with only a few of those French errors of contempt for foreign tongues:

    I. Love's Spontanity and Surprise

    II. Virtu and Pompicity: Serious Love, Serious Life

    III. Love: Fatal, Fetal, Fecal

    IV. Bombastique Purity

I no longer think it odd that people attack in others their own weaknesses. We brood about what we're not, what we don't have and can't do. I don't think that the saying "If you can't do, teach" is right. Rowena quoted Aquinas (I assume correctly):"Teaching is an active life." Well, it isn't day-trading, football, or serial killing, but yes, it's real work. Still, as forgers are not as good as the painters they copy, so professors are not usually up to the great texts they profess. Journalists don't—or shouldn't—pretend that we're as accomplished as the people we interview and rake over our resentment. Reporting, like forging and teaching, is a craft, not an art (although, since the *Times* let Maureen Dowd off the leash, not a few of my colleagues have come to regard themselves as not-so-miniature novelists and historians).

Where was I? Oh yes, Rowena, the Professor of Moral Philosophy.

I'd skimmed a couple of her books after finding my own name in the index. And why was it there? Because Rowena liked to illustrate subtle analysis with "living examples. . . . I want to be down in the dusty arena, not preaching from moral Mt. Zions." For demonstration, no name was more fully indexed in her books than "Plotnik, Rowena." There it was after Parfit, Plantinga, Plato, and Plotinus, among Paul, Pater, Putnam, and Proust. Unindexed, but otherwise ubiquitous, were Suffering Rowena, Passionate Rowena, and, foremost, High-Minded, Responsible Rowena, Moral Philosopher Rowena; Rowena loving X, remembering Y, caring for, that is, improving, Z.

Rowena, the Great Scholar, cited articles, reviews, conference papers, and books by "Plotnik, Rowena,".a lecture "given in Melbourne and revised in Canberra," "a conference paper presented in Cambridge to an unusually responsive group," "a review-article of my early work on counterfactuals in *Ethics*," "a particularly thoughtful critique by

Davidson's best-known student from which I've greatly profited," although, "as it turns out, it seems that a review of my journals reveals that I'd sketched out much of what he suggested, I remain grateful for his generous attention." This is the Rowena who approached speakers after their talks, congratulating—by revealing her "almost-total agreement" with—them, then, opening her rucksack, depositing a pile of "related" rowenian offprints. Few heterosexual males were immune to the flattery of this vulpine blonde a quarter-inch of muzzle away from beauty; and not a few found themselves—sometimes within hours of their presentation—propelled by her muscular legs into more intimate awareness of her powers. That this physical and psychic prodigality did not advance her more rapidly in the profession was due to the cruel telegraphy of academic gossip. It took Rowena years of—to her—incomprehensible setbacks to realize that she'd better turn down the burners.

6.

The moral significance of love was Rowena's great theme. She was devotee, practitioner, and explainer of love: "I was so lost in passion, I couldn't work. . . . I lay across John Krylchek's belly thinking about Hume. . . . My ex-husband, the journalist, Eddy Dortmund, looked at me disconcertingly; he had no idea what I was getting at." (Maybe not then, Rowena.)

In copulation, Rowena lost herself—or at least her partner—in the topology, mechanics, and acoustics of love. There were strategic scratches, programmatic bites, timed slaps. One was here, there, on the edge, on the floor. There were hums, screeches, arias, moans. A museum, a parade, a curriculum. It didn't, however, take long to graduate. Within weeks, I realized that this *professeuse d'amour* was so deeply self-directed, self-involved, self-important, and self-centered that, fucking and being fucked by her, I felt not a tithe of what I felt with Jean (and other women I've known). Rowena had flickers of attentiveness, flickers of pleasure, flickers of amusement, flickers of excitement, but not a second of whatever it is which gives as it receives, receives as it gives.

7.

*Collège de France* lectures are open to the public. I walked over to the Rue des Écoles, beating my way through clouds of Gaulois fumes, and sat in the back of the auditorium. It is a high-backed shell of a room, and the back, where I sat, was not far enough from the podium. My row was just about eye-level with the speaker. It didn't disturb me, partly because I thought it unlikely that Rowena would recognize me. The fifteen or twenty pounds that I've put on since I last saw her at her lawyer's office had gone not just to my middle, but my cheeks, and my mustache and head were now gray. Besides, Rowena was myopic.

When she entered, I turned away, just in case. The lights were on during her talk, and we were on the same level, but I didn't believe that she'd see or recognize me from the podium, and if, by some rowenian power, intuitive or pheremonic, she did, what of it? Why not give her the small pleasure of an ex-husband's homage?

The lecture was "Love's Spontaneity and Surprise" and dealt—as far as I followed—with the mental agility which love energized, the on-your-toes readiness to deal not only with a lover's least word and gesture but the enlarged attentiveness to the world which love supplied. "For lovers, everything is surprising, but nothing is a surprise. . . . Spontaneity, a freshness, an originality of both action and reaction, word and audition, is the genius of love. It is the reason so much art, so much insight and so much invention occur in love's zone." This is what I jotted down as Rowena semi-sang the words in the hoarsely melodious voice that had not much changed since I'd first heard it thirty-odd years ago. Its cadence and paratactic balance seemed to mesmerize most listeners, so that even those who understood as little as I did of her talks often said that they'd been enchanted by them. I, though, had long ago broken the spell of Rowena's voice and syntax. Then, too, I was busying myself with the contradiction of her paean to spontaneity and her own nature, the least spontaneous, most doggedly, nervously, even fanatically unspontaneous I know.

Years before the answering machine appeared on everyone's table, Rowena had found ways of avoiding the surprises of telephone calls. Anybody who was in her apartment knew that it was his job to pick up the phone and screen her calls. And her friends and relatives also knew that Rowena was to call them, not they her. So with doorbells: even the UPS man knew he should leave packages at the door if no one answered the initial ring. Rowena would no more go to the door without her makeup than the queen of England would open Parliament in shorts. Rowena would not participate in a seminar or conference unless the papers or questions were submitted beforehand in writing. As for any spontaneous or surprising movement from her night's partner in passion, Rowena would check it with, "Keep that for the zoo."

In the middle of some section to which I was not paying attention, I heard my own name and saw Rowena's sleeveless—still rather beautiful—arm tossed over rows of heads and heard something to the effect that "The attendance of those we used to love, and who loved us, has the force of involuntary memory, the vividness of that past which is, as Proust and Faulkner taught us, not only not past, but more vital, more pure, more profound and powerful than the confusing, buzzing, encompassing present." And then, blowing a kiss with her fingers across the swiveling heads, she said, "Thank you for being here, dear Eddie."

Even as I shrank from the exposure, I knew that somehow or other, she'd been prepared for either my presence or that of someone else from that past which is not past. Had someone told her I was in Paris? Had she, or a friend, seen me in the street? I had no idea. All I know is that she'd supplied her audience, all but one member of it, with the "spontaneous" intimacy that guaranteed the success of this initial lecture. The rest of the talk I did not hear. I was sunk in anger, then in debate about what to do about it. Should I leave immediately or should I just go up to Rowena, wait for her admirers to disappear, and take her for an apéritif and whatever might follow?

8.

The arm, not quite so lovely up close, shorn gray bristles in the pit and flaps of unsustained flesh where there had been fullness, was flung my way and ready for embrace or a handshake. "Eddie, what a fine surprise. How good of you," and, as I shook limp fingers, "If I'd known, we could have had a Cinzano. Give me your number."

"What a shame, Row," I said. "I'm on assignment."

"Here?"

"Afraid not. This was pure self-indulgence, a nostalgic detour."

The blue eyes, not quite so dense under the dyed gold mop, took in the lie as I intended they should. "Ah yes, self-indulgence," she said with a lilt of melodious menace. "Another time, another place."

9.

That was the last time I saw Rowena, although, as I said, two years later, I did see her picture within the obituary headlined "Philosopher Plotnik Struck By Bus After Jog in Central Park." That the most spontaneous event of Rowena's life was its final one moved me more than I'd have guessed.

# II

# PLACES

*Many writers, some of them travelers, some not, are identified with different parts of the map. Their readers tend to visit these places. Although much of what the writer described is gone, the description rebuilds the place for the haunted reader. Hundreds of writers since Dickens have described London, and God knows there's precious little left of the city Dickens knew, but more travelers today go in quest of Dickens's London than, say, that of Margaret Drabble or Martin Amis. Ditto for Joyce's Dublin or Faulkner's half-mythical Mississippi.*

*Those for whom place is crucial feel that an undescribed one is somehow incomplete. In the summer of 1966, when we were teaching together in Buffalo, the Northumbrian poet (as he called himself), Basil Bunting, showed me a letter he'd just written to Ezra Pound urging him to come back to America from Italy "because there are so many underdescribed places here waiting for you to describe them."*

*Much powerful place writing comes from exiles hanging on to the places of their past for dear life. (Joyce's Dublin was reconstructed in Trieste and Zurich.) For some writers, only new places are written about, sometimes more richly in travel writing than in fiction. I don't think it matters much where Dostoevsky's novels and stories take place, but his vitriolic account of Paris is a comic wonder. There are brilliant flashes of place in Henry James's fiction, Paris in* The Ambassadors, *Venice in* The Wings of the Dove, *but it's in his travel essays that you'll find most of his energetic place writing.*

*In my own fiction, place is as important as, say, occupation is in Malamud's. Part of this has to do with the fact that I've spent most of my adult life in Chicago and the first twenty-seven years of it elsewhere. Until I went away to school in North Carolina when I was six-*

teen, I lived in New York and have deeper feelings for its streets, parks, and apartment houses than for those of the Chicago I also love. Another part has to do with the wanderlust which gripped me sixty years ago and which, even now, is part of me. Reading was its source: none of my friends traveled and my parents' account of their single 1935 week in Paris did not thrill me. I first went abroad as a Fulbright scholar in 1949 when I was twenty-one. After three years in Europe, I spent ten in the United States getting a doctorate and working as an instructor and assistant professor to support a family on low wages, so there was no money for travel except to towns where I lectured for a few extra dollars. Since then, I've spent about a tenth of my life abroad, mostly in Europe, but also in Africa, Asia, Latin America, Australia, the Caribbean, and the Pacific. I like to feel that I'm at home more or less anywhere in the world, although of course I know that I'm less equipped than most people to handle solitary time in foreign or, for that matter, domestic wilderness or ocean. That is, on most of the earth's surface, I wouldn't be at home at all.

The largest section of "Places" is on Chicago, the city in which I've spent most of my adult life.

# Where the Chips Fall

MARCH 2000. LOS ALTOS, CALIFORNIA.
Oh for a tithe of Gogol's ability to describe places before and after such changes as the stationing of a regiment in a sour, somnolent, dusty village where a cart drawn by a grim nag or a hen crossing a road on eight inches of piled dust was an event.

The Santa Clara County village incorporated as Los Altos in 1952 was, if not sour, dusty and somnolent, little more than the scarcely inhabited valley beside the Los Altos hills to which Paul Shoup, a Southern Pacific executive, offered San Franciscans, just recovering from the terrible earthquake, free railroad excursions and picnics by the tracks. By 1911, there were fifty homes and a few office buildings in the area. After World War II, this Valley of Heart's Delight—the promotional name—grew, but the "regiment" which transformed it and the rest of the peninsula between San Francisco and San Jose was the silicon chip

Silicon Valley is as mythical—and as real—as Combray or Yoknapatwapha County, as Dickens's London, Joyce's Dublin, Bellow's Chicago. The heart of its young heart is daily sounded in the *Palo Alto Daily News*'s "100," the stock list of the leading technology companies, of which 60 are based in it. From Acuson PA (Palo Alto) and Catalytica MV (Mountain View), through Informix MP (Menlo Park) and Microcide MV to Sun Micro PA, and Veritas MV, the list stands for a concentration of technical genius and financial power that makes the Ruhr Valley of the 1930s or the blast furnaces and storage tanks in crescent around lower Lake Michigan in the 1950s seem like gigantesque, obstreperous, overgrown industrial humps of flaming filth.

Los Altos, where this writer is living for a charmed year as an odd-man-out literary fellow of the Stanford-based Center for Advanced Study in the Behavioral Sciences, is one of the quieter, more elegant precincts of this valley. From 1960 to the present, its population has risen from just under twenty thousand to under thirty while the county population has more than doubled to 1.7 or 1.8 million. The mean income of its more than ten thousand households is $140,000, the average price of a three-bedroom, two-bathroom condominium $800,000—and soaring. Rents are intergalactic: the latest reported in the scandalous lingua franca, Domicilese, is $6,500 a month for a pleasant hacienda in a gentrifying section near Mountain View. (Rented by two married law professors, a successful appeal was made to the Stanford Law School to almost double its usual housing subsidy of $3,000 a month for it.) In his final State of the University address, Gerhard Casper, the marvelous president of Stanford these past eight years, spoke of the menace housing costs were to the recruitment of graduate students, professors, and staff. The effect on the already subverted California public schools is even greater.

Blue-and-white metal signs affixed to streetlight posts declare that Los Altos is a Street Watch Community in which any suspicious person or event will be immediately reported to a Police Department fortified with "the latest in Mobile Data Terminals," a "fully customizable public safety software system that provides wireless access to national, state and local data-bases, priority dispatching, incident report, car to car and dispatch messaging and more!" This software, along with the efforts of the newly acquired police dog, Disco, seems to be doing its job well. The *Palo Alto Daily News* Police Blotter reports such heinous crimes as "Transient arrested for public drunkenness in front of Borders Books," "Noisy dispute between mother and daughter near le Boulanger," and—what is the place coming to!—"Computer hardware missing from a software firm." Indeed, much police work seems to be a quest for police work. So a friend of mine, a distinguished economist, reports that he was recently "ticketed and fined over $100 for making a right turn without stopping at an isolated corner" near his condominium "though there was no vehicle or pedestrian in sight." He was on a bicycle.

Twenty-five restaurants—French, German, Italian, Japanese, Chinese, Mexican, American, and Cosy—flourish in the flowering tree- and bench-lined streets. Somewhat less crowded than their cousins in Palo Alto, Redwood City, and Menlo Park, they flourish because the population of entrepreneurs, technicians, Stanford faculty, and retired seniors has neither time nor inclination to prepare home dinners and is looking for any way to spend its growing fortunes. Draegers, the Jockey Club of supermarkets, does, however, offer gourmet take-outs as well as seventy brands of olive oil, a tundra of imported cheese, a massif of California and imported wines and micro-brewery beer, and to me, most tempting of all, twenty types of bread warm from valley bakeries.

Regiments and such other Gogolian worms in village tranquility as the quarrels of longtime neighbors or their suddenly wakened martial or marital ambitions are as antiquated in this sleek and silent valley as the abacus, but worms there are. Technology companies may not be labor-intensive and do not devour the carbon fuels which in the old industrial revolution befouled the planet's air and water, but their widely distributed prosperity generates tremendous individual hunger for luxury, amusement, transportation, and service, the satisfaction of which generates further demand. So the traffic thickens and the gorgeous green hills erupt with palaces and palatial complexes. A labor shortage—unemployment is a semi-mythical 1.6 percent—has created an often delightfully insouciant, occasionally sullen and dismissive service class. So in the Safeway market where we usually shop, a sweetly daffy young woman, before tabulating my purchases, opens my *San Francisco Chronicle* to read her horoscope and bemoans that its prediction of an amorous evening is, given her manless life, unlikely; her delight in my wish that I were forty years younger and could supply the need eases the mounting savagery of the six patrons waiting behind me.

Indeed, the patience threshold at gas pumps and checkout lines here seems to this Chicagoan exceptionally low. Can it be that the sense—as they say—of entitlement in the new rich is unmodified by their awareness that those around them may be ten or a thousand times richer yet?

But where are the rich rich of this fabled valley? I can't tell the difference between designer and ordinary t-shirts, and billionaires can drive only one Lexus at a time. Has the twenty-something t-shirted Pakistani American sitting with the gorgeous Korean American girl at a corner table just scored nine hundred million dollars in an IPO or is he spending a hundred or two hundred dollars for dinner as the 1950s "man in the gray flannel suit" put his last savings into a necktie that might clinch a job interview? Or is she buying the dinner, part of her interview with him for a job in the company she started last month? Did he or she arrive by skateboard or Lexus, and which mode of arrival would signal their status? There's nothing in the manner, clothes, voice, gestures, or company which tips off this reporter to bank account, occupation, or mode of life.

(Henry James would be as distressed here as he was by the absence of striking distinctions in the United States of the 1860s and 1870s.)

Occasionally a friend will encounter one of the comparatively venerable wealthy, a Packard, say (not the old car but the family), who complains that his foundation controls only 11 percent—a billion or so dollars' worth—of the company wealth. Another friend, who rents a charming Atherton house—pool, sauna, riding ring—from an osteopath's assistant who's in Malaga living on the rentals, told the mother of one of his daughter's public school classmates that his car was in the shop and was casually invited to use "one of the Porsches in the barn, the keys are hanging on the board." A Woodside family erected a three-story haunted house for their son's ninth birthday party. By their deeds, ye shall know them. Perhaps. In any event, ye shall not know them by look, voice, dress, vehicle.

A DEMOCRACY OF PLUTOCRATS

This form of society does not show up in Plato's *Republic*. (Will Plato be confused one day with Palo Alto as Ford and Freud were fused in Huxley's dystopia?) Or perhaps the locals should be called Cavalier Democrats. A sign in the launderette on Los Altos's main street reads "Please do not wash horse blankets in machines." This is not a problem for my wife and me, but bicycling the hills here does pose problems of chivalry: the bike lanes may well be occupied by horses as—at least financially—distant from Gogol's nags as they are from us prole cyclists.

≈≈

As I write this little report in February, the sun is glittering on the bushes, and cherry blossoms are waving from yards and roads. (It's as if a convention of beautiful girls has been airlifted into town.) A rainbow—why not?—arcs over the soft, lapping hills. Below, the Hoover Tower stands over the Stanford campus, the concrete axis of world-transforming, Stanford-centered ingenuity. Does it evoke that affection for one's village bell tower that Italians call *campanelismo*? I suppose so, although the tower is not part of a structure dedicated to transients' imploration of the Eternal but houses one of the most conservative research institutions in the world, whose often first-rate and Nobel-winning scholars champion market theories sprung in the year of the American Revolution from the brain of the Scottish moralist Adam Smith. This suggests deference to

Beneficent rather than Benevolent Destiny, a kind of reasoned Luck which is probably the proper logo of Silicon Valley, whose prosperity and Tuscan beauty sit atop one of the hugest and least stable of earthly faults.*

* Ah, fortuna! "Silicon Valley is a train wreck," reported a dot-com CEO in the April 7, 2001, *New York Times.*

*I've been playing tennis for sixty-five years and am about as good now as I was my second or third year. In the middle years, I was somewhat better, so that when a small portion of this Wimbledon piece appeared in the* Chicago Tribune, *the by-line indicated that my ranking was 1,345,262. I realize now that that ranking was too high.*

*I will not add footnotes to this piece. Many things have changed in the nine years since. Two days before I write this note (January 29, 2001), Jennifer Capriati won her first grand slam tournament, beating the ingenious and dogged Martina Hingis in straight sets. Jennifer was cheered on by her father, who, speaking to a reporter before the match, talked of the ineradicable scar left in their family by the sad events which followed the tournament reported here: the 1993 citation for shoplifting a ring from a Tampa kiosk, the 1994 arrest for possession of marijuana, the abandonment of and then return to "the tour," and the difficult climb back to the top ten. To someone who remembered the exhausted child of 1992, the triumph in Melbourne was cheering.*

*As for England's climb back from the post-thatcherian grimness of 1992, that is a more complicated story, one beyond my competence to describe.*

## Wimbledon, 1992

1.

If, like me, you know Wimbledon only on television, you don't know it. You know an airless abstraction, a moving picture lumpy with dramatic close-ups and indigestible commentary. The tension, pace, grace, the look, smell, feel, and noise of the actual event are different.

Pace. Take the two worst of the 128 male singles competitors, and watch them warm up. You can't believe the speed of their drives whipping two inches from the net cord, the clear *bung* of racket on ball, the silence of the bounce on grass. Balls are scooped off this green silence like thread picked off a carpet. And what a carpet. (Are ten thousand nearsighted midgets with magnifying glasses and razorblades employed to cut every grass blade to the correct millimeter?)

As for the serves, you haven't seen anything. I mean you almost don't see them. Not just those of the big servers, Ivanisevic, Sampras, Rosset. Take anyone, Thoms, Pescosolido, Grabbe, Boetsch, Zoeke. Never heard of them? No, and probably never will, unless you're a devotee of the fine print of early-round losers. But here, watching them serve, you think, "This guy's the next champ. Who can return his service?"

Anyone here can. The reaction time of these players, the coordination of eye, arm, and that part of the brain that says, "Drive it out of reach," constitute an intelligence unrecorded on IQ tests. The unreturnable service is smashed into an unreachable corner of the green rectangle, where it's scooped up and crashed crosscourt into some other unreachable place, where . . . and so on.

What television doesn't register is the labor and strain of this serving, returning, smashing, angling, dropping. These players aren't playing. They're working. Their faces are grim, tense. They breathe hard, they sweat, and like Monica Seles, the Great Grunter, they grunt, groan, heave, sigh, squeal.

Remember that bubbling, joyous child, Jennifer Capriati. At sixteen, her face is dense with age and struggle. Her great shoulders carry the world on them, the world of expectation and frustration, victory and defeat, defeat of and defeat by other unchildish children, deprived of childhood by money-hunger and publicity, ambulatory conglomerates whose lips are still stained with mother's milk.

Twenty-five of the 128 women competitors here, many of them teenagers, already have earned more than $1 million from tennis alone. Martina (this was before the appearance of Navratilova's namesake and usurper, Hingis)—like mountains, the great ones have only one name—has earned $17 million and God and Peat Marwick alone know how many more in endorsements, cars, silver trophies, and freebies. So when you see these children from all over the world (fifty-five countries were represented in the 1992 tournament), you're seeing human money machines.

These machines are ballerinas, athletes, and competitors of tremendous will, skill, discipline, and endurance. Just being here means they're winners, yet all but eight of them, two singles and three doubles winners, will leave as losers. Every one of them has suffered enough defeat to put most of us on the couch for life, but they go on, tournament after tournament, year after year, winning and losing, at least those whose knees and shoulders don't buckle, whose backs and hearts don't break, whose heads don't burn out in the fierce tennis tropic. (That graybeard of American tennis commentary, Bud Collins, told me that Papa Capriati told him that Jennifer might burn out, but she would be a rich burnout, fixed for life.)

Television also deprives you of the setting of these matches. I don't mean the ivy on the Centre Court walls, the green and purple ballet of the ball boys and girls, the croquet court amidst the white picket-fenced garden enclosures where international corporations entertain clients, the green-jacketed officials guiding you with courteous firmness to just those seats where *you* can sit, the midway of marquees where you buy and eat Dutchies (hot dogs), drink champagne and Pimms, and spoon up seven strawberries in Devonshire cream (for $3.50), but all the movements, noises, smells, and feelings, your own climb to a seat, your neighbors' breath, the heat, the wind, everything that sets off and contrasts with the flashing super movements of the athletes constructing in front of your eyes the way they're going to beat each other's brains out. And there's the ceremony: the ritual of the change of linesmen, the offering of the ball boys and girls—arms extended, yellow ball wristed to the player at a nod—the calls of the umpire ("Time." "Play."), the metal click of the scoring board, the players in white shirts and shorts. All this sets off— and veils—the combat.

Even matches recorded as "routine" or "a straight-set victory" are usually far tougher combats than those words suggest. I watched Ivan Lendl, playing with brilliance and power, come within five crucial points of losing to a twenty-one-year-old German named Arne Thomas who walks like a Skid Row bum but is as quick and savage as a tiger on the court.

2.

Anyway, here you are in this beautiful little theme park of English Privilege, eight miles southwest of Trafalgar Square. Lloyds of London has lost $2 billion this year, Sheffield steel is no more, United Newspaper is ending *Punch*, the London Zoo is threatened, the royal family's in even more trouble than yours and mine, and England has every possible industrial and postindustrial disease. But Wimbledon, *Wimbledon* is flourishing.

The tanned, blue-eyed faces of the county families are in their old seats snooting it over the rest of us while we watch these superb, expensive athletes enact allegories of struggle and survival intended to recall that England's "green and pleasant land" is still the England of Marlborough and Churchill, Shakespeare and Newton, Dunkirk and Agincourt.

### 3. 🐝 GETTING THERE

In the first place, There isn't There. That is, Wimbledon—the Lawn Tennis Championship—isn't in Wimbledon. At least, the tube station is neither Wimbledon nor Wimbledon Park, but Southfields. (Wimbledon—from *Wubba Dun,* place of the Saxons—was the old site of the tournaments.) The name, though, Wimbledon, now has the resonance of Lourdes, Campostella, or Canterbury, a place to which pilgrims come because of ancient sacrifice and miracle. Wimbledon differs from those places in that sacrifice and miracle are reenacted at the same time every year. Perhaps that's why some of its pilgrims are more intensely devout than most of those Chaucer put on the way to Canterbury.

Wimbledon is more Disneyland than Canterbury, although the Disney pilgrims, like Canterbury worshippers, are more than gawkers. In Walt's sacred precinct, the pilgrims are also the players. And, too, Wimbledon is harder for ordinary people to penetrate. Entrance involves that stoical English form of genuflection to life's difficulties, the queue. For hours and hours, Wimbledon pilgrims stand on a slowly moving line hundreds of yards long, waiting five, six, or seven hours for luckier ticket-holders to leave and make room for them. As they approach the gate, they become a more intimate part of the day's events: public address systems relay accounts of the matches; touts, leaning on signs warning against them, offer to buy—and thus, covertly, to sell—tickets; police and Wimbledon security people maintain the lines; late editions of the *Mail* and *Mirror* report the matches and gossip of the morning.

Eleven thousand general admission tickets at £6 are put on sale every day. These do not admit you to either Centre Court or Court No. 1, but they still leave God's plenty to watch on seventeen other courts. Each day the crowd is larger, movement from court to court slower, official calls for "Silence, please" more frequent. Many spend time at the shops, purchasing expensive t-shirts and sun visors, eating, drinking, gabbing, ogling the beautiful, rich, and famous. The worshipful, bovine stoics stand behind the white rail in front of the Centre Court entrance to watch seeded players escorted to and from dressing rooms and matches. Those on the lists of companies renting marquee space drink, eat, gossip, and do business in their fenced enclaves. The largest and most exclusive enclave is for the members of the Lawn Tennis Association, many of whom wear their green blazers. Occasionally they take reserved seats to watch a set or two, but until the quarter final rounds, few sit out a whole match. As the days go on, the green of the jackets, more sober than the bright grass of the courts or the burnt richness of the ivy, drabber than the sleeves of the ball boys and girls, takes on, with the other official color, mauve, a ludic power, symbolic of this system of controlled excitement, an assurance that the combat of the players will not seriously challenge tradition. Like so much else in English life, Wimbledon allows the ordinary person a sense that he can purchase privilege, as long as he doesn't stretch it. With my press badge, I, too, felt the pleasant twinge of privilege and superiority: while others waited on lines, I was admitted. But for every twinge of such pleasure, there was a pinch of resentment: my badge read "Rover," which meant that I was not a full-fledged reporter. If I wanted to go to Centre Court or Court No. 1, I had to go back to the Press Office to pick up a special ticket, and that could be taken away if there were not enough seats for the reporters who described the matches in daily dispatches. I could pass from superiority to inferiority in seconds, more or less like a player who can lose caste with one swish of his racket. A winner, he goes on to the next round, to money, coverage, rating points; a loser, he packs his stuff and waits for the next tournament. One afternoon, on the Southfields platform, I stood next to a fine-looking, ebony-colored teenager in tennis whites being consoled by his Caucasian coach. The coach took a notebook from his pocket, consulted it, and said, "Friday, Singapore. One night. Then Bangkok." Multitudinous miles would wash out the stain of a first-round Wimbledon loss. A match here, an exhibition there, a tournament, a win, a few more points on the computer, and before you knew it, Wimbledon would roll round again.

The crowds didn't have this worry. For them, Wimbledon was not only a fine outing but a class endorsement. Thousands of Englishmen, colonials, ex-colonials, and foreigners managed to say, "I was at Wimbledon" or "I saw Budge beat Von Cramm back in" whenever. The charming, spirited girl who spent fifty-odd hours a week behind the desk of my shabbily genteel hotel in Earl's Court had been to Wimbledon two years earlier and felt that my daily trip there brought luster to her and the hotel. (She arranged for me to use the hotel typewriter and fax machine for my two dispatches to the *Chicago Tribune*.) After going to Wimbledon, an Englishman doesn't add a suffix to his name, as a pilgrim to Mecca adds *haj*, but there is some of the same sense of separation from inferiors, and it appears on the spectrum of pride somewhere between passing an A-level and finding a £5 note in the gutter.

4.

Wimbledon is not only an expression of English class and privilege, it is itself a sort of English class machine. Within the twelve playing days of "the fortnight," the pre-selected tennis players eliminate each other in the struggle for position, power, money, and celebrity. At the end, there is a king of men's singles, a queen of women's singles, and royal dukes and duchesses of doubles. Many millions of people around the world are absorbed in these semi-mythic struggles. Very few annual events are reported so widely, and each year the players become more and more familiar, as they are absorbed in the greatest and most inevitable human story: growth, maturation, and defeat, spiced with the subsidiary stories of comeback, burnout, and senatorial wisdom. Each nation has special interests, and it may be that Wimbledon not only reenacts but actually transfigures national imagery. It could be said that the triumphs of the young German players, Boris Becker and Steffi Graf, in the late 1980s enabled many to accept the old enemy of World Wars I and II as a partner in the new Europe. The Germans had been Wimbledonized.

Wimbledon is a way of making foreigners English. In recent tennis history, some foreign players have expressed resentment at chivvying formalities and regulations. They have been taken for a ride by the English gutter press, been broken and then remade by it. Two of the four recent finalists, André Agassi and Monica Seles, turned up their noses at Wimbledon, refused to play in the tournament, and were made to feel that they were not complete tennis players. In 1992 they spent time trying to explain their defection, and at least Agassi won the affection of the tennis-loving (at least tennis-attentive) public.

The best known such rebel was John McEnroe. His absence from Wimbledon ceremonies, his sulky reluctance about complying with others, his "un-English" complaints and curses, made him a devil hated by people in England who knew nothing else about tennis. He was one of the people to whom English newspaper readers had an immediate reaction, usually negative, often furious. But for years McEnroe has been a has-been, that is, someone one can pity instead of hate and envy. He's also softened. He not only submits to the conventions he used to despise, he instructs younger players in them. The Wimbledon Process turned him into an angel. In 1992, no one but England's Jeremy Bates received more support from the fans. The bad boy in McEnroe was—to borrow the ancient papal pun about the English—Anglicized and angelicized. Now he has a special place, that of the American free to express English resentment of class rigidity. The people calling out his name are not saying "John," but "Jawn." He is the idol of "the yobs," anti-hero of the 1992 tournament.

Let's see him in action. In Round Three, after a magnificent match with his pal and act-alike, Pat Cash, the Australian, he played the almost unknown Alexei Olkhovskiy, who'd come from the Nowheresville of the qualifying rounds (from which the seventeen-year-old McEnroe had come in 1977). Two days earlier, Olkhovskiy had decapitated—no, better, dispatched—the number one seed, Jim Courier. McEnroe knew he might be in for a tough match. With the spigots of his rage and brilliance open all the way, McEnroe let him have it.

First, he arrived five minutes late and through the wrong entrance. Then, warming up, he hit a few beauties out of the Russian's reach. The match started. Mac zinged a terrific backhand at Olkhovskiy's head. Olkhovskiy put it away, a winner. Okay, so that's what Mac's up against. Olkhovskiy started to serve. Mac held up his hand, tossed his head at something in the stands and spoke to the umpire. The umpire, a deferential gentleman named Sultan Ganji, politely requested an astonished woman behind Olkhovskiy to stop fanning herself. Olkhovskiy double faulted. Still, he won the game, and they were even on service. McEnroe felt the heat, not the sun's 90 degrees, but the heat of someone trying to take over what he owned, this tennis court, this match. He threw his racket on the ground, then threw it against the canvas court cover close to the knees of the first-row spectators (including this one). Code violation? Not from Mr. Ganji, who would as soon have told the queen that she'd passed wind as to cite the furious ex-champion for an abuse. Including abuse to him, for McEnroe told him, "You're not doing your job." The job for McEnroe meant the enforcement of absolute silence on the court. You'd think McEnroe was doing theoretical physics. He cannot bear noise, even the cheers of his supporters. He yelled for silence in the "peanut gallery." Then, amazingly, he told himself to shut up. Yes, himself. He'd opened the second set with a double fault and said, "That's a fine way to start." Then, walking back to the service line, he told himself, "Shut up, for God's sake." Astonishing.

What Olkhovskiy, the umpire, the linesmen, ball girls, and fans were seeing and hearing—all of us had been yelled at—was a half-mad competitor driving himself and letting himself be driven to—but never over—the brink.

More. McEnroe let himself display his rage because such a display is a tactical part of his game. As modern architects often don't conceal a building's shafts and tubes with steel and concrete skin but display and color them, so McEnroe's display of rage and hatred is a structural part of his game. It certainly helped wear down Olkhovskiy, who finally realized it and requested Mr. Ganji to cite McEnroe for "racket abuse." Turned down, he took it fatalistically: "They don't cite stars." In the press conference (where he's also expert, self-deprecating, amusing, caustic), McEnroe approved of Olkhovskiy's complaint: "He was looking for an edge." (The day before, Baroness Thatcher, a sort of McEnroe in skirts, hadn't been as generous to John Major in her interview with David Frost about Maastricht.)

Compare McEnroe to the British hero of the 1992 championship. This was Jeremy Bates, the 109th-ranked player in the world. A brave sport who looks like a bastard brother of Prince Charles (by the kitchen slavey) and who has the mildness, competence, and decency of John Major, Bates played "out of himself" and beat players far ahead of him in the rankings. England was enchanted. Here was the heroic bloke, back against the wall, showing the world what the ordinary Englishman could do.

What he could do was lose the way an Englishman loses: graciously. For a week, though, Bates was a dream of himself, playing marvelously (perhaps stimulated by the prospect of marriage a month after the tournament). He was Prince Hal in his *Henry V* incarnation, beating back the insulting tennis balls sent him by the Dauphin. His third opponent was French, Thierry Champion. Bates triumphed while the stands and the country went wild. The next Frenchman, though, was seeded, and his marvelously English-French name was Guy Forget. Born in Casablanca, Forget was not about to do the Humphrey Bogart thing and let the gallant hero take off for the quarterfinal match with McEnroe. For two and a half sets, Bates had Forget on the ropes. One serve would have done it. He threw up the ball—and let it drop. In the press conference afterward, he said, "I heard a sneeze or something." Thrown off, he served a dumpling. Forget murdered it. Deuce. Two points later, a Forget drive hit the net cord and hopped over Bates's racket. In the fifth set, Forget wiped him out (only to lose in the next round to an especially diabolical McEnroe).

Said Bates in his press conference, "The example I have set for British tennis is that the whole thing is mental. Anybody can do it if they believe in themselves."

The BBC ended the day's coverage with a montage of great Bates moments, the victories over Michael Chang, Javier Sanchez, and Thierry Champion. On the audio, Elgar's "Land of Hope and Glory" lolly-popped away.

5.

A few spectators come to Wimbledon as if they're going to play on the courts themselves. They're wearing white shorts, tennis shirts, expensive sneakers. Some of them carry rackets. A very attractive costume it is, and many players are exceptionally attractive specimens. An extraordinary number are blonde. Perhaps it has to do with hair bleaching in the sunny climate of the game. Despite the notorious remark of the Dutch player Richard Krajicek that "80 percent of the women players are fat, lazy pigs," these athletes, men and women both, are exceptionally fit and well built. Many have star looks as well, and champions, whom one may re-gard as odd or homely at the beginning of their careers, in time establish themselves as new ideals of beauty. (In her autobiography, Chris Evert speaks of growing up conscious of being unattractive. After four or five years, the Chrissy look was another beauty standard.)

I speak here for the *homme moyen sensuel*. There is clearly an erotic el-ement in the attraction of women's tennis. Krajicek's remark—for which he wasn't bright or mature enough to apologize properly, giggling that he meant that only 75 percent of the women were pigs and that he was re-ally angry about their thinking that they should be paid as much as men players—points to this erotic component of tennis. I doubt that few men are not aware of the legs and breasts, shoulders and rear ends of the women players as they stretch and bend and run. The physiology of the game arouses physiological as well as athletic responses in the onlookers. The breathing, the perspiration, the cries, grunts, and squeals come out of the same physical repertoire as those of sex and love. The combat itself is erotically rousing. Many athletic contests see the athletes uni-formed, their bodies disguised with pads and other protective gear. Oth-ers reveal so much of the body that there's little to hope for, to be surprised about. Tennis, with its virginal whites, ever briefer over its hundred-year history, still veils "the private parts," still *suggests*.

Then there is its combination of grace and strength. There are hun-dreds of beautiful moves in tennis. Many of them are rituals—showing new balls to your opponent—and the tension between these formal movements and that extra exertion, even if clumsy, which wins points, is as thrilling as such moves are in love-making.

I don't say that eros is a major component of a good match, especially a good quarter-, semi- or final match, but it is in the Wimbledon air. These young, nubile athletes, some of them rich and famous, all of them hungry to be, create a romantic soup out of which emerge the exciting struggles.

## 6.

Tennis was introduced to England by a good French poet who was also a French prince and the father of Louis XII. Charles D'Orléans was captured at the Battle of Agincourt in 1415 and spent the next twenty-five years in England. At one of his residences, he had a tennis court laid out. Back then, it was a handball game, a *jeu de paume*. Tennis remained a royal or noble game for most of its existence. At some point, though, rackets were introduced, for by the time *Henry V* appeared on the stage in about 1600 (the date of the bad quarto), rackets were part of the game.

> When we have matched our rackets to these balls,
> We will in France, by God's grace, play a set
> Shall strike his father's crown into the hazard.

(Hazard: a goal-like opening.)

Modern tennis was invented and patented by one Major Wingate, who returned from India intent on creating a game which could be played by both men and women. Three years after the patent, the Wimbledon tournaments began.

A century later, the Wimbledon Machine is a remarkable and complex assemblage, an expensive and carefully detailed production, a Festspiel, like Oberammergau's. The difference here is that the tournament producers don't know who the stars will be. The similarity is that it doesn't matter. The champions have different names; all are engraved on walls, in silver, in books, but what counts beyond this year's winner is Wimbledon itself, the idea of the tournament, the English tournament waged by athletes trained not only to perform physical marvels but to be representatives of the English idea of winning.

This, of course, involves hypocrisy. Under the celebrated Kipling quotation which urges the good sport to treat victory and defeat as "similar impostors," Wimbledon promotes purity and virtue. White is the costume, sportsmanship the mode, deference the attitude. And, sure enough, one player after another buys the credo, wears the white costume, bows to the Duke and Duchess of Kent, and suppresses or sublimates the competitive rage and hatred in his or her heart.

In our democratic age, the exclusive old game, once played by kings and princes,* has, like so much of its aesthetic equivalent, *Masterpiece Theatre*, been shaped by its feudal notions of class. As knights in tournament were concealed by their armor, so the white costumes of Wimbledon conceal the class and, usually, the ethnic and religious background of the players. It is their skill and valor which will knight them.

Unlike theater, which depends for much of its glory on language, tennis, like music, crosses national boundaries. For spectators who don't require the violence of body-contact sports, it is the sport which best sublimates the competitive ferocity worked up by rage, envy, resentment, hatred, and sheer bafflement at life's insults and injuries. In the past quarter-century, tennis tournaments have become increasingly popular. Popularity has fattened the purses, and the fat purses have increased the popularity (in part because they have brought more and more excellent athletes into the game). Yet more than any other popular game, tennis is saturated by class. It is a climber's game, whose rituals and courteous performance standards are modeled on those of the British upper class, the English public schoolboys and girls who became "our hunting fathers" and remote mothers. Despite the occasional Nastase, early Connors, and McEnroe, it's unlikely that tennis will see a Mike Tyson, an athlete who crosses the boundaries of his sport to act with some of the same ferocity outside as in it.

So far there haven't been any drug scandals on the tennis tour. The game's skills aren't enhanced by drugs or bodybuilding steroids. The game requires eye-hand coordination, fluid and controlled power, and, more and more, strength and endurance. (Even with tiebreakers, tennis games are theoretically endless.) A Wimbledon singles champion has to play seven matches in fourteen days. No other major sport sets so great a

---

* As the royal Prince Albert, George VI played in a first-round doubles match at Wimbledon. An excellent social player, he was outclassed by the quasi-professional amateurs and was so humiliated by the experience that—my guess is—it soured his beloved eldest daughter, Queen Elizabeth II, on the sport. Her only recent appearance at Wimbledon was at its centennial, when, fortunately, the women's singles title was won by her countrywoman Virginia Wade.

test of endurance. It is a tribute to the supervision of the governing bodies that the game has altered so little since Major Wingate started it.
Rackets, balls, costumes, and even scoring have been somewhat altered,
but not the brains and physiques of the players.

Although there are many indoor tournaments and exhibitions, tennis
is essentially an outdoor game. The Tour goes on all year, but in northern
winters, it goes to temperate, tropical places. The brief outfits don't
change, although slacks and sweaters are worn on the rare cold days.
(The subject of many Charles D'Orléans poems is the "pleasant time" of
year when "le temps a laissé son manteau du vent, du froideur et de
pluie," that is, tennis weather.) Boxing, a sport which exposes even more
of the body, used to be staged outdoors, but more recent outdoor fights
such as the Ali-Foreman "Rumble in the Jungle" revealed the danger of
compounding the injuries caused by human fists with those caused by
heat. (It was the heat as much as Ali's strength and skill which overcame
Foreman; part of the skill was "using" the heat.)

The usual setting and climate of tennis are paradisal. More than the
cost of laying out a court, this is the reason the game isn't much played in
or near urban ghettoes. The only American black male champion,
Arthur Ashe, was the son of a park policeman who had access to courts.
Ashe has written brilliantly about the "whiteness" and "classiness" of his
demeanor and style and wonders what will happen to the game when an
Ali shows up in it.*

7.

The techniques of mass media make orderly what appear to be such un-
controllable social situations as riots and battles. The free-swinging cam-
eramen of "live" television "instinctively," "unconsciously" select the
most telling and dramatic shots: a woman standing in front of a trashed
store with arms stretched out, her head bent into the angle of painted
crucifixions; the throwers of bricks and Molotov cocktails looking like
Davids fighting the Goliaths of capitalism; "processions" of looters,
and, finally, weepers holding the fallen bodies of loved ones in the iconography of the *Pietà*. Human beings have a relatively small repertoire of

---

* This brilliant man was stricken with and died of AIDS. At the U.S. Open in 1992, many
players wore insignias which marked their commitment to combating the disease, commitment secured by the man whose old social stigma, blackness, had been largely overcome but whose new stigma was a threat to all, particularly to the young, sexually active
people who play his game.

gestures and expressions, and great emotion does narrow the repertoire, but I think it more the theatrical sense of photographers and their editors which standardizes the appearance of riots. The visual shorthand expresses and elevates the human condition into the sacraments of public entertainment by restoring to familiar norms passions and struggles which threaten them.

In the past quarter-century of televised Wimbledon, a billion people have mastered its iconography and now regard it as a precious annual staging of the struggles, losses, and triumphs of their own lives.

8.

If, as Pater said, "All the arts aspire to the condition of music," perhaps all sports transfigure the conditions of bloody combat. It's a mark of humanity to transform its fiercest acts to make them tolerable. (The slaughter which feeds us is countered by extending our hands with utensils, roasting our meat, dividing our day into mealtimes, and making meals themselves into occasions of conviviality and, sometimes, sacrament.) The most dangerous Western sport, boxing, is bound with more rules than Gulliver was by Lilliputian cords: the sixteen-ounce gloves, the oxymoronic square ring, the three-minute rounds, the separation at knockdowns, the injunction against low blows, the initial touching of gloves, and, more often now than not, the embrace of loser and winner. Tennis is much further removed from blood, but it remains a face-to-face combat and thus requires social transfiguration. As commercial interests take over more and more of the tournament, it may be that more and more attention will be devoted to the transfigurations than to the sport. At that point, Wimbledon will sink beneath commentary and Devonshire cream.

# James, the Traveler

Henry James's first memory was of the Napoleon column in the Place Vendôme. It was 1845; he was two years old and had made the first of the trans-Atlantic crossings which made him as international, at least as Europeanized, an American as literature has known.

Travel became a central part of James's life. In the earliest of the pieces printed in the collection of his travel writings, he writes from Lake George (August 10, 1870),

> I find so great a pleasure in traveling, and maintain so friendly and expectant an attitude toward possible 'sensations,' that they haven't the heart to leave me altogether unvisited.*

These sensations become "impressions," the material of the writer. For them, James would write thirty-six years later in the preface to his finest travel book, *The American Scene*, "I would in fact go to the stake." By this time, the "sentimental tourist" who wrote the early American and European pieces *(A Little Tour in France)* had become the "restless analyst" whose impressions were organized by an intelligence as darkly amused as Mark Twain's but qualified and complicated by a deeper sense of what social life should be. This sense had been developed not only by long residence in the old world but by working out the extrapolations of a gregarious life there in his fiction.

It is hard to believe there was time in such an intensive literary life for the ships, trains, carriages, horseback rides, and—especially—long walks of a traveling life. But the literary life is, to a large degree, dependent on

---

* Henry James, *Collected Travel Writings*, vol. 1, *Great Britain and America;* vol. 2, *The Continent* (New York: Library of America, 1993).

the scenic and human variety of travel for the perspective which gives it and the characters it conjures up complexity and depth. If the early travels are superficial and "sentimental," full of churches, paintings, and scenes, pieced out with historical and literary recollection, they quickly—in the late 1870s, the time of *Italian Hours*—acquire depth and shadow. James comes to understand the questionable enterprise of traveling itself.

> A traveler is often moved to ask himself whether it has been worthwhile to leave his home . . . only to encounter new forms of human suffering, only to be reminded that toil and privation, hunger and sorrow and sordid effort are the portion of the mass of mankind . . . there is something heartless in stepping forth into foreign streets to feast on "characters" when character consists simply in the slightly different costume in which labour and want present themselves. . . . I know that . . . half the time we are acclaiming the fine quality of the Italian smile the creature so constituted for physiognomic radiance may be in a sullen frenzy of impatience and pain.

James knows what all but the least sensitive of travelers uneasily knows: that the world which is his pearl-rich oyster can barely endure his physiognomic radiance. James travels no longer just for pleasurable sensation but to understand, to express, and thus to make more life than he "takes."

Discriminate, discriminate. Express, express. All right, the English may be "the handsomest people in Europe," but James is not blinded by these "regular faces and tall figures." He sees the "hard prose of misery" in "the battered and bedraggled bonnets of the women, which look as if their husbands had stamped on them . . . as a hint of what may be in store for their wearers. . . . [T]wo-thirds of the London faces . . . bear . . . the traces of alcoholic action. The properties of flushed, empurpled, eruptive masks is [*sic*] considerable."

James lived among the comfortable and leisured and was repelled by "the rabble," but he did not avoid individual members of it, indeed, sought them out. He had—this is a surprise—an ear for speech, although in the sixteen hundred pages of these volumes there is too little sign of this Dickensian / Twainian gift. In 1904, James visits a Pennsylvania prison—the "huge house of sorrow" reminds him of a club—and talks "for a long time" with a murderer, half-expecting him to ring for coffee and cigars; but we don't hear the murderer. James is struck by the odd male intimacy of the prison, not the colorful speech and lurid events which fill most travel narratives. It is the unexpected symmetry of behavior showing up in unexpected places which fascinate this mature traveler.

The prison visit is a part of James's greatest travel book, the one not written in parts and assembled with snips and tucks later on, *The American Scene*. It was written after he finished the last of his three great novels on Americans in Europe, *The Golden Bowl*. Returning to his country after twenty years' absence, he traveled from coast to coast, stopping in St. Louis, Indianapolis, Gary, and Chicago. The book, though, is centered by observations of Boston, New York, Philadelphia, Washington, Charleston, Palm Beach, and St. Augustine. These eastern cities supply everything the restless analyst needed. That, I think, was loss, shock, the tragedy which, since the Civil War, had burned out his affiliations and patriotism. James, as American as any American writer has ever been, sees a country driven to near madness by commerce, its men emptied of any but commercial drive, its women burdened by having to supply all that counts of meaningful life.

His own birthplace in Washington Square was gone. It had given way to "another" fifty-story skyscraper.

The multitudinous sky-scrapers standing up to the view, from the water, like extravagant pins in a cushion already overplanted, and stuck in as in the dark, anywhere and anyhow . . . are triumphant payers of dividends. . . . The vocabulary of thrift at any price shows boundless resources, and the consciousness of that truth, the consciousness of the finite, the menaced, the essentially invented state, twinkles ever, to my perception, in the thousand glassy eyes of these giants of the mere market.

In this "great lonely land, . . . everything was still to come," and so America "points . . . the homely moral that when you haven't what you like you must perforce like, and above all misrepresent, what you have."

The vision of commerce and mendacity annihilating the decency and dignity of "civil creations" comes as James strides the orange groves of tiny Los Angeles, a remarkable prevision of the Hollywood that was about to build its dream factories. It makes this great American's American book the bleakest, if most gorgeous, account ever given of the country. Limited, narrow, out of touch, perhaps, but in the odd way of great art, it is also the redemption whose absence it describes.

# Going and Coming: On Celati's Adventures in Africa

Life has long been thought of as a journey—the *cammin di nostra vita*—and much literature centers on actual or imaginary journeys. "Muse, help me sing about that complicated man who after he'd plundered . . . holy Troy was forced to travel in misery along the coasts of men, the victim of their customs good and bad, while . . . his heart ached to redeem him and to bring his crew home safely" (Homer, *Odyssey*, 1:1–5). The most profound travel literature springs from the departure, and then the—always more difficult—return home. So there's the *Odyssey*, the Old Testament's account of Jewish exile from and return to Palestine, the New Testament's letters of the traveler Paul (whose return is to a spiritual home), and Dante's fabulous psychological, spiritual journey through hell and purgatory to the home of his Creator in paradise. (Less exalted, closer to the actualities of terrestrial movement, is the modestly magnificent epic *The Long Walk* [1956], Slavomir Rawicz's account of seven prisoners in a Soviet labor camp who in 1941 and 1942 walked thousands of horrific, perilous miles through Siberia, China, the Gobi Desert, and Tibet and over the Himalayas to British India and freedom.)

Some of the world's greatest and most important travelers have been Italian, and I don't mean those like Dante,* whose voyages aren't under-

---

* Dante would have been the greatest of travel writers. Not only is he a pithy "reporter" of infernal, purgatorial, and paradisal sights, sounds, tastes and smells, but his constant comparisons to earthy equivalents are stunningly apt, or, better, transformative. I just picked up the *Purgatorio* and opened, at random, to Canto 23, which begins with Dante looking through foliage, *"le fronde verde,"* like a hunter *"chi dietro a li uccelin sua vita perde"* ("who wastes his life going after birds"), then talking with his old friend Forese "Bicci" Donato, who compares the modest women of Sardinia with *"le sfacciate donne fiorentine / l'andar mostrando con le poppe il petto,"* "the brazen Florentines who walk around showing off their breasts." In the next canto, Dante compares the movements of starving gluttons to *"li augli che vernan lungo 'l Nile / alcun volta in aere fanno schiera, /*

taken by boat, plane, train, horse, or foot, but those like Marco Polo and Columbus, Amerigo Vespucci and Matteo Ricci, who, for one reason or another, underwent the physical, stress-heavy excitements of long land and sea-tethered journeys.

Gianni Celati is the most recent Italian literary traveler.* Like such other traveling men of letters as Goethe, Dickens, Stevenson, Gide, Waugh, Greene, Moravia, Parisi, Naipaul, and Theroux, he travels not because of obligation or externally imposed necessity. "Why are you going?" someone asks Andre Gide as he begins his voyage up the Congo. "I'll know when I get there," says Gide (*Voyage to the Congo* [1927], p. 1). This is the keynote of the literary traveler.

Travelers frequently have assignments: so Alexis de Tocqueville goes to the revolutionary young American country to help his friend Beaumont investigate its prisons; Johann von Goethe heads for Italy to escape his overdetermined ministerial life in Weimar; and Gianni Celati goes to Africa to help his friend, Jean Talon, research a documentary film about the Dogon priesthood. The essential drives of these travelers, however, are the desire to test their physical and mental powers in the break from the monotonous routine of familiar life, sheer curiosity about other places and people, a semi-mystical life-hunger which Germans call *Wanderlust* and, finally, for the literary traveler, the need to find in new worlds and stressful motion new forms and turns of language.

The literary traveler is not a specialist. Gide makes a point of this in *Voyage au Congo:* "How fortunate the sociologist who is interested only in manners and customs, the painter who cares only for the country's appearance, the naturalist who occupies himself with insects or plants. How fortunate the specialist!" (p. 16). Fortunate because specialization limits the risk of the pure traveler for whom everything is up for risk, whose chief risk is just this and the menace of what Jean-Paul Sartre called "the nausea" of—mental—freedom.

In the books of the best literary travelers, tension derives not just from the actual, almost always surmounted dangers or from the urgency

---

*poi volan piu a fretta e vanno in filo."* Dante may never have seen the Nile, but he'd surely observed birds flocking, then flying in files along the Arno or the Po. It's the eye for both real and imaginary groupings which would turn most travel writers—to use a cliché Dante would scorn—green with envy.

* Gianni Celati, *Adventures in Africa*, trans. Adria Bernardi (Chicago: University of Chicago Press, 2000).

of a mission reported in coherent narrative, but from whatever literary
brilliance the traveler-author can strike from new acquaintances, scenes,
events, and his self-interrogating self. If there is a progressive, ever-
deepening rhythm of discovery, then his book will have the shape of a
*Pilgrim's Progress*, a *Gulliver's Travels*, or an *Alice in Wonderland*, or of a
Robinson Crusoe's slow re-creation of a middle-class English world that
will supply his needs until his return to its model. (John Coetzee plays in-
geniously with the Crusoe experience in his *Foe*.)

The mention of Robinson Crusoe alerts one to another, almost ubiquitous, element in good travelers' books: the discovery of a foreign
friend or friends in whose life the traveler plays a more or less significant
part and whose fate moves him. In Gide's two Congo books, the friend is
a small animal, a sloth whom Gide names—after the native term—
Dindiki. Dindiki's death is the emotional highlight of the voyage and the
books. The emotional center of *The Long Walk* is the excruciating death
of Kristina, the delicate Polish-Ukrainian girl whom the seven male es-
capees protect, adore and, heartrendingly, bury. Gianni Celati describes
several new acquaintances: Moussa and Mohammed, two of the boys
who stick to the travelers like unshakeable colds and try for tips and their
own adventurousness to guide and procure; the proud semi-official
guide, Boubacar, whose metronomically measured pace is the most as-
tonishingly artful element of his guidance; the able, charming woman,
Batouly Sarr, who desperately, vainly wants to leave her burdensome
Dakar life for Paris. Finally and always, there is Jean Talon, the docu-
mentarian, who is not only Celati's eccentric friend but, increasingly, the
obstacle to his exploring adventurousness. None of these, however, is
described as Celati might have described them in such a fiction as his *Il
paralitico del deserto* (1987). They are animated elements of the essential
landscape. That landscape is the process of discovering another, an
African form of space, of time, of *life*. The process is the book. This one
reaches its almost epiphanic climax in its very last sentences:

> . . . one knows that when one's left behind a window, he tends to feel
> that he's missing something, even if he has everything and he's wanting
> for nothing, and this lack of nothing perhaps counts for something, be-
> cause one can also be aware of not needing anything at all, except some
> of the nothing he truly lacks, some of the nothing that cannot be bought,
> some of the nothing that does not correspond with anything, the nothing

of the sky and the universe, or the nothing that the others have who do
not have anything.

The nothing that the others have who do not have anything.
This *nothing* is an *uncommodity* which will not be advertised in the
brochures issued by African ministries of tourism, but then this "text-
book case of African tourism," as the author mocks it in one of the re-
frain lines which help hold the book together, is, like all the best traveler's
books, not a tourist book but a book of self-transport, self-investigation,
self-transfiguration. That this Italian "tourist" has the nose, eyes, ears,
curiosity, endurance, common sense, and uncommon literary power
which can experience, then verbalize sights, sounds, and odors, makes
the book one a good tourist might well pack before heading for Mali,
Mauretania, and Senegal. The faces, markets, savannas, and characters
are African meat on which both tourists and stay-at-homes can feast, but
they're feasting on an Africa that does not appear in the pages of specialists or the films of even the best documentarians. The best-cooked meat
of *Adventures in Africa* is Signor Gianni Celati himself, the spirited, the-
orizing sexagenarian author-adventurer whose abundant life is aug-
mented and enriched but constantly called into question by the poverty
whose nothingness he begins to see as a form of that unpurchasable possession which other, very different Western intellects have called *grace*.

## An Indiana Library

On a brutally stormy November 1995 night, I gave a reading at the Michigan City, Indiana, library. The rational expectation was that nobody would bother to leave a warm home to hear an old writer read one of his stories, but twenty-five or thirty people ventured through the storm to come to the beautiful, warm library to hear Bill Olmstead interrogate me shrewdly about my work and life, then hear me read the story and talk about it and anything else on their good minds. My thought was, "How marvelous a human communion, surrounded by the books which hold what sustains and is the best of what transforms us from clever animals into citizens, people in active touch with what's been and what'll be." In this small Indiana town, thoughtful men and women care enough to build a beautiful library, a center of the mental power which turns this ball of whirling dust into a radiant speck of—who knows?—some infinite grid of significance. Here, twenty-five or thirty people, young and old, of different ancestries, religions, and education, assemble to take in the small accomplishment of one of their own, a specialist in story, that deepest human organization of observation, knowledge, imagination, affection, and language which brought the species from apish struggle to civic and esthetic consciousness. Bless you, Michigan City Library.

# My Chicago

Chicago?

That was where Great-Uncle Herman fled from hawk-nosed Aunt Milly to be fetched back to the connubial jail by my grandmother, her younger, sweeter sister. I loved Uncle Herman. Who else cackled over egg bins at the grocer's, sucking the yellow and white stuff through pinholes he made in the shell? Who else let me win a figure ring from whose belly button I would—years later—remove a diamond for my fiancée? So early, I had the sense of Chicago as a refuge from New York troubles.

⤞⤝

Age six, parents away for a rare week, I was left with Ida—who whacked me with metal corset stays—and Mary, my usual caretaker. Ida, pointing to a front-page picture, told me to tell Mary, "Your boyfriend's been shot in Chicago." (The "boyfriend" was John Dillinger.) So menace was part of that strange greatness on the distant lake.

Chicago was also where Colonel McCormick came from, he of the highfalutin' accent which editorialized among Strauss waltzes on one of my favorite radio programs.

Was I in seventh, eighth, or tenth grade when *Life* featured a page of solemn men in black robes under the headline "Is the University of Chicago the World's Greatest?" To one who knew only Columbia, NYU, and Harvard and ended up at Chapel Hill, this was a bolt from a different blue. What went on out there in the city of pig squeals and gangsters?

Chicago fact and fiction accumulated before I actually set eyes on the place. I'd seen Chapel Hill and Waterville, Maine, had worked in a department store in Evansville, Indiana, a radio station in Orlando, Florida, then, after a year in Cambridge, Massachusetts, had gone to Versailles as a Fulbright Fellow. After that, I worked in Heidelberg and Frankfurt, married, became a father, saw Brussels, Belgrade, Beirut, and Berlin—but not Chicago. Then, back in the United States, en route to Iowa City, I changed trains there. I walked out of the old La Salle Street Station, up State Street and down Wabash. I saw the Palmer House, the El, the broken faces of failure, the striding suits of success, felt the speed, thrust, racket, variety, and power of a great city, not New York, not Paris, something else, I didn't know what.

Eighteen months later, I drove up from Iowa City with other graduate students for the Modern Language Association Convention. We were looking for jobs. I stayed with my friend Tom Higgins, a pianist, then paying his bills as a bellhop at the Hotel Del Prado. He told me that he'd just been stopped on Lake Shore Drive by a cop. Knowing the city, Higgins held out his wallet, a five-dollar bill clipped to his driver's license. The cop's hand moved to the lapel of Tom's camel's hair overcoat, which someone had left behind at the hotel. The official fingers rubbed appreciatively. "Gettin' a little big for five, Higgins," said the Chicago guardian. Tom doubled the offering and was absolved. Ah, Chicago.

After ten humiliating interviews persuaded me that I was an unhireable zero, I retreated to the Art Institute and stood before *Sunday Afternoon on the Grand Jatte*, as suspended in fixative color as the butterflies, dogs, boats, and forty-seven people—I counted them—strolling, lolling, fishing, and staring in Seurat's great canvas. Chicago had its consoling beauties.

In an elevator, I asked a lady with an MLA badge for an interview. "Send me your life," said she. (The word she used was *vita*.) Weeks later she wrote, offering me a year's job at Connecticut College in New London. The next spring (see part I), Don Justice wrote that he'd just turned down the year's best academic job at the University of Chicago. "The city intimidates us," he wrote. "So does the University." Three days later, I got a telegram asking me to come for interviews. I borrowed the fare and met the men—no women then—who were to be my friends and colleagues. That day, my chief sponsor, Norman Maclean, drove me into the city, telling me how it was both entwined with and removed from the university. Too excited—or insensitive—to be intimidated, I was wowed by everything. In addition, they would pay me $4,800, $1,300 more than I was making at Connecticut College.

In August, I drove my newly purchased fourth-hand Chevy past the blazing mills of Gary and the dumb white Standard Oil vats of Whiting to South Chicago. In front of the South Shore Country Club, cops stopped cars until a huge Cadillac, license plate number 1, eased out of the gate. "Who's that?" asked I. "His Eminence," said the cop. "The Cardinal." I advanced a grade.

In 1955, Richard Daley the First was, like me, just beginning his municipal career. He prospered, grew great; I hung on, held on, taught classes, wrote books, raised children, made friends, moved every few years, always within twenty minutes' walk of my office. I met, watched, and listened to some of the world's most interesting and talented people. Some were colleagues, students, neighbors, friends. I knew joy, grief, excitement, fatigue, intrigue, nobility, treachery, triumph, defeat.

Much life, much death.

Back in the days when I played cards with Uncle Herman, I held up a spoonful of my favorite dessert and announced, "I love Brown Betty." Said my father, "You can't love what can't love you."

But I did love Brown Betty, and, despite burglaries, break-ins, stolen cars, broken bones, disappointment, bewilderment, exhaustion, fear, and rage, I not only loved and love Chicago, but felt and feel that I was and am somehow a loved part of it, an old fixture now, like a wind-shaken but still standing locust tree or a replastered, repainted, rewired, retubed three-flat that stands amid slum clearance or gentrification. Uncle Herman's temporary refuge has become my permanent one.

# The Chicago Writer's City

I.

I think it would make more sense to talk of the Chicago Dentist's City.* We'd have clearer research lines: numbers, income, training, relationship to technicians, laboratories, instruments, use of precious metals, comparative dental care in different regions, surveys of attitudes toward dentists and dentistry, toward fluoride, x-rays, prosthesis. We could learn a great deal about the city that way.

Then there's the Undertaker's Chicago; the Physicist's Chicago; and— exceptionally rich in clues—the Garbageman's Chicago.

A city contains so much, is so much. You can spend a useful life studying a hundred-celled creature. A thousand devoted students have not exhausted Chicago.

I notice that the rubric "The Chicago Writer's City" comes in the syllabus between "Neighborhoods" and the "Chicago School of Sociology: Ecology and Ethnography," and that later you go on to compare Chicago and Calcutta, discuss Chicago's politics, housing, employment, crime, and then "Old Images and New Realities." This last is where the Chicago Writer belongs.

No matter how close to the facts—as he sees and feels them—he writes, the writer's words themselves conjure up images. Images are also facts, or at least, realities, the sort which help us organize perceptions of other realities, other facts.

Social scientists are, I understand, in the business of organizing facts into pictures of reality which will not easily be refutable, and certainly

---

* This talk was given to a graduate seminar taught by Professors Morris Janowitz and Gerald Suttles at the University of Chicago. I wish I'd read Suttles's excellent *The Man-Made City* (Chicago: University of Chicago Press, 1990) before I'd given it.

not by myths and legends no matter how venerable and cherished. Most writers, too, want to make irrefutable work, although their facts and fictions may have more to do with sensations, true and false impressions, tones of voice, and scenic tension than with *how much, how many, how frequent.* Neither historians, sociologists, nor reporters, they are still governed by standards of verisimilitude, authenticity, and sincerity.

No adult writers today begin, "Once upon a time." Most adult stories deal with specific times, specific streets, recognizable, if unusually explored, people and worlds. They construct events which evoke familiar sorts of reactions, and although they aim to deepen or even subvert them, they know that nothing menaces their work more than disbelief in what they've set down. (There are differently rigorous standards for farce and fantasy.) "This could not be" is not what a writer wants to hear from his readers, yet even the most conservative novel alters the range of the reader's actuality. "There are more things in heaven and earth than are dreamt of in your philosophy, Reader," says almost every writer. If the believability contract is broken, he loses his reader. It doesn't mean that a clever writer can't persuade his Horatio that a fish is talking or a wind is making love to a high-rise, but it must be clear that these "facts" aren't part of the world of biology and physics but of psychology or style.

What most of us want from imaginative writers is a mental freedom which, through certain literary charms and conventions, brings a special emotional experience. The lives of characters in a novel are both slowed and speeded up; above all, they are made exceptionally coherent. Narrative tricks instruct readers more at ease with quantifiable fact how to take in the abstract, evocative, fact-world of fiction. Why this world affects people so deeply has, I think, much to do with a desire to be at least momentarily free of ordinary obligations, the old human way of losing one's own loss and fear in stories about others'.

What is at issue here is how the "real" Chicago, the complex immensity covered by the seven letters grouped into three syllables, relates to its fictional portrayals.

The sociologist is trained to persuade by eliminating from his articles his own temperament and eccentricities. The imaginative writer is trained—or trains himself—to express everything in him which is eccentric. His temperament is not an obstacle to clarity; it is his material, his gold mine. The reality filtered through his temperament and talent is what counts for his readers. A writer who accepts other writers' views of his material is either plagiarist or parodist.

Social scientists require the apparatus of their profession to align themselves with acceptable investigative, expressive, and recording techniques. Almost everything the story writer chooses to set down must be separated from familiar truth, if only by his vocabulary, imagery, choice of scene and event, the rhythm of his assemblage, the syntax of his attitudes.

Does this credo of eccentricity and dissociation mean that novels, let alone novels with a Chicago setting, can't be classified? Of course not. The minute your realize a book is a novel, you've classified it, and of course "Chicago novels" narrows the classification.

## 2.

In 1935 Lennox Gray received his doctorate at the University of Chicago with a dissertation called *Chicago and the "Great American Novel": A Critical Approach to the American Epic.* Gray surveyed approximately five hundred Chicago novels by two hundred different writers which were in large part set in the city. He grouped them chronologically and by subject: Chicago as a portage, a fort, a trading post, boomtown, an agricultural metropolis before and after the Civil War and the Great Fire, the industrial city, the white city and the black, and the modern city (up to his day). Nobody has issued a comparable volume on the Chicago novels between 1935 and today, though I suspect that it would be an even more useful book than Gray's splendid and almost totally unread work.* Gray's title allows you to see his thrust, which is that Chicago has somehow been seen as the most American of cities and the most appropriate setting for that literary unicorn "the Great American Novel." Its centrality, its transformations, its exceptional individuals, especially its transgressors and overreachers and the myths built on and around them, its tradition of being untraditional, its ethnic variety, its inventive clamorous commerce and industry, its old status as junction and port, and, finally, its tradition of literary vaunting and self-explanation make it the ideal "writer's town."

Whether or not it is more of a writer's town than New Orleans or Bordeaux, Worcester, Massachusetts or Worcester, Worcestershire, is a complicated question. If, say, a group of Brontë-like sisters grew up in Worcester, Massachusetts, it might become more a writer's town than,

---

* There are shorter surveys, including an excellent article by Michael Anania, "A Commitment to Grit," in *Chicago* (November 1983): 200–207.

say, Moline, Illinois, or Kansas City, Missouri. Yet it is a fact that so many writers seem to have had something to do with Chicago that about eighty years ago H. L. Mencken was able to call this city the "Literary Capital of the United States." Mencken's extravagance was widely circulated and probably stimulated what it described. "In Chicago," he wrote, "there is a mysterious something that makes for individuality, personality, charm. . . . Find a writer who is indubitably American in every pulse beat . . . and nine times out of ten you will find he has some sort of connection with the Gargantuan abattoir by Lake Michigan."

This sort of rhapsody with its "mysterious something" and its "American in every pulse beat" is easy to grasp by unthinking and unliterary people, but on page after literary page, as Gray shows, it represents the note struck about this city: Chicago is the real America, the place where individuality—America's sap—runs clearest.

Fourteen years before Mencken's hyperbole, William Dean Howells, writing in the *North American Review,* spelled out the Chicago connection to the Declaration of Independence.

> The republic of letters is elsewhere sufficiently republican, but in the metropolis of the Middle-West, it is so almost without thinking, almost without feeling; and the atmospheric democracy, the ambient equality, is something that runs like the prime effect in literature of what America has been doing and saying in life ever since she first formulated herself in the Declaration.

This is less hyperbolical, but few can get away with such personifications today. Howell's remarks make us suspicious: America either says nothing or says so much that you can't summarize it with such phrases as "ambient equality" and "atmospheric democracy." Nonetheless, the imagery of Chicago is a product as distinct, saleable, and potent as the products it puts into boxes or reduces to electronic blips. If we play a sort of parlor game—one that might help us decide where we want to spend the rest of our lives—and free-associate with "Chicago" and, say, "Los Angeles," we come up with two very different sets of imagery. Los Angeles suggests make-believe, Disneyland miniaturization, Hollywood illusion, San Simeon pretentiousness. Southern California seems a sort of Polynesia on wheels, a technicolor fragility menaced by a creeping Sahara and grinding tectonic plates, these being nature's revenge for its exceptional bounty of climate and beachlife. The Chicago profile is rugged, raucous, scarred. The word "real" comes to mind, although there are elements of theatrical farce in the midst of violent reality. Fires, riots, strikes, blood in the streets, yes, but then a municipal government whose manipulated vote totals, machine politics, and corrupt officials suggest both farce and sinister injustice.*

Chicago politics should be reviewed by drama critics. Its stock characters include the boss, the corrupt alderman with a heart and pocket of gold, the deal-maker, the syndicate *pezza novanta*, the amiable voluptuary cardinal whose treasures are not exclusively celestial. Chicagoans, most Americans in fact, are entranced by such characters. They expect, they want, maybe they need their fix of fraud, con, toughness, slaughter. Chicago is not Disneyland but a national Oberammergau played with real nails and blood.

3.

Chicago grew as journalism did. The eastern centers of journalism needed explanations of the noisy industrial mess swelling along Lake Michigan. Chicago drew and developed writers to supply the need, then to deride and subvert it. Much of this work was done in newspaper columns. George Ade, Finley Peter Dunne, Ring Lardner—an ex-sportswriter like many of the mythmakers—Ben Hecht and Mike Rokyo were the best-known newspaper creators and critics of Chicago comedy and pathos. Their heroes and—rarely—heroines were the abused and the abusive, the Paddies, Mikes, Vitos, Big Als, Fast Eddies, and Crazy Janes who ran the city or fronted for those who did.

The novelists, at least the ones who will be read for a while by more than dissertation writers, historians, and nostalgic grandpas, underwrite the columnists' imagery and myths. Even when their novels spring from historical characters and events, it is the coherence and energy of their imaginative transformation which survive. Dreiser's financial genius, Cowperwood, is based on the traction tycoon Yerkes, but he is Yerkes plus Dreiser. For Dreiser's heroes, Chicago begins as a dream, turns into a field to be plowed, a stage to fill. Stimulated by their conception of boundlessness, his heroes overreach and fall. Wealth isn't enough, power isn't enough. What they ultimately want is explanation. "If he had not

---

* In December 2000 I reread this piece amidst the shenanigans of the Gore-Bush election. Ex-secretaries of state and presidential candidates, hired or volunteer guns, make the ward captains of old Chicago look like Boy Scouts.

been a great financier," writes Dreiser of Cowperwood, "and above all, a marvelous organizer, he might've become a highly individualistic philosopher. . . . His business, as he saw it, was with the material facts of life, or rather, with those third and fourth degree theorems and syllogisms which control material things and so represent wealth."

Material. Stuff. The real. Again and again these dominate Chicago writing. The sheer mass and variety of matter pouring into the industrial city requires ever subtler, ever more abstract shorthand to register and manipulate it. (The futures markets have some of the abstract intensity of medieval philosophy.) The enchantment, complexity, and fatality of matter have been for more than a century a Chicago theme. It agitates such soft novels of the 1890s as Henry Blake Fuller's *The Cliff Dwellers* (1893) and Robert Herrick's *The Gospel of Freedom*.

> Chicago is an instance of a successful, contemptuous disregard of nature by man. . . . [In] Chicago, man has decided to make for himself a city for his artificial necessities in defiance of every indifference displayed by nature. Along the level floor of sand and gravel cast up by the mighty lake, the city has swelled and pushed, like a pool of quicksilver, which, poured out on a flat plate, is ever undulating and alternating its borders as it eats its way further into the desert expanse. Railroad lines, like strands of a huge spider's web, run across the continent in all directions, willfully, strenuously centering in this waste spot, the swampy corner of a great lake.

The railroads haul in both promise and threat. The threat—spelled out by Edgar Lee Masters in *Children in the Marketplace*—is quasi-Marxist: what's hauled in, the material of wealth, "has become you."

Again and again, novels describe Chicago as the emblem of mastered nature, again and again they measure out the penalties for this mastery. (Long ago, Mrs. O'Leary's cow was seen as bucolic revenge for Chicago's transmutation of the western plain into agri-business.)

Of course, some version of this theme is as old as Genesis and stands for the uneasiness humans feel about the transience of what composes and satisfies them. Wealth and power, the enchantment of matter, get their modern celebration and epitaphs in Chicago novels. Even in the Chicago sections of non-Chicago novels you hear the death song of material wealth. F. Scott Fitzgerald's richest, most arrogant and destructive characters often come from Chicago. In *Tender Is the Night*, the Swiss psychiatrist in charge of the broken Chicago heiress, Nicole Warren, tells Dick Driver that he knows such Chicagoans and has often treated their victims. Nicole's father, a millionaire meat packer, is, like Cowperwood, a transgressor. The boundaries he's crossed are those of kinship: his incest with young Nicole has driven her mad. After years of treatment, a cured Nicole herself turns into a ruinous transgressor. Her beauty and intelligence, but above all her wealth, help ruin the people who saved her, and her rich girl prodigality ruins those much further away.

> Nicole bought from a great list that ran two pages and bought the things in the window besides. Everything she liked that she couldn't possibly use herself, she bought as a present for a friend. She bought colored beads, folding beach cushions, artificial flowers, honey, a guest bed, bags, scarves, love birds, miniatures for a doll's house and three yards of a new cloth the color of prawns. She bought a dozen bathing suits, a rubber alligator, a traveling chess set of gold and ivory, big linen handkerchiefs for Abe, two dozen leather jackets of kingfisher blue and burning bush from Hermes—bought all these things not a bit like a high-class courtesan buying underwear and jewels, which were after all professional equipment and insurance—but with an entirely different point of view. Nicole was the product of much ingenuity and toil. For her sake trains began their run at Chicago and traversed the round belly of the continent to California; chicle factories burned and link belts grew link by link in factories; men mixed toothpaste in vats and drew mouthwash out of copper hogsheads; girls canned tomatoes quickly or worked rudely at the Five-and-Ten on Christmas Eve; half-breed Indians toiled on Brazilian coffee plantations and dreamers were muscled out of patent rights in new tractors—these were some of the people who gave a tithe to Nicole, and as the whole system surged and thundered onward, it lent a feverish bloom to such processes of hers as wholesale buying. . . .

In later writers, the extravagance of the rich (see the birthday party for the Great Dane in Bellow's *The Dean's December*) is more a subject for bemused farce than indictment. *Tender Is the Night* comes out of the American Depression and, like most books of the time, finds very little comedy, let alone absolution, in epic indulgence.

Chicago writers such as Farrell and Nelson Algren spend few pages on the rich; they love and celebrate the defeated poor. Farrell—one of the few Chicago writers actually born in the city—tracks the degradation of poor Irish Catholics. His description of their communities makes Joyce's Dublin look like Periclean Athens. His Chicagoans are sunk in oppression, ignorance, bigotry, boredom, mindless violence, and mindless discipline. Now and then, a whiff of poetry stirs one of them. It may come from a lake breeze, a kiss, or a fight, but there is almost no hope that it will alter, let alone transfigure, a life. Only at the end, in the form of regret or pathetic nostalgia, does poetry stamp out a Farrell character, but the poetry is shallow, the regret inarticulate, and the nostalgia the "garlic of low cuisine."*

The Chicago of Algren and of the columnists who tried to write and think as he did is a Sancho Panza–Chaplin Chicago, full of tough little guys making verbal music out of abuse and loss. The Algren character just wants to make it through the day with a small stake, but his world is run by those who think he's trash. As they push him around, he tries to hold on yet finds nothing but bottles, needles, and the broken bodies of other losers. He hates winners, those who own what he thinks he wants, those who judge him, the swaggering princes of life who stifle what really counts for him, the poetry of defeat. Chicago is both the setting for this poetry and the setting for what kills it. It breaks and shelters those it breaks. Algren's famous personification of it is the girl with the broken nose whom he happens to love.

Ten or fifteen years before his death, Algren knew his material had thinned out. The new king of the Chicago heap, a much greater writer, found poetry all over the city, in Dreiserian winners as well as Algrenian losers, in the be-Sulkaed finaglers in Loop law offices as well as the tough old Jews in the Russian Bathhouse on Division Street. Like so many Chicago writers of the past ninety years, Saul Bellow has been associated with the University of Chicago, but unlike many of those writers— Phillip Roth, Austin Wright, Thomas Rogers, Robert Coover, James Purdy, Kurt Vonnegut, Douglas Unger—he wasn't a transient for whom a few years of school time were kept as a special icon of carnival or Paradise. Born in French Canada, he spent most of his life in the city about which he always complains and always loves. Bellow's heroes are also overreaching border-crossers, but their borders are sensuous, intellectual, and spiritual. His books are education novels and his heroes are

---

* Some of Farrell's later characters escape as he did, moving past Washington Park to the grey towers of the University of Chicago.

educated by great men and books as well as the thugs, lawyers, business-
men, con men, and splendid ladies of the city. The Bellow hero is heavy
with memory. The Chicago of the twenties presses on the Chicago of the
sixties, the seventies, the eighties, the nineties. (There are geniuses of
memory as well as of fact and theory.) No writer has written longer or
better about this city than Bellow, and as he has changed, so have his versions of it. In early Bellow, people scoot up and down the town, working
in coal yards, haberdasheries, Loop department stores. Wherever they
work, they classify, analyze, transform fact into theory, need into poetry.
One fellow delivers relief checks in the ghetto. He can't locate his Mr.
Green but finds what he's really after, which is *what things mean.*

> He had four or five blocks to go, past open lots, old foundations, closed
> schools, black churches, mounds, and he reflected there must be many
> people alive who had once seen the neighborhood rebuilt and new. Now
> there was a second layer of ruins; centuries of history accomplished
> through human massing. Numbers had given the place forced growth;
> enormous numbers had also broken it down. . . . Rome, that was almost
> permanent, did not give rise to thoughts like these. . . . But in Chicago,
> where the cycles were so fast and the familiar died out, and again rose,
> changed, and died again in thirty years, you saw the common agreement
> or covenant, and you were forced to think about appearances and reali-
> ties.

Much wonderful literature invokes a material world which is then penetrated and seen as the cipher of something else. In the later Bellow stories, meanings aren't conclusions. The odd juxtapositions of memory
create a kind of understanding which passes meaning by. It's as if material Chicago is its own explanation, a fulfillment beyond the words which
provoke it. Here is Woody Selbst, hero of the long story "The Silver
Dish," which, like Henry James's *Golden Bowl,* is a good deal more than
itself. An old Woody remembers his dying father, who once tried to steal
the dish from the pious lady who was helping young Woody. He also remembers when he worked at the 1933 Century of Progress World's Fair
pulling a rickshaw,

> wearing a peaked straw hat and trotting with powerful thick legs, while
> the brawny, red-faced farmers—his boozing passengers—were laugh-
> ing their heads off and pestered him for whores, he, although a freshman

at the seminary, saw nothing wrong when girls asked him to steer a little business their way, in making dates, and accepting tips from both sides. He necked in Grant Park with a powerful girl who had to go home quickly to nurse her baby. Smelling of the West Side, squeezing his rickshaw puller's thigh and wetting her blouse. This was the Roosevelt Road car. Then, in the apartment, where she lived with her mother, he couldn't remember that there were any husbands around. What he did remember was the strong milk odor. Without inconsistency, next morning he did Old [*sic*] Testament Greek: the light shineth in the darkness—to fos en te skotia fainei—and the darkness comprehendeth it not.

Bellow's Chicago, his Chicagos, are not the last, only the most vivid pictures so far of this city. They are authentic and full of fact yet don't belong as good social reports do to the world of evidentiary fact. Like Dreiser's Chicago and like the smaller portions of the imagined city registered and in a sense owned by—though not stored away in the vaults of—other writers,* they constitute bodies of evidence for some other case, one which has to do with the level of imaginative power existing at different times in this one place.

* In the summer of 1984 the distinguished magazine *TriQuarterly* published a special Chicago issue. A critic of this issue, James Hurt, writing in the September 14, 1984, issue of *The Reader*, takes off from a description of the city in a piece of my fiction to describe the latest "alternatives to the Hog Butcher line" of Chicago writing. There is here, says Hurt, "a kind of compromised laughter, a survivor's cynicism" but also "sweetness and the awareness of human possibility." He quotes Dave Etter's version of Sandburg's poem "Chicago": "City of the bent shoulders, the bum ticker, the bad back. City of the called third strike, the blocked punt. City of the ever-deferred dream. City of the shattered windshield, the loose wheel, the empty gas tank. City of I remember when, once upon a time. City not of 'I will' but of 'I wish I could.'"

# Books and Chicago, Chicago and Books

## 1.

When in 1996 that witty but taciturn presidential candidate, Robert Dole, asked the American novelist Mark Helprin to write the crucial speech in which he'd define himself for the electorate, we book people, Democrat and Republican alike, were comforted. An insecure lot, used to turning our heads to see what new phenomenon is passing us in the race for public attention, we grip whatever reassures us of our importance. The old shibboleths—"The pen is mightier than the sword," "In the beginning was the Word"—sometimes seemed more like epitaphs than reassurance. After all, how could we compete with Netscape and Michael Jordan, virtual reality and *Mission Impossible*? Where do we figure in this televisual, digitalized, info-chipped world? Can even the most sacred paragraphs excite and unify the millions who seem to respire with one great set of lungs when Jordan drives a basketball through the net? (We are reassured that he too has become a man of thoughtful words and that he will only play for Coach Phil Jackson, who selects books for every Chicago Bull.)*

## 2.

Forty thousand book people gather this June in the city of Jordan and Jackson. We're told that more books are sold and read than ever before. We know that bookstores have become social institutions where attractive people, surrounded by thousands of books and periodicals, are attracted to each other over coffee, music, and poetry readings. The

---

* A somewhat creakier Jordan suited up in November 2001 for the Washington Wizards; a somewhat grayer Jackson had led the Los Angeles Lakers to successive championships. *Sic transit gloria verborum.*

bookstores, both more selective and more open than the health clubs and church socials where people used to meet, spell out the unexpressed message, "We belong to those who think, who are curious, who love what is, what was and what will be. By the way, you up for dinner?"

3.

Eventually everything may end up in the World Wide Web, but as of now, almost everything that counts ends up—as Mallarmé once said—in a book. Books are still the ultimate world seal of approval.

Books will be hard to replace: their portability and reproducibility, the margins and end pages on which readers can scribble comments, even the inscribed spine which makes for rapid identification and retrieval and which, aligned with other spines in a home library, reveals an owner's mind and character better than any other possession. A screen which summons any text along with illustrations and commentaries from cyberspace may be wonderful but has the sort of transience and tension of a movie. (Downloaded and even bound, that electronic text is—well, a book.)

Even if present-day books were replaced by cyberiana, the essence of the book would be unchanged. It would still contain the deepest, most varied, beautiful, and amusing human expressions, wisdom, comedy, tragedy. That this least sensuous of the media—clever scratches on a plain surface as against the delicate, difficult "scratching" of violin music or the vigorous, intricate motion of human bodies on stage or screen, in marble or paint—is so powerful is a tribute to the supremacy of mind.

4.

A large percentage of the human population is, even today, more or less illiterate; but no percentage is wordless. Taciturnity, yes; sign language, yes; almost subhuman grunters, yes; but humanity is verbal and much of the verbal treasury is booked.

5.

The American Booksellers Association meets in Chicago, this prototypical city of industrial capitalism, the city of Globex and the Merc, a city notorious for extremes of more than weather, of organized crime and superstring theory, theatrical politics and a hundred theaters, a city of the deal and of architects and musicians, of social, legal, economic, and theological theory, great sports, and great con men. It is the city with the longest unbroken line of literary realism in America. From Mrs. Kinzie, the author of *Wau-bun*, through Joseph Kirkland, Hamlin Garland, Theodore Dreiser, James T. Farrell, Nelson Algren, and Saul Bellow to the penmen of today, Chicago's neighborhoods, social and ethnic castes, skyscrapers, sewers, beaches, airports, politicians, lawyers, criminals, and uncommon common people have been given voice, definition, and hyper-vivid existence by writers.

Our mayor, Richard M. Daley, is not famous for verbal felicity, but he invited Saul Bellow to speak at his inaugural and, with his cultivated wife, gave a wonderful seventy-fifth birthday party for him at the Art Institute. On that occasion, the present writer wondered aloud if he were in fifteenth-century Florence or twentieth-century Paris. He knew of no other large city mayor who'd celebrated the birthday of a great American writer.

The mayor's mayoral father, Richard J. Daley, was considered a prime offender against the English language. His more celebrated Yogisms include "Together we must rise to ever higher and higher platitudes" and "The policeman isn't there to create disorder; the policeman is there to preserve disorder." This Mayor Daley often drove to work with Judge Abraham Lincoln Marowitz (named by an immigrant mother who'd learned that this biblically named president had been shot in the temple, a word, she knew, that American Jews used for *synagogue*). Judge Marowitz reports that one day, Mayor Daley asked him about Stephen Douglas, whose monument they passed each day on the way to City Hall. Several years later, when the Oxford University Press asked around Chicago for someone to introduce a new biography of Douglas, Mayor Daley volunteered and gave a brilliant, literate, deesless-and-demless talk about Douglas and the politics of the 1850s.

6.

That May Wednesday when Senator Dole was giving his speech in Washington, its author, Mark Helprin, was speaking at the University of Chicago about art and the novel. I was unable to hear him because I was talking to a class about another novel, Stendhal's *Red and Black*,* perhaps the greatest of all accounts of the collision between power and senti-

---

* This was Albert Gore Junior's favorite novel. Since the only A student I had in my summer 1969 class at Harvard was an Albert Gore Jr. and since the novel we read was *Red and Black*, I've wondered if he was my student. (My attempts to find out have been in vain.)

ment. I told the class that I was just beginning to understand and agree with a statement—Susan Sontag's—which had once amazed and annoyed me, namely, that the finest product of the French Revolution had been this novel. One hundred and sixty-six years after the book's publication, it struck me that this brilliant, beautiful work had subtlized sensibility in a way new to human life. If the book has lost some of the revelatory shock it had in 1830, it compensates by leaving the finest of all accounts of post-Napoleonic France, its political, religious, and erotic tension displayed in the lives of some of the most marvelous characters ever invented. This, I suggested to the class, was power, the lasting power of literature which ultimately defines all that counts.

# A Glance at Bellow in Chicago, 1993

On February 3, 1993, pocketing the same recorder—and perhaps tape—with which I'd bungled an interview with Janet Lewis fourteen months earlier,* I met Bellow at the Quadrangle Club. He'd just come from teaching *Little Dorrit* and looked tired. Between his long, grooved white head and his sporty blue and white striped shirt, checked sport coat, and dark slacks, there was a large, sad space. Until, that is, recalling Dickens's description of Mr. Rugg, "Pancks' friend, with his hair like a worn-out hearth broom" and his daughter "with her face full of little yellow buttons," his face shed fatigue, lines, years, and one felt the boyish joy in the big laugh bursting from the full-lipped mouth, the gapped front teeth.

We went upstairs for dinner in the dark, paneled library: ten white-clothed tables rich in silver and glasses. Alone there, we were rich also in service, waiters recommending and serving us grilled tuna and a California chardonnay. In this manorial splinter of the university, Bellow felt safe. For years now, he'd been edgy about the danger of Chicago's streets and alleys.

We hadn't eaten by ourselves for a long time. There was much joking, remembering, analyzing. He said he was writing a novel about "a ninety-two-year-old man in Miami Beach who edits a magazine called *Brillig*. He has a girlfriend named Chickie McNellis." (We both roared at this new entry in the great Bellow directory, which, seven or eight years later, was absorbed into—but mostly lost—in the novel *Ravelstein*.) "They're trying to have a baby." (More roars. At the time, I didn't know that the Bellows had been trying to have one.) I told him about a classics student here whose ambition was to be the last mistress of David Grene, Bellow's

---

* Lewis died, age ninety-nine, in 1998. (See *One Person and Another: On Writers and Writing*.)

octogenarian colleague and team-teacher in the Committee on Social Thought. Another roar.

We talked of our children and grandchildren. His granddaughter, Juliet, was "reading Alice Walker and Toni Morison. She hasn't read a word of mine." Daniel, his youngest son, had left a reporter's job to bind skis in Colorado before taking exams for public policy schools. "With my Depression mentality, my thought is, 'You don't quit a job.'" The tone, if not the thought, was affectionate: he'd spoken with Daniel that morning. Thirty-odd years ago on St. Patrick's Day, the evening of Daniel's birth, I'd had a steak with him in the Cornell Lounge on 53rd Street. He'd wondered what a man on the edge of fifty was doing having another child. (No Chickie McNellis thoughts then.)

Melon and ice cream finished, he said, "We'd better get down to it."

"It" was the interview, the obligation. For years now, Bellow has done many of them. One aspect of Western success is this form of self-spillage, self-creation. Bellow has used most interviews to think out loud, more to set up new fiction than to explain and celebrate what's been. Baking one's own madeleine. Yet each interview is a sort of robbery, a threat to what counts. This interview was for a book we'd planned as a contribution to the University of Chicago's centennial celebration.

Downstairs, in the empty little Periodical Room, I tested the machine, pressed buttons, and began asking questions.

Two hours later, back home, I pushed the Play button. Except for the sentence which had tested out, there was nothing. Blank. I called Bellow. When he hears trouble in a voice, he's immediately sympathetic. "We'll do it again later." But he was off to Cincinnati in the morning, I to East Africa a few days later. We would have to do it between my return and his early March departure for two months in Paris.

When I came back from Africa, I called him. He was down with a virus; Paris was postponed for a week. In the rush of departure, there'd be no time. "Send me the questions, I'll write something while we're there."

Which I did. Paris brought him two fine, free months. Between lectures (at the Institute Raymond Aron, in Portugal and Budapest), he wrote—rewrote?—two hundred pages, walked the beautiful streets, and drank wine in the cafés with Janis. This interlude of urban ease led to a decision to accept an offer from Boston University that had been on their table for several years. "I'll live out the rest of my life in the East." In Boston, yes, but more, in Vermont, where, a few years earlier, he'd built a house and then a one-room studio through whose glass sides a wood pours greenness.

In any case, there was no time to tape the interview. "Besides," he said, "I hate the tape recorder. And you do too, or it wouldn't have failed. Send me the questions. Ask Janis to police me. I'll get it to you the first week in June."

I write this at the end of the third week in June. He's had the questions, Janis has been alerted, but I will not pester him any more. (Janis was to conduct the fine interview which appeared in *An Unsentimental Education*, edited by Molly McQuade in 1995.) A few days ago, he had his seventy-eighth birthday; he needs every moment for what counts.

What I do here, then, is set down what I remember of our taping session back in February.

Bellow said he first came to the University of Chicago in 1933 because it was nearby, and it was what his father could afford. He commuted from the northside to 51st Street and walked to the university through Jackson Park. (Did he mean Washington Park?) "You could walk anywhere then." Isaac Rosenfeld and Oscar Tarkov, his friends from the neighborhood and Tuley High, were here. "We were confident of our ability to learn everything." But "I was lost in the huge classes." He remembered Norman Maclean lecturing through clenched jaws as if reluctant to spare a word and then Walter Blair's Shakespeare class, "which I loved." (Walter, who died at ninety last year, remembered the young Bellow, "bringing me a Rooshian novel which I had never read.") After that first year, "My father had no more money, my mother had died, I left and went to work. Then I got interested in Africa and went up to Northwestern to study with that wonderful man, Melvin Herskowitz." Then it was "back here to study with Robert Redfield. . . . It was wonderful then, good old Bohemian Chicago. I got in with Gertrude Abercrombie [the painter] and her crowd. I worked for the WPA, wrote biographies of Anderson and Dos Passos. He'd been born here; I claimed him for the Midwest. They must be in a file somewhere." New York lay ahead. "I'd nearly gone years before. Sydney Harris and I wrote a book when we were fifteen and tossed a coin to see who would take it to New York. Sydney won and hitchhiked there. I think he saw Covici." (Pat Covici, who became Bellow's friend and publisher. Years before, he'd had a bookstore in Chicago.) "The people I knew here were Nathan Leites and Edouard Roditi. Roditi put us on to French literature. After that, the war, the Merchant Marine, New York."

I met Bellow in Chicago in late 1956 or in January 1957. I invited him to teach my class for a week that spring. "I took my first airplane flight for your class." (The class discussed a new story, "The Conversion of the Jews," by my fellow instructor, Philip Roth.) Afterward, when Bellow came down to Chicago from Minneapolis—he was teaching at the University of Minnesota—we'd met downtown at Pixley and Ehlers for coffee and sugar doughnuts among the Randolph Street bums. Sometimes we met at Jimmy's for beer and a burger. It was here he told me that writing *Augie March* was "like giving birth to Gargantua." We also met at my house or at the Cogans', where there was dancing, schnecken, and coffee. Zita Cogan had been a girlfriend from the old neighborhood. He used to climb the fire escape to see her. Her mother, a gamy old Communist, had sold stockings door to door but now spent time urging Saul to go to Russia, where "you can be a real writer." Bellow talked Yiddish with Zita's husband, Bernie, a jeweler who owned a complete file of Leavis's magazine, *Scrutiny* (which he later gave to Bellow's—and my—then friend Edward Shils). One semester Bellow taught at Northwestern. I drove up to his cramped hotel suite and read a version of *Henderson the Rain King* while his second wife, Sondra, drove baby Adam around Evanston until the writing stint was over. Their marriage was breaking up. A year or two later we had a gloomy talk about it: he said he thought about getting a gun and doing some damage to Jack Ludwig, his friend, the horn-maker. Bellow needed money. I arranged a Mandel Hall lecture in which he flayed Thomas Mann's work. He bought a car with the proceeds. In 1961, Shils and I worked to get him on the Chicago faculty. Oddly, there was resistance; luckily, not enough. He arrived in the fall of 1962 for the first of his thirty-one years with the Committee on Social Thought.

⇜⇝

Many questions hung—and still hang—in the air. Why hadn't Bellow ever bought a house in Hyde Park? Like many here, he could have gardened, which he loved to do. The two apartments he did buy were given up in divorce settlements. Perhaps that was behind the advice he gave his dear friend Allan Bloom to keep renting: "Why buy a cow when you can get milk delivered to the door?" Bloom's death in October 1992 was a terrible blow. Bellow had nurtured Bloom's success—he told me it was "a discipleship built for two"—then seen him through his illness. ("I couldn't have made it without Saul," Bloom told me a year or two before he failed to make it again.)

Twenty years earlier, of the lesser death of a minor Chicago poet, Bellow said, "Death is so big and Henry [Rago] was so little."

Perhaps the gloom of his Chicago dead had as much as anything to do with his leaving the city. Maybe, but on the hapless tape he'd said nothing of that.

*This piece of fiction—like the miscellany's two others—has been broken off a larger work and slightly tailored for this book.*

## Chicago, in the Depths of Feeling

Like most New York City kids of my class and generation, I didn't travel very far from home until I went away to college. I knew New England and had spent time with relatives in central Pennsylvania, and that was it until I went to college in North Carolina, which was The South to me until, after graduation, I took a bus to Florida, where a girl to whom I was more or less engaged lived and where I worked until her mother told me that her daughter could never marry a Jew, drove me to the station, saw that I bought a ticket on the Silver Meteor to New York, and, to my surprise and disgust, gave me a peck on the cheek as she hoisted my bag into it.

1.

I didn't see Chicago until after I'd spent three years in Europe, where I married Jean, became a father, discovered my vocation, and started practicing it. My Chicago base was Les Reilly, a pianist I'd met on the *Queen Mary* going over to Cherbourg in 1949. I was headed for a Fulbright teaching assignment in Versailles, Les for the Institute Cortot to study piano with Professor Jules Gentil. In Milwaukee, he'd studied piano ten years "with a pupil of a pupil of Leschititzky" but felt he couldn't take the next musical step until he had Europe under his belt. Hemingway and Fitzgerald had cooked that moveable feast in the twenties, and for years the young were ravenous for it. If the travel industry paid ten dollars to the estates of those two writers for every reader who took to sea and air for a bit of that feast, their heirs would be richer than Gates and Buffet. People like Les and me could be driven crazy with desire by words.

On that almost sleepless Atlantic trip—in whose four and a half days I made out—not the phrase of that day—with, indeed *fell*—its standard participle—for Gerda Ebel and Maidi Fuchs, I didn't notice Les un-

til the the third day out. In a Tourist Class talent contest, he played the
Chopin *Berceuse* and won twenty-five dollars and a bottle of champagne.
The bottle was emptied into our glasses and the money used to buy two
more.

Les's physiognomy was all thrust: though he was small, 5′5″ or 5′6″,
his blue eyes bulged, his teeth bucked, his ears Clark-Gabled like small
tables from his bright, orange-red head. His voice was loud and could
rise to hysteria; it was also capable of a variety of snorts, a gamut from
contempt to dismay. In both manic and depressive modes, he was for me
a comedian. We walked the Paris streets diagnosing *viva voce* the defects
of the locals, assuming of course that English was beyond them.

That first evening, on the *Queen Mary,* a dozen young passengers
drank around the Steinway while Les played Gershwin, and his wife,
Angela, black eyes so bright they looked as if they belonged to a special
electrical system, belted out—another standard participle of the day—
lyrics in the Ethel Mermanian torch fashion of the Milwaukee bars where
she'd sung to support them.

In Paris, the first week the three of us lived in a rathole on the Rue Budapest, near Gare St. Lazare. Then I took off for a Versailles *pension* and
they settled into a fuliginous Pigalle apartment a floor below an embit-
tered lady pianist who, when Reilly practiced, batted insanely away at the
piece he was playing. Every couple of weeks, I'd come into Paris, we'd
have dinner, and Reilly would play for me what he was studying; I'd sleep
on their floor and take the early train back from the Gare des Invalides for
my morning Anglais classes at the Collège Jules Ferry. In December, I
met Jean Ayers, who was taking the *Cours de Civilisation,* the money-making supplement the Sorbonne cooked up for *étrangers.* From then on, I
stayed not with the Reillys but at the apartment on the Rue Verneuil that
Jean shared with Bryna Johannson, an older—all of twenty-six—girl
who worked at the U.S. Cultural Center on the Rue St. Honoré.

Angela was pregnant. "In Milwaukee," Les proclaimed *viva voce* in
the Paris streets, "We were barren as mules. Three days into the Atlantic
and boom, connection."

Paris was our Atlantic: in May, Jean, two months' pregnant, went
back to Old Lyme to explain her Old World life to her parents. Meanwhile, I applied for jobs all over Europe and found one in the English
Section *(Anglistiksabteilung)* of the University of Heidelberg. I was to
teach two classes in American literature. The pay was auditors' fees

*(Ohrgeld)*, about two hundred dollars a semester, so I found a lucrative supplementary job with the U.S. Occupation Army. No sweat. I was a clerk in the Staff Message Control, editing mind-killing communiqués about personnel changes and supply problems from all over the European Command. In August, Jean flew back to Germany wearing the diamond engagement ring my parents gave her the day she and hers came into New York to meet them, and days later we were married in the baroque chapel of Heidelberg Castle by an army chaplain. Our ancient landlady, a granddaughter of the philosopher Schelling, was our maid of honor, and the best man was her boyfriend, Goetz Speicher, a thirty-year-old student in Alfred Weber's seminar who, as a Nazi submarine officer, had been imprisoned in an English prisoner of war camp where the—as he said—"Nazi poison was drained by reading Hölderlin."

The Reillys didn't come to our wedding, but, two months later, Les showed up at our door with photos of naked Angela giving suck to baby Rita. These he displayed to anyone encountered in our Hauptstrasse hang-out, the Schnookeloch. One day, a thoughtful-looking sociologist at the adjoining table studied them and asked Les what gender the baby might be. "Female," said Les. "A beautiful little girl named Rita Camille Johannson Reilly." "So sorry," said the sociologue. "I hope you'll have better luck next time." In Paris, Reilly had suffered every sort of pianistic insult—the skepticism of Professor Gentil, the mimicry of his upstairs neighbor, and most recently, the proclamation of an Englishman met in the local *estaminet* that no one named Reilly could concertize in England (adding as consolation that Reilly might, just might get work moving pianos on stage). The sociologist's dismissal of the world's newest Reilly roused Les to question the fellow's own lineage. There were ever-louder exchanges, then threats, shoves, punches, china-breakage, and, finally, banishment from the Schnookeloch.

Six weeks after that, a letter came from Angela telling us that Les had broken down, "so sick we called the priest from St. Augustin to give him last rites." Upstairs, the mad pianist had somehow intuited the proceedings and banged out, "over and over," wrote Angela, "the Chopin *Marche Funebre*. Maybe that did the trick. Two days later, Old Lester got out of bed, yelling for cognac. Then off to confront Gentil, who, probably to get rid of him, would that I could, gave him a pass mark. We're on our way back June 3 to Rudy Ganz's Chicago Musical College. Seeya in *Dick Tracy*."

2.

In 1955 I went to Chicago to do a piece for *Esquire* about the death of Enrico Fermi and the election of the first Mayor Richard Daley. I looked the Reillys up in the phone book, called, and accepted Les's invitation to stay in their basement apartment five blocks west of the lake in Hyde Park. During the day, Les had classes, nights he was a bellboy at the Del Prado Hotel, where, in addition to tips and salary, he picked up stray change, half-bottles of scotch, and, most recently, a discarded camel's hair overcoat not more than a size too big for him. He drove a growling '47 Hudson down the Outer Drive to and from the college, where he studied piano with a pupil of a pupil of Schnabel.

The dark apartment, an American clone of the one in Paris, stank of urine and defeat. Approaching it, you could make out tiny faces staring—desperately, I began to think—through the barred windows. Inside, a frazzled Angela chain-smoked Kools, drank dollar-a-bottle muscatel, washed diapers—drying on lines all over the house—and cursed her life of Reilly.

Jean and I had wondered what held them together. "They're always battling." "Not quite 'always.'" During the four days I stayed with them, I discovered their frenzied, careless sex life. God knows what got into the heads of their three little daughters. I peered warily into any room I entered to avoid the sight and sounds of copulation.

Love noise, smoke, urine, fatigue, and Beethoven saturated the dark rooms. Les was working on the Opus 101 in A, to which, until then, I'd never listened. He played it—I thought—marvelously. His pianistic weakness was memorizing, a drawback to a concert career, but not to fine performance. Les was a fair technician—his own appraisal—and had exceptional—ditto—musical intelligence. There were phrases in his Opus 101 few pianists could match. (My view.)

He showed me the sonata's shifts, transpositions, developments, symmetries. Playing the section over which Beethoven had written "lyrical, full of the innermost sensitivity" (or "deepest feeling": *mit innigsten Empfindung*), Reilly was a great master, or so, sitting on a broken sofa beside a bottle-sucking, fecal-stinking daughter, I believed. That music somehow altered my feeling for the waterbound, steel-proud city. *With the deepest feeling.* I fell for the place, the sea-sized lake reflecting the belt of glassy skyscrapers on shore, the endless neighborhoods, bohemian and black, Spanish and Polish, Litwak and hillbilly, marked by stone avenues and stippled by little green parks, and, every now and then, a stunning building or enormous factory that took your breath away. You felt every sort of human career and emotion pumping here, every human type, every trick, every sublimity.

*Mit innigsten Empfindung.*

Dodging outbursts of lust, nostrils tense with excretory fumes, I'd walk to Promontory Point, overlooking the great lake which smashed green-water fury against the protective stone tiers rising from its brim. From there, you had a grand view of the Loop's skyscrapers. The tallest buildings looked like masts of a great schooner, though one embarked not for Cythera but for Wealth and Power.

## 3.

My twelve-thousand-word piece on Fermi and Daley contrasted the end of the heroic scientific era of the thirties and forties with the stirrings of a new municipal era. I interviewed Daley, a solid, jowly man with sharp blue eyes and imperfect grammar, who exuded expertise, confidence, and strength. I couldn't get him to talk about himself, only about the city— its dwindling tax base, the state's legislative miserliness, the suburbs' exploitation of the city which nourished them. Grim about each difficulty, the thick-necked, jowly man in the blue suit, shirt, and tie couldn't, every now and then, keep back a burst of girlish giggling, the sign, as I read it, of joy in the municipal and national system he'd worked out to improve the city he so loved. Riding back to Hyde Park along the gorgeous lakeshore, I found myself unjournalistically crazy about that dese-and-deming, giggling, oddly brilliant man.

The next day, I interviewed a physicist who'd collaborated in Fermi's world-changing sustained reaction experiment under the old squash courts of Stagg Field. A skinny, peppery man in his late forties, he talked about the tension of that December afternoon, then, changing gears, described the Saturday softball games the physicists played. "Terrified when Fermi pitched that if we swung too hard and hit a ball into that head, Hitler might win the war."

No one could be more different from the mayor than this passionate atomic physicist, but I felt a kinship of power and of intelligence there. Later, back at the Reillys', listening to Lester playing the thoughtful chords of the Opus 101, I fused the two of them into my feeling for their city.

4.

Reilly was playing with exceptional passion. That morning, driving back on Lakeshore Drive, he'd been pulled over by a cop. Without looking, he did the Chicago thing, handing his license, clipped to a five-dollar bill, out the window. The cop, "a bruiser," reported Les, pushed it aside, reached in the window, and fingered the camel's hair overcoat. "You're getting," he said, "a little big for five there, Lester." Reilly, princely with five, coughed up a ten.

Angela often laid into him about his driving—"You don't dream, you don't masturbate, you don't sightsee, you d-r-i-v-e!" She hated the Hudson. "That oil-leaking whale." Today, the denunciation, fueled by the lost tenner, was followed by an oratorical condemnation of the life he led and the one to which he'd condemned her. Les responded in kind, which led to shrieks, slaps, blows, and then, Venus knows how, furious, furniture-shoving copulation—with the little girls and I retreating to the kitchen.

5.

The piece I wrote was a mess. Felker, the *Esquire* editor with whom I worked, said I should change the names and turn it over to Rust Hills, the fiction editor. Somehow a farcical note had fused or—Felker said—been confused with a soppy romantic one, that *Empfindung* which I had for the city.

6.

Les and Angela are dead. Three more children and several miscarriages later, she broke apart in a sea of muscatel. Les, teaching piano in an Oklahoma City community college, married the young assistant registrar—"I am her her Paris and her Greece," he wrote me—had two children, then was divorced by her and moved back to Chicago. Driving there, he skidded into a truck and crushed an index finger, which ended his piano playing.

In Chicago, he bought and sold pianos, wrote about concerts for neighborhood newspapers, and did a "corrective edition" of Debussy's *Suite Bergamasque* for a new music publisher, taking so long to do it that he got no other assignments. He lived on a small academic and a larger veteran's pension plus a few dollars for playing—he was up to this—Gershwin, Berlin, Kern, Rodgers, and Porter in a local club. (That lasted until Watergate, when even older patrons wanted other sounds.)

Every few years, he got to New York. If I was there, I'd take him to the best restaurant in which his ever-shabbier clothes and ever more depressed, ever louder and odder self would not be embarrassingly conspicuous. I'd listen to the latest installment of his saga, the scholarships, graduations, jobs, and then, the bolt-out-of-the-blue deaths of two of his children, his own stays in veterans' hospitals for electric shock depression treatments. There were also stories of new enthusiasms, mental, medical, musical, and sexual encounters (rubbing against women on buses, hand-jobs in the listening cabins of Tinklin' Tunes, even a couple of lengthy—at least protracted—relationships with other gifted castoffs).

7.

It was Rita, whom I had not seen for forty-five years, who called to tell me that "Dad died in the elevator" of his dingy Chicago apartment house. "Heart attack."

"He had lots of heart, Rita."

"And a tough time letting his kids know about it."

She told me when and where the funeral service would be.

I could—should?—have flown to Chicago for it, but I didn't. I hadn't been there for six or seven years, and now, some ugly disinclination to pay respects to a dead friend kept me away. The day of the funeral, I telegraphed flowers and wrote an email letter to Les's children about what a special man and friend their father had been. That evening, I sat in my workroom with a snifter of cognac listening to Artur Schnabel playing the Opus 101 and let myself have the luxury of breaking down in the "rather lively and with the deepest feeling"—*etwas lebhaft und mit der innigsten Empfindung*—section of the beautiful Allegretto.

# III

## THE IS OF WAS

*The 2000 Subway Series between the New York Yankees and the New York Mets opened with "the ceremonial first pitch" delivered by a white-haired, stooped Don Larson to a somewhat more robust looking, but clearly arthritic, Yogi Berra. In this now oldest of democratic countries, whose anti-feudal principles celebrate perpetual renewal, the level playing field, and equality of opportunity, the desire for rootage and historical perspective erupts in strange ways. Instead of a Stonehenge, we have five-hundred-year-old Indian arrowheads and million-year-old dinosaur bones. For our Parthenon, we have Williamsburg, baseball stats, and celebrations of survivors, war veterans, sports heroes, and even, occasionally, writers, painters, and composers. That Don Larson's pitch bounced its way toward though not into Yogi Berra's glove pleased us far more than if he'd somehow or other winged in one of the fastballs which Berra had called for in that famous "perfect game" almost half a century ago.*

*Those of us in my corner of the American scene see, each year, more of our contemporaries turning into the marble of literary history. Most of us collaborate in these exhibitions. Little that we read and less that we hear tells us what our insides tell us is the truth about the past we know. We write our corrective reviews or letters, appear on programs with more or less brilliant biographers and historians from whom we often learn much that surprises us even as we sense that when our friends and enemies or we ourselves are mentioned there's something missing, and that the museum of history must be full of forgeries and fakes.*

*In fact, our own version of the actuality we knew will often be as far from it as the Don Larson and Yogi Berra of 2000 from the Larson and Berra of 1956.*

*In this section, there are some versions of this theme in pieces about several biographies and autobiographies. It ends with a short story that handles the theme in a more oblique manner.*

# Over the Hill

Autobiography and memoir writing are senior precincts. The presumption is that having made it over the hill, you've had the good view and are willing to describe it for other climbers. No longer active, you have little to lose, less to conceal. Yeats called this "withering into truth."

Writing about your past is a familiar way of rounding it out. If you've done it with style, your readers will make adjustments for geriatric vanity and score-settling. Indeed, they may relish them as revelations of your crusty character.

The Free Press has published the autobiographical memoirs of two stalwarts of the modern conservative movement whose peculiar icon, Ronald Reagan, was peculiarly assessed in Edmund Morris's biography.* These stalwarts, Norman Podhoretz, longtime editor of *Commentary* magazine, and Thomas Sowell, the economist, are intellectuals, and Reagan doesn't play a central role in their stories, but the success he represents and embodies does. Their life *Kampf,* like his, was, as they tell it, against the grain. Like him, they began on the left; like him, they began poor; like him, they started far from the centers of power. Now seventy, their chief work done, they are senior fellows of conservative think tanks, Podhoretz at the Hudson Institute, Sowell at Stanford's Hoover Institution.

Born in Brooklyn to impoverished Jewish parents, Podhoretz spoke as much Yiddish as English and had so thick an accent that a teacher insisted he take a remedial speech class. For this, as for almost everything he describes, Podhoretz is grateful. The class not only cleared up his ac-

---

* Thomas Sowell, *A Personal Odyssey* (New York: Free, 2000); Norman Podhoretz, *My Love Affair with America: The Cautionary Tale of a Cheerful Conservative* (New York: Free, 2000).

cent but opened the way to fellowships which, he believes, would have been otherwise denied him. It also opened up the wondrous English language, with which he's had a lifelong affair almost as intense as the one which gives the title to his book. Educated at Columbia and Cambridge, Podhoretz served in the U.S. Army, where he encountered some of the "ordinary guys" who are the "true backbone" of his beloved country. At thirty, he was made editor of the magazine whose credo was that the Jews of America—all of them and not just the intellectuals—belonged in and to America. They were not living in *galut,* the diaspora, waiting to be brought home by the messiah or by David Ben Gurion: they were home already.

Sowell, born in North Carolina to poor black parents, was raised in Harlem by a great-aunt he for years believed was his mother. His upward struggle was slower and tougher than Podhoretz's. Intelligent, full of curiosity and ambition, Sowell saw that almost every attempt at realizing himself was blocked by the low expectations and sheer racket around him. Tenacity and a remarkable, almost arrogant self-reliance saw him through Howard, Harvard, and the University of Chicago (the last the only school he respected). Drafted into the Marine Corps, his bristling toughness developed a carapace of rational calculation which, in retrospect, he thinks of as "thinking like an economist." Like Podhoretz, he has one daughter and a son named John. His favorite editor is Podhoretz's wife, Midge Decter; he's written for Podhoretz's former magazine and is cited in Podhoretz's book. Also like Podhoretz, he regards himself as a hard-nosed, difficult, independent man.

Being admirable and difficult men is one thing; being admirable writers is another. These two autobiographies are cut to the same roughly chronological pattern, and each ends with a litany of thanks for the luck which helped bring their authors where they are. Podhoretz thanks America for granting him "the inheritance of the English language," for sending him to great universities, for letting him "make a modest but decent living," for opening "the way . . . to meet and mingle . . . with some of the most interesting people of my time," for handing "me a magazine of my own to run," for seeing "to it that I would live in an apartment in Manhattan much like the one in which the affluent parents of some of my classmates at Columbia had lived," for arranging for him to "build a country house on the east end of Long Island," with a study door that clicks shut, unlike the doors of the crowded Brooklyn home in which he grew up. Only the last has something of the individuality which almost everywhere enriches Sowell's book. *My Love Affair with America* is soft-core Podhoretz. At his best as scrapper and polemicist, his well-known attacks on Bellow's *The Adventures of Augie March* and an anti-Semitic essay of Gore Vidal were full of bite. His accounts of them here are toothless—the fights are long over. His retelling of old political warfare sags with tedium. Nor does gushing at the glories of English and American literature inspire addition to them. Only when he writes about his narrow, egocentric relatives and early days in Brooklyn is there any of the flavor that distinguishes Sowell's book, although even here the taste is of poorly warmed-up leftovers.

> . . . his teacher, like most of her colleagues, was a middle-aged Catholic woman of Irish ethnicity and (in the lingo of those days) an "old maid." Probably representing a majority of the teachers in the elementary division of the New York City public-school system of the 1930s, they were something like (and may even have seen themselves as) secular nuns. . . . This was the very height of the age of the "melting pot."

Poor, even ungrammatical, stuff. Young editor Podhoretz would have red-penciled it from the pages of *Commentary*.

Sowell's book is better because he does not establish character by proclamation but in action. He's a storyteller. In some stories, he's the dupe, in others the duper. So he tells of a Marine Corps boxing match in which he swings wildly, missing his opponent but causing him to trip and get counted out. In Sowell's next match, he is beaten to a pulp; his opponent tells him later, "the reason he dared not let up on me was fear of that 'one punch' that could turn the fight around." Mostly, it's Sowell's crabby stubbornness that's at the heart of the stories, and to no small degree, of his life. He can't bear the lazy habits of students, masked at Howard by victimization cant and at Cornell by the contempt of engineering students for unquantified thinking. He ends up resigning from both schools. In the academy and in government—where he had a job with the Labor Department—he encounters indolence and timidity which prevent him from doing or completing his work. This leads him to swear off government programs, and he resigns from the department. There are people he admires, often those who've taken chances on and believed in him, a foreman at a machine shop, his false Mom's daughter, his siblings, his Chicago teachers, George Stigler and Milton Friedman, and then his beloved children (one of whom, a very late talker, becomes the center of his pioneering study of late bloomers) and second wife. His litany of gratitude is a neat summary of his life: "it now seems in retrospect almost as if someone had decided that there should be a man with all the outward indications of disadvantage, who nevertheless had the key inner advantages needed to advance."

Two distinguished conservative seniors, two books, but only one with any claim to distinction. As there is political morality, sexual morality, and social morality, so there is esthetic morality. That's why Podhoretz's book sullies not only the character of its author but of two distinguished friends who praise his book so extravagantly that they themselves are demeaned by it. Daniel Patrick Moynihan is quoted on the jacket as saying "Not, surely, since *The Education of Henry Adams* have we had so profound, yet lively account of a life of ideas," and William Buckley says, "Never (that I know) has a single lifetime borne such literary and philosophical fruit." For shame, gentlemen. It would have been a greater act of friendship to have reminded the poetry-loving Podhoretz of the words of William Blake: "Never seek to tell thy love / Love that never told can be." Thomas Sowell understands this.

# On *Atlas on Bellow*

I.

In the acknowledgments section of his biography of Saul Bellow, James Atlas quotes a somewhat greater biographer, Samuel Johnson.

> We know how few can portray a living acquaintance, except by his most prominent and observable particularities and the grosser features of his mind, and it may be easily imagined how much of this little knowledge may be lost in imparting it, and how soon a succession of copies will lose all resemblance of the original.*

Johnson knew few of those whose lives he described and none nearly as well as Boswell knew him. (Which, considering their few days together, was not all that well.) Would he have been as pessimistic about the unreliability of history and biography if he'd read Boswell's book? Probably more so. The truer, the more vivid the portrait, the more repellent to such a subject.

I'm not as pessimistic about discovery as Johnson was. So, for instance, well as I knew Bellow before reading Atlas's biography, I think I know him better now.

Know him?

I mean that I know more about the places he lived, what his parents were like, what others thought of him, what he said about many things, including me. (To my surprise, I learned that I was once mentioned in his will and that, perhaps after one of our arguments, was removed from it.) It doesn't mean that my view of Bellow now is Atlas's. By no means.

Atlas also knows Bellow and was helped by him in the course of writ-

* James Atlas, *Bellow: A Biography* (New York: Random House, 2000).

ing his book.\* He writes that he immersed himself in his records and acquaintance far more than he'd done for his prize-winning biography of Delmore Schwartz (whom he'd never met). He wonders, though, if familiarity and labor have produced a better book. I think this is a better book, largely because Bellow is more brilliant, interesting, and accomplished than Schwartz. (Indeed, Bellow's version of a Schwartz-like character in *Humboldt's Gift* is far more amusing and touching than the one in the Atlas biography which was—we learn in Atlas's new book—inspired by it.)

Better, truer; more interesting, more touching.

The first two distinctions don't matter in works of fiction. So the uproar over Bellow's *Ravelstein* doesn't bear on its power as a novel or, on the other hand, on the pain it gave and gives some who saw themselves "portrayed" and perhaps "betrayed" in it. They do matter, however, for biography. Would Boswell's *Life of Dr. Samuel Johnson* be as good a book if it were a work of fiction, if, say, the Johnson in it hadn't lived or had been a totally different man? It would not be. The understanding a biographer establishes with his readers includes the sense that he is telling as much of the truth as he's been able to gather about actual people and events. If that understanding is compromised, it constitutes an esthetic betrayal different from—and, in my view, worse than—the "betrayal" of a fiction writer's acquaintance in his fiction.

I'm one of the many Bellow friends Atlas interviewed and whom he cites in *Bellow: A Biography*. Much that I know and feel about Bellow is not in the book because I didn't tell Atlas about it. Some of it would have somewhat altered his portrait of Bellow; none of it would have altered it significantly.

Most of the book's citations from me are from letters Bellow wrote me or I him.† Such citations constitute the sort of record biographers and other historians have drawn on since good history has been assessed as a function of it. If I'd given Atlas access to my journals he would have

---

\* Although Bellow told me that he "opened himself" to Atlas, who then turned away from him. I said that Atlas probably didn't want his work to be compromised by affection. After I wrote Bellow not to read the book, he answered that he wouldn't, that there was "a parallel" between it "and the towel with which the bartender cleans the bar." This image of biography as the soak of spilled drinks is the sort of thing Bellow has invented for most of his eighty-five years.

† Most of our letters are filed in the Special Collections of the Regenstein Library at the University of Chicago.

found another source of Bellow matter which would have expanded, if not deepened, let alone altered, his view of his subject. The subject of every biography has had millions of thoughts and experiences which have never—thank God—been recorded. The gulf Johnson wrote about is uncrossable.

The difference between modern history-biography and, say, what constituted their equivalent in Thucidydean Athens or seventeenth-century Europe is enormous. Scholars don't believe that Pericles delivered the oration which Thucydides attributed to—that is, wrote for—him, although he probably delivered a speech that resembled it. Our problem with a presidential speech today is not the actuality of the words pouring from the presidential mouth but who wrote and even who conceived them. We're content that our conception of Periclean Athens is to no small degree that of Thucydides, but the historical standard is different for modern events and people, those who leave their tracks in letters and diaries, interviews and film.

Atlas uses such archival materials and such biographical techniques as interviews, and he is far more aware of the hazards as well as the advantages of such usage than, say, Vasari was in his verbal portraits of fifteenth- and sixteenth-century artists (some of whom he knew). A good journalist, Atlas has a nose for bias and such vested interest as the desire of ordinary people to be part of the record of extraordinary ones. He also raises the question of how his long biographical labor affected his book. Did he, like his mythical namesake, get so weary of "holding up" the "bewilderingly complex" Bellow world that the exasperated weariness created a portrait as far from actuality as Thucydides' Pericles was from the "actual" Pericles?

2.

I've known Bellow for forty-five years. For many of those years, we've been close friends and have said things to each other that we may not have said to other people. We have also quarreled, disagreed, and not seen each other for months and even years at a time. Our politics have been different, and the difference counted—perhaps more for him than for me. Nonetheless, we are close enough so that a few days before I wrote these words, we could tell each other on the phone—the first time we'd spoken since my wife and I stayed with him and his wife in their Vermont house two years ago—things we'd have avoided saying earlier. We are old men now, and I believe that we thought it possible that we wouldn't see or talk with each other again. In that conversation, I told Bellow that I'd read much of Atlas's book and that he shouldn't be concerned about it. I said that Atlas had built a crate large and secure enough to deliver the marvelous sculpture within.

A few hours later, I finished the last hundred or hundred fifty pages of the book. In them, I detected weariness complicated by judgmental anger. Atlas had interviewed many people who'd been hurt—or said they'd been hurt—by Bellow. Partly as an attempt to maintain his independence of and objectivity about Bellow, partly from his sense that he'd surrendered—his verb—his life to another man, a man whom he'd been seeing in part through the angry eyes of others, Atlas had become harsher and harsher in his assessments. I wrote Bellow telling him that although what counted—the portrait of a remarkable person becoming over decades ever more remarkable—was intact, I believe that it was deformed by Atlas's querulous anger, if not by sanctimonious contempt, and that he and Janis (Bellow's wife) would do well not to read it. "Hector and Andromache," I wrote, "don't need to know Thersites's version of their lives."

This was perhaps as unfair to Atlas as I thought he was, at times, to Bellow, but then Atlas writes that I am Bellow's "old and faithful friend," the "Boswellian explainer of the great man to the general public," so any unfairness to him has been—clairvoyantly?—subverted.

3.

Very well. As friend of subject and author, I am disqualified from reviewing Atlas's—I'll risk two adjectives—fascinating, sometimes brilliant book.* I will instead talk about Johnson's concern: the gulf between actuality and its representation in biography, conversation, and history.

I've read a number of books and hundreds of articles about people I've known. There are few, though, from which I've not learned often surprising, even shocking, facts, none in which I haven't felt at least some distance between what was written and what I knew. At times, as in the case of *Bellow,* my complex admiration for the central portrait has complicated and deepened my admiration for the friend portrayed. Reading remarks Bellow made or wrote years before I met him made me realize even more how remarkable a person he was and is.

---

* See Atlas's well-done interview with me, originally commissioned by George Plimpton for the *Paris Review,* in *Chicago Review* (Fall–Winter 1999).

More than twenty years ago, the day after I finished reading the manuscript of *Humboldt's Gift*, I had lunch with its author and told him that it
was difficult for me to think that the man across the table was the same
man who'd written that profound, delightful, beautiful book. The man
eating a sandwich and drinking tea talked with me about ordinary as well
as extraordinary things, but nothing out of his mouth came close to the
depth and beauty of what was on its best pages, and I said something like,
"Yet there's less distance between you and your work than between any
writer I've known and his."*

Atlas's biography has narrowed that distance for me. For all the
schmutz that accumulates about and spatters the central portrait, it
emerges as that of a great man becoming great in the course of a long life
of activity, acquaintance, introspection, and expression. There is more
original power in the intelligence recorded here than in 95 percent of biographies. Atlas does not have the mimetic power of Boswell or of a
writer he rightly praises here, Mark Harris, author of a delightful book
about Bellow called *The Drumlin Woodchuck;*† he does not have the stylistic or analytic gifts of Samuel Johnson or Richard Ellmann, but what he
does have is access to hundreds of brilliant Bellow observations and
analyses outside of Bellow's books. Atlas's *Bellow* is like a match, Atlas's
contribution being the assemblage and, perhaps, the wooden stem, Bellow's the sulphur which, rubbed, ignites and fires the wood.

4.

The day the galleys of this book arrived in the mail, I saw my sister-in-
law, who, days earlier, on a trip with her husband to Israel, had swum in
the Dead Sea. She said that there were all sorts of perils there, the crystalline spears one dodges to get to the viscous water, which deposits a
salty scum on one's skin, and the water's semi-impenetrability, so that if
one somehow managed to dive into it, ascending would be dangerously
difficult. I felt an analogy to the perils of biography. The subject is himself
almost impenetrable, guarded by fearful suspicion and his own complexity; even after getting access to him, the progress is difficult, and biogra-
pher-readers are left with the scum of his resistance to their penetration.

---

* No one seemed more different from his work to me than Samuel Beckett, whom I saw
about once a year between 1977 and 1987. See the portrait of him in *One Person and Another* (Dallas: Baskerville, 1993).

† This is a book dedicated to me in which I play a minor role.

I've thought and talked about Bellow—and now this biography—with a few friends who also know him. Each sees Bellow in a somewhat different way; all condemn Atlas's version more than I. (I credit Atlas for collecting and organizing the materials which enable us to know more about Bellow; they blast him for his inability or unwillingness to understand him.) One friend, a novelist, thinks that Atlas not only misunderstands Bellow's radical independence but resents it. So he sees a politically correct Atlas piling up criticism along familiar—to Bellow critics—misogynist, conservative, and racial lines. He thinks that Atlas is shocked by Bellow's anarchic "cocksmanship," and when I suggested that Bellow had a grand streak of bad boy, if not outlaw, in him, he found a different way to express his own view: "He's a transgressive monkey. And a great con man."* He makes Bellow into a version of a character in his own fiction, a brilliantly anarchic, half-crazed sexual adventurer.

A former woman friend of Bellow's talked of his powers of devotion and charm. She detests Atlas's portrait, especially the account—to which she feels one of her letters has contributed—of his love-making.† "He made me feel wonderful. I still love him." (She hasn't seen him in ten years.)

I myself have written about Bellow as a man simpler in many ways than other people, one who early in his life discovered his powers and let them set his course. More important than what happened to him—and I'm persuaded by Atlas that such things as the death of his mother help explain later behavior—were these exceptional powers: an extraordinary memory, an extraordinarily acute and cultivated sensorium (visual, musical, olfactory, tactile), and—let's call it—emotional power (unusual ability to empathize, sympathize, love, hate, and also be detached). Like most of us, Bellow is many things, but unlike most of us, he's more of a piece and has been that way a very long time. The piece is stamped "writer," indeed "great writer," and the pressure of that stamp isn't like most other professional pressures.

5.

What I've mostly wanted to hint at is the difficulty of writing, reading, and being the subject of other people's descriptions of oneself and to

---

* We both remember Bellow's early portrait of the terrific Chicago con man Yellow Kid Weil.

† On the order of John F. Kennedy, one of whose "girls" is said to have described the relationship as "the greatest 30 seconds of my life."

spell out what Johnson said was the distance between the real, the remembered, and the written version of reality, the deformation of the
"was" in the "is." Yet such versions are what we have of the past, the history and biography with which we're left. One work of history can challenge or even refute another, or it can add to, refine, or subtilize it. Even
memories rub against each other. Yet I do not subscribe to the notion (of,
say, Peter Novick's splendid book, *That Noble Dream*) which tries to dis-
pose of the actuality of objectivity. I don't think that we should abandon
the recording of actuality as an ideal or ever think that there's no crucial
difference between what we believe is actual and what we know we've
made up or lied about, yet what we get when we describe something or
someone is, at its driest and purest, metamorphosis.

The greatest—at least the most delightful—investigator of such
metamorphosis, Marcel Proust, claimed that only in what he called "involuntary memory" does the past ever reemerge with its original—and
even more than its original—power. (Beckett's comment about this was
that Proust showed that the only real paradise was a lost one.) Sensuous,
unsummoned memory is clarified as reflections in a clear pool are, free of
the dust particles and blinding light of an actuality which makes what's
reflected almost impossible to see.

Atlas's *Bellow* is a work built around voluntary, elicited, and recorded
memory. It is a version of actuality that may be read, sometimes with
shivers of recognition, by its subject and his acquaintance. It has a truth
of its own, somewhere between the original actualities, the complex feelings and memories of those who supplied the author with data and the
author's own gifts and feelings. The portrait of the great man who is its
subject will be difficult to dislodge. Luckily, the man has left a far more
powerful self-portrait, that of the mentality behind his beautiful books.

# Bertrand Russell

Scene: Pembroke Lodge, the estate given to the former prime minister, Lord John Russell, by Queen Victoria ("the giant paperweight that for half a century sat upon men's minds," H. G. Wells). Time: 1883. Persons: Frank Russell, eighteen, on school holiday from Winchester, and his eleven-year-old brother, Bertie, educated at home under the supervision of the widow, Lady Russell, mother of his long-dead father (who'd barely survived his young wife). Frank has just given Bertie his first lesson in Euclid; Bertie asks him why he should simply accept the axioms. That's the way it is, says Frank, and if you don't like it, no more lessons.

Bertie did like it, and, decades later, wrote of his "delight in the power of deductive reasoning . . . the restfulness of mathematical certitude" and, above all, "the belief that nature operates according to mathematical laws, and that human actions, like planetary motions, could be calculated if we had sufficient skill," an insight which suggested to him that he might be, after all, intelligent. "This was," he wrote in his autobiography, "one of the great events of my life, as dazzling as first love."

Intelligence.

For almost all his almost century-long life, Russell expressed and stood for intelligence. At first, it was concentrated on mathematics and logic. His decade-long attempt—with his old Cambridge tutor, Alfred North Whitehead—to distill the axiomatic foundation of mathematics was perhaps his single greatest intellectual effort. (Not his most remunerative: he calculated that he and Whitehead had made "minus fifty pounds"—their contribution to publication costs—for the *Principia Mathematica*.) After that, the intelligence spread over a hundred fields. Here are some Russell titles: *ABC of Relativity, Authority and the Individual, The Conquest of Happiness, Leibniz, The Democratic Ideal, Common Sense and Nuclear Warfare, Education and the Social Order, Foreign Policy of the Entente, German Social Democracy, Impressions of America, Marriage and Morals, Portraits from Memory, The Problem of China, Satan in the Suburbs* (fiction), *The Status of Women, War Crimes in Vietnam, Why I Am Not a Christian.* There are thousands of articles, speeches, lectures, letters. Russell stood for Parliament, founded and helped his second wife run a pioneering school, spoofed, oracled, and debated on radio and television. Galvanized in his nineties by the Vietnam War as he had been in his seventies and eighties by the fear of nuclear destruction, he played a role in an international tribunal (somewhat less gloriously than the one he'd played during the Cuban missile crisis of 1962, when Khrushchev used him as a public conduit). Explaining, clarifying, coordinating, mocking, rejoicing, condemning, Russell appealed to enlightenment, was enlightenment.

Yet.

Scene. Isola Bella off the Sicilian coast. Time: Russell is eighty. Persons: Young painters, children and grandchildren of Russell's friends. A picnic, fish grilled on hot stones, wine, music. Earl Bertie chases and kisses the girls. "I'm as drunk as a lord, but then I am one."

"Philosophers and mathematicians in love are exactly like everyone else," Russell wrote one of the many women in his life, "except, perhaps, that the holiday from reason makes them passionate to excess."

It was partly "glands," partly solitude, the unendurable "loneliness of the human soul" that drove Russell from the isolation of his orphaned childhood to the joys of sex and companionship. Whether it was talking with the Apostles (the twelve self-selected Cambridge Talkers), enchanting the children at his school, bringing his students at Chicago, California, Harvard, and Oxford home for good whiskey and talk, organizing protests of every sort, or vainly trying to settle in with his wives and children, Bertrand Russell lived as gregariously as his eighteenth-century counterpart, Voltaire. He surrounded himself with intelligence and welcomed it when it sought him out. From the logic-obsessed genius Ludwig Wittgenstein,* who broke with him over his "vomitous" popularizing to the woman who thanked God for his work only to be told that the remark suggests "that He has infringed my copyright," Russell existed for others in courtesy, wit, receptive comprehension, clarification, charm, and erotic liberty.

---

* He is the subject of a wonderful biography by Raymond Monk, which, unlike Caroline Moorehead's life of Russell, brilliantly examines the philosophical work.

That his work is now read largely for the beauty of his style or for its historical interest, that the causes he championed are either dissolved in the stream of modern life or ignored as crank irrelevancies, that two of his four marriages ended in bitterness and that his children were somehow broken seem to ratify the gloom, pessimism, and irrationality which existed near the core of joy, passion, and clarity he celebrated.

Caroline Moorehead's biography chronicles the scandals—political, sexual, domestic, and intellectual—which broke out of and around this remarkable man.* Drawing on newly available letters from his wives, mistresses, friends, and publishers as well as conversations with his survivors, it is a sort of descriptive menu of the Russell cuisine. Among its finds is this bit of a letter to Gamel Brenan, one of the many women Russell loved (though, in this rare instance, probably didn't sleep with):

> I wish I believed in a timeless Platonic world where whatever has held a momentary existence in the stream survived timelessly in heaven. The moments of ecstasy in love, of sudden intellectual insight, of intoxicating glory in storms on a rocky coast. . . . I should like to think of them as forever part of the universe. But that is mysticism and folly, born of old fear. If we must die, let us die sober, not drunk with pleasant lies. I should like to end gloriously . . . like a Shakespeare hero; it is shocking to think that as the bomb bursts I shall be wondering how to find the money for next month's bills.

* Caroline Moorehead, Bertrand Russell: A Life (New York: Viking, 1999).

## Misunderstanding Carnap

As I understand it, a hypostatization or substantiation or reification consists in mistaking as things entities which are not things. C A R N A P, *Meaning and Necessity*

Twelve year olds with stomach cancer.
Precisions of fog.
Unending conclusions.

In odd months
making arrangements
sensed disorder
quarreling

Spring drained primary colors

Took two weeks at the shore
painted cactus at the pole,
ate plums in Martha's
Vineyard.
Then,
tubes dry,
brushes stiff,
packed country anger
and returned
to distressed urbanity.

# W. C. Fields

Paid for seeing a learned pig—1 shilling. THOMAS JEFFERSON,
*Diaries,* 1786

Freak shows, minstrel shows, burlesque, variety and Wild West shows,
showboats, circuses, rodeos, dime museums, music halls, olios, vaude-
ville: live entertainment before nickelodeon and bioscope, radio and
movies, television, digital and virtual reality. What we do in our spare
time may not require all that much of us but—perhaps for that reason—
it becomes part of the interior which supplies us with the boundaries of
physical possibility, with the images of extravagance and desire, horror
and disgust, delight, thrill, and, best of all, insight, comic, pathetic, and
tragic, into our lust and looniness. The learned pig Jefferson paid a shilling to see, Houdini's escapes, Ziegfield's girls, Tarentino's films slake
that thirst for diversion—what role does it play in the maintenance of
the gene pool?—that as much as anything distinguishes humans from
reptiles. Why is it that millions, maybe billions of us keep the face, voice,
costume, walk, and almost the meaning of a hundred princes of diversion in our interior gallery? Take the subject of this biography.* Does
anybody reading this not instantly conjure up—and smile at—what's
behind the eight letters W.-C.-F-i-e-l-d-s, the sardonic drawl, the swollen
diction, the swagger, the battered top hat, the flip of the whiskey jigger,
the straw hat on the cane, the snarl at children, the mutter at the connubial termagant, the sales pitch delivered to the naïve or swallowed when
delivered by the most obvious of con men? Why?

Perhaps because Fields and his few peers have worked ways of being

* Simon Louvish, *Man on the Flying Trapeze: The Life and Times of W. C. Fields* (New
York: Norton, 1997).

and performing which incarnate so much of what we see and are that it's inadequate to say that they "mean" this or that. They don't mean, they just are (or were). After Fields's death in 1946, the English novelist J. B. Priestley, who'd seen him juggling before World War I, described him moving "warily, in spite of a hastily assumed air of nonchalant confidence, through a world in which even inanimate objects were hostile, rebellious, menacing, never to be trusted. . . . They were not, you see, his things. . . . He did not belong to this world, but had arrived from some other and easier planet." Simon Louvish, the novelist who teaches film at the London International Film School, quotes this eulogy, but his biography spends five hundred pages placing Fields firmly on this planet.

᠅

William Claude Dukenfield, born and raised in Philadelphia, the son of an English emigrant who fought in the Civil War, and an American of German ancestry, left school in the third grade but stayed more or less peacefully at home working in a department store, racking balls in a pool hall, and delivering newspapers. At fifteen, "the juggling urge first asserted itself," his model, Paul Cinquevalli, Prince of Jugglers. Fields was good but no Prince. Terrified of dropping his cigar boxes, "desperate" about his act failing, he one day realized what every great entertainer learns.

> I had heard a man say he liked a certain fellow because he was always the same dirty so and so. You know, like Larsen in Jack London's 'Sea Wolf'. He was detestable, yet you admired him because he remained true to type. Well, I thought that was a swell idea so I developed a philosophy of my own, be your type! I determined that whatever I was, I wouldn't teeter on the fence.

The birth of an artistic creation is a wonderful thing to see. The most thrilling paragraph in the autobiography of Fields's detested younger rival ("that goddamned ballet dancer"), Chaplin, describes the minutes in which he found the small derby, big shoes, and baggy pants which turned him into—Charlie. Fields told an interviewer, "So long as I have this personality . . . it wouldn't matter whether my tricks or my sketches were no good."

Intelligent, how intelligent Fields and so many of the other unschooled comics were. Many spoke and wrote brilliantly. Fields was even learned, and not just in the history and practice of his trade. Years later, Eddie Cantor, another up-from-the street comedian, wrote about working with Fields in the Follies. One evening he noticed that Fields's theatrical trunks were filled with books. Fields told him that "you didn't know anything until you started to read," and from then on, he gave Cantor books to read at night—Dickens, Hugo, Dumas, George Eliot, science, history—then in the morning quizzed him about them. Cantor called him "Professor Fields." When, years later, David Selznick was casting *David Copperfield*, Fields lobbied for the role of Micawber and played it wonderfully. Why not? Micawber was one of the Dickensian models of his personality. Fields varied and expanded this personality as he expanded and refined his routines and sketches. He kept notebooks, dictionaries of invented words ("Philanthroac: One whose mission in life is to take care of drunks who don't want to be taken care of"); he enriched the speeches of his film and stage characters, Egbert Souse ("Souzay, accent acute," he corrected the ignorant), Larson E. Whipsnade, and Eustace McGargle. Louvish has found the notebooks and the old scripts (including those of lost films); he traces the genealogy of jokes and skits; he quotes contemporary critics of Fields and quotes Fields on those with whom he competed and worked. (One of many surprises: the over-the-hill D. W. Griffith made a comedy with Fields; they appreciated each other's talent.)

If the most interesting part of the biography deals with the development of Fields's art, there is plenty about his life. There's the pretty twenty-year-old chorine, Harriet Hughes, whom he married and sent back, pregnant, from their tour in Australia. (He said he wanted his son to be president so he had to be born in the States. It's clear that he'd had his fill of Harriet.) He seldom saw her or his son again although for years sent her monthly checks and vitriolic letters. Mistresses, friends, producers, actors, and, yes, his dogs have their day in the biography, but it is not a narrative that one reads with bated breath. (Such biographies are rarer than good novels.) What Louvish does do splendidly is distinguish Fields from his invented character and reveal the hard work which made him the great comic expression of pomposity, prejudice, sloth, fear of domestic aggression and tyranny, the consciousness of being smaller, clumsier, and more cowardly than we want to be, in short, one of our great cleansers, a part of what many of us carry around until we drop off the planet he, happily, inhabited before we did.

# Hannah Arendt and Martin Heidegger

Much of this story has been known since 1982, when Elizabeth Young-Bruehl published her biography, *Hannah Arendt: For Love of the World*. Since then, Elzbieta Ettinger has been allowed—by the Heidegger family—to paraphrase and characterize if not, unfortunately, to quote from the letters in the German Literary Archive in Marbach.* Using them, she has written a coherent account of the relationship between two extraordinary people who met, loved, separated, and reunited around and within some of the most horrible events of what is in some respects the most horrible of centuries.

In 1924, the eighteen-year-old Hannah Arendt came to Marburg and attended the lectures of the mesmerizing revolutionary philosopher Martin Heidegger. Intelligent, beautiful, learned, emancipated but naïve, timid but ready for grand experience, she was enraptured by the small, dark, peasant-garbed, thirty-five-year-old philosopher. Marburg was his first professorial post. It had been acquired with difficulty, largely through the effort of Edmund Husserl, the Jewish phenomenologist who held the chair at Freiburg which he would soon yield to his student, collaborator, and rival. Heidegger would dedicate *Being and Truth* to Husserl him but withdraw the dedication after the Nazis came to power. He ignored Husserl's illness and death, not even writing a condolence letter to his widow, who had also been his intimate friend and supporter.

Marburg was "a foggy place" whose "soft, flabby" air worked to undo the health Heidegger built up at Todtnauberg in the Black Forest hills where his wife had had a cabin built for him. There he skied, chopped wood, carried water from the well, wrote by oil lamp, and relished the

---

* In 2000 the family gave permission to scholars to quote the letters. We know more than we knew when I wrote the piece, but little that alters what's here.

solitude indispensable to turning metaphysics upside down. From Marburg, though, he wrote his friend, Karl Jaspers, in June 1924, "there is nothing happening, no stimulus at all."

A few months later this had changed. "The hidden king . . . in the realm of thinking" had spotted the brilliant young Jewess taking in the intelligence which (she wrote forty-five years later) was "completely of this world" but "so concealed in it that one can never be quite sure if it exists at all." He invited her to his office. She came in a raincoat, a hat pulled low on her face, her yeses and nos barely audible. He wrote "Dear Miss Arendt" how much he respected her mind and soul, how he hoped that she would be faithful to herself and also understand the frightful loneliness of a man exclusively devoted to the scholar's pursuit of truth. Ettinger calls this letter (which she was forbidden to quote) "a subtle caress . . . lyrical . . . seductive." Four days later, a second letter came to "Dear Hannah," and two weeks after that, "a brief note" made it clear that the professor and his student were lovers. "A total giving of oneself to one person," "the continuity of my life." These are two of the many ways Hannah Arendt described what Heidegger was to her. Twenty-five years later, she would write her husband Heinrich Blucher about a postwar meeting with Heidegger and his wife Elfrida in which "he never denied that during all of twenty-five years, I was the passion of his life."

In the small university town, however, the lecturer on "Truth as the Unhidden" (the *Unverborgenheit*, the *aleithea*) did everything he could to hide what was happening. Assignations were made by mail (although Arendt was never to write him anything but innocuous cards signaling approval of his precisely timed arrangements), signal lights blinked on and off in rooms. It was wearying, demoralizing. The passionate young woman was played like a yo-yo by the edgy, smitten philosopher. Then, "because of my love for you, to make nothing more difficult than it already was," he sent her away. She went to Heidelberg to study with Jaspers and write a doctoral dissertation on the concept of love in Augustine. She had one affair, then another, but every now and then, a letter would come from Heidegger summoning her to a train station here, a house there. Heidegger convinced her that she "could find happiness with another man while still loving him." She married one of his students, Günther Stern. Heidegger came to see them. He and Stern left together, Arendt hiding in the station for a final glimpse of her old lover.

It was 1929. The air was thickening with the bloody nationalism and racism of the Nazis. On a visit to the Heideggers, the blonde Stern had stood on his hands for five minutes, his athleticism so delighting them that they suggested he join the Nazi Party. He said, "Look at me and you'll see that I belong to those you wish to exclude." Hearing this and other stories, Arendt wrote Heidegger about mistreatment of his Jewish students and colleagues. The response was a sarcastic account of all that he'd done for Jews who'd badgered him for favors. Had he been an anti-Semite in Marburg (that is, when he'd made love to her, a Jewess)? This was the spring of 1933; he was rector of the University of Freiburg, and, in April, gave the infamous Rector's Address which described Adolph Hitler as the expression of that Being which broke through the filthy crust of history.* Four months later, Arendt left Germany.

In the black years that followed, she knew exile, poverty, a heart so lacerated by Heidegger's deception and mendacity that she thought she'd never love anyone again. In 1936, her first marriage long over, she met Blucher, who would enable her to both love and to be what Heidegger never allowed her to be: herself. In 1941, they managed to get out of wartime Europe and in America began building a life which saw her become one of the world's most renowned public intellectuals. Her first open discussion of Heidegger came in 1946, when she described him as "the last (we hope) romantic . . . whose complete irresponsibility was attributed partly to the delusion of genius, partly to desperation."

Arendt kept in touch with Jaspers, who, like her, understood the infantile, despicable, cowardly, and temporizing elements of this "mystagogue-cum-sorcerer . . . who occasionally succeeds in hitting the nerve of the philosophical enterprise in the most mysterious and marvelous way." (This is from Karl Jaspers' "Letter to the Freiburg University Denazification Committee, Dec. 22, 1945.") Arendt told Jaspers of her affair with Heidegger. "How exciting," he said, and then wrote Heidegger that she was coming to Freiburg.

Heidegger came to her hotel and "recited" his life as a tragedy in which she had played a role for two acts. After that—she wrote Blucher—they had what was the first honest talk of their lives, so moving to both of them that it began another phase of their fifty-year relationship. Until then, Heidegger had never treated Arendt as a grown-up. For several

---

* Two years later, although the rectorship had been resigned, Heidegger described in his *Introduction to Metaphysics:* "the inner truth and greatness of this movement ["Nationalism Socialism"] (namely the encounter between global technology and modern man)." Martin Heidegger, *Introduction to Metaphysics* (New Haven: Yale University Press, 1959), 199.

years after the war, he would not acknowledge that she was a writer and thinker of consequence. Then, in the last years, he became her supporter, acknowledger, and true friend, and she the *flugelman* of those who redeemed his reputation. he had, they said, been deceived by the Nazis; he'd resigned the rectorship after one year; the Nazis isolated and ignored him; then, after the fall, he was again humiliated: his house was requisitioned by the occupying power, his library was threatened, he was forbidden to lecture, he was forced to sweep rubble from the Freiburg streets. Arendt said how much her work owed him; Heidegger said she was the one who understood him best.

The last romantic? The last two romantics, as Elzbieta Ettinger methodically relates their story, one whose power springs from their complexity and the terrible events which formed so much of them. What a film it could make. I see the lovely, half-Jewish actress Winona Ryder as Hannah; as for Heidegger, perhaps Anthony Hopkins, if he could work up the fusion of mental power and conscientious obscurantism, plus a swinishly arrogant, peasant remoteness, the kind the poet Paul Celan hinted at in "Todtnauberg," a poem written after visiting the philosopher there. As he inscribes the visitor's book, Celan wonders whose name appeared before his Jewish one and hopes that his host will manage to utter the words which will acknowledge, if not absolve, the diabolism of the Nazi years. (I am spelling out what is more cryptic, and thus generous, in "Todtnauberg.")

> die in das Buch
> —wessen Namen nahms auf
> vor dem meinen?—
> die in dies Buch
> geschriebene Zeile von
> einer Hoffnung, heute,
> auf eines Denkenden
> kommendes
> Wort
> im Herzen . . .

# Jung

I took on this review assignment as a way of countering my ignorance of
Jung, an ignorance that included a cavalier dismissal of him as the brilliant Freud disciple who'd betrayed not only him but reason itself to become the champion of every sort of mystic, sometimes fascistic, sect,
practice, person, doctrine, and toy: parapsychology, Tarot cards, racism,
UFOs, the occult, Zen, spiritualism, numerology, J. B. Rhine, mandalas,
you name it. This assignment, which Jung, I've learned, might have called
an *enantiodromia*—a return to one's opposite or "immersion in the destructive element"—has led to an appreciation which does not exclude
the detestable but includes much more. Now it doesn't seem absurd to me
for Jung to be coupled on cultural menus with Freud, if not as "the Swiss
Tweedledum" to "the Viennese Tweedledee" ( Joyce), at least as intellectual ham and eggs, a coincidence of opposites which has affected the behavior and thinking of more twentieth-century human beings than all its
dictators, philosophers, and poets put together. I owe the reassessment to
Frank McLynn's biography, whose factual density and balanced arraignment of Jungian exposition and anti-Jungian argument is a model of its
kind.*

That kind is closer to intellectual biography than to a Boswellian portrait in action, a Straychean unhorsing of *Eminent Victorians,* or a no-holds-barred *bildungs*-life full of thuggery and glitter such as Kitty Kelly's excellent *His Way: The Unauthorized Biography of Frank Sinatra.*

There was glitter and thuggery aplenty in Carl Gustav Jung. He
knew the great figures of the twentieth century. He became rich, famous,
and scandalous, had fascinating opinions about almost everything, and
conducted his continuous self-education in books, public lectures, and

* Frank McLynn, *Jung* (New York: St Martin's, 1997).

conferences financed by some of the world's richest people in some of the loveliest places on earth.. He married a rich woman whom he quickly instructed in his polygamous needs. He tried "every conceivable trick" to thwart the "tide of . . . little blessings" she produced—they swelled an already overpopulated world. (He complained about her to his paternal confidant, Sigmund Freud: "The life of the civilized man certainly has its quaint side.") The reluctant progenitor taught his four daughters and son how to carve wood, hew stone, build ships and houses; he took them on hikes in the Bernese Oberland and, amidst authoritarian decrees and cutting remarks, let them pretty much decide what to believe, where to go, what to do. Their freedom was his, freedom from years of schooling and mind-bending clinical years under Bleuler (the inventor-namer of schizophrenia) in Zurich's Burgholzi Hospital. By marrying Emma Rauschenbach, Jung was able to make his own schedule, see only the patients he cared to see, write his books, and travel with that season's incarnation of his *anima* (ideal woman) to his beloved England or America, where his superb English and boisterous charm made him enormously popular, and later to Africa and India (though never to Rome, Freud's favorite city).

Powerful, half a foot taller than five-foot-seven Freud, Jung was a bully, dominating conferences, shouting people down, heckling and punching out opponents, dismissing patients as bores. He ate hugely, drank good wine, slept with and discarded women who didn't serve his *anima*, attacked establishments ("Small is beautiful"), championed individuality (especially his own), and, in short, had the sort of life which generates stories. McLynn is less interested in them than in Jung's ideas, but one story, the dominant story of Jung's life, he tells in detail, the story of his relationship to Freud.

For Freud, the young Swiss Protestant was the gateway to the Christian world's acceptance of psychoanalysis. For Jung, Freud was the genius who put the unconscious on the map, and, as well, the first man to whom he could really talk. At their first meeting, March 3, 1907, Jung talked "non-stop" for thirteen hours. Freud later told Ludwig Binswanger, "When the empire I have founded is orphaned, no one but Jung must inherit the whole thing." In 1909, invited by the enterprising president of Clark University, the two went to America together. (Freud saw his first movie in Manhattan.) Already the tensions between them were clear. In New York harbor, at the ship's railing, Freud, after predicting that America was due for a surprise (psychoanalysis), told Jung that he himself was "the most humble of men and the only one who isn't ambitious." To which the sardonic Jung replied, "That's a big thing to be—the only one." They were separated by years (nineteen), temperament, training, religion, and ideas about sex, family, and marriage. (Freud was strictly—and to Jung, suspiciously—monogamous; he later spread the rumor that Freud slept with his wife's sister.)

They were separated even more by their theories and practice of psychoanalysis. For Freud, neurosis was rooted in repressed memories which therapy, powered by emotional transference, revealed and relieved. His patients were mostly under thirty-five and Jewish. Jung's patients were successful Protestant burghers who wanted more out of life than success. He saw their neurotic symptoms as signs of the collective, universal unconscious out of which great myths and stories also came. A patient's significant dreams revealed the collective, of which he could then relieve them. (When he learned that the African Elgonyi never dreamed, he was devastated until he decided that they'd entrusted their dreaming to the British who ruled them!) Unlike the Freudian analyst, a sort of tabula rasa on whom the patient projected his previously repressed passions and to whom he transferred what he'd been blocked from expressing, the Jungian analyst faced the patient, saw him not five times a week but once, and, if it were called for, opened up his own life to him. These differences deepened until the familiar, ugly forms of ingratitude, betrayal, and rage became war to the death.

McLynn describes the long war, the wives, friends, and mistresses who took one side or the other or who switched from side to side. (The most significant of these was the beautiful Jewish therapist Sabrina Spielrein, a Jung *anima*, who became a Freudian therapist and later died in a concentration camp.) At Freud's death in 1939, Jung published an abusive repudiation of the man and his work ("In Memory of Sigmund Freud").

Jung lived another twenty-two years, pronouncing on gods and men, technology (monstrous), alchemy (a key matrix), Heidegger (a detested rival in Nietzschean interpretation), Hitler (a recrudescent Wotan on whom Germans projected their suppressed diabolism), Americans (ruthless and naïve, their sports inspired by Red Indian ideals of heroism and thus without the spirit of play), interstellar travel (undertaken when man's inhumanity to man was at its worst), capital punishment (necessary so that the punisher can recognize his own criminality), Franklin Roosevelt ("a limping messenger of the Apocalypse"), American universities ("animus incubators" whose coeducation ruined femininity), simulated madness (a form of mental illness), and the various subpersonalities he called "complexes," the keys to psychosis.

Gather ten thousand Jung *aperçus*, discard, say, the worst 25 percent and you'd have a remarkable book. (Or so thinks this ex-skeptic.)

Until the end of his eighty-six-year-long life, Jung lived it up. He carved Latin mottos and quatrefoil clusters into his Yeatsian stone tower at Bollingen, dominated the Jung conferences at Eranos, summoned his maenads for secretarial and amorous duties. One of them recorded his last words: "Let's have a really good red wine tonight."

# The Outsider Inside

At twenty-five the Russian-Jewish writer Isaac Babel became a correspondent for YugROSTA, the southern section of the national wire service. He was assigned to the First Cavalry Army, led by the famous Cossack general Semyon Budyonny.

Since 1917, wars of the sort being fought in Bosnia, Chechnya, and Azerbaijan had been tearing up Eastern Europe. Red armies were beating back the White forces of Admiral Kolchak and General Denikin, and, in the south, Poles were trying to regain territory taken from them 150 years earlier. Sorties, pogroms, and battles stripped and torched the towns and villages of Galicia, Volhynia, the Ukraine, and Poland.

Near-sighted and asthmatic, Babel mounted a horse for the first time in his life. He kept military records, interrogated prisoners, wrote reports, and sent dispatches to *The Red Cavalryman*. Every night, from spring until mid-September, he wrote in a diary what he saw, smelled, heard, thought, and felt. Years later, the diary was left with a Kiev friend, and so, when the secret police arrested him on May 15, 1939, eight months before they shot him to death, it escaped the confiscation of his papers. The diary was given to Babel's widow in the 1950s, published in Russian in 1990, and now appears in a well-translated and edited English version.* It is worth reading, and not just because it is the raw stuff from which Babel cooked the thirty-five sketches and stories of his masterpiece, *Red Cavalry*.

In 1916, Babel's literary protector, publisher, advisor, and friend, Maksim Gorky, "sent him out into the world." He became "a soldier on the Rumanian front, then served in the cheka, in the *Narkompros* (Peo-

* *Isaac Babel: 1920 Diary*, ed. Carol J. Avins, trans H. T. Willetts (New Haven: Yale University Press, 1995).

ple's Commissariat of Education), in the Food Detachments of 1918, in the Northern army against Yudenich, and in the First Cavalry Army. . . . I was a printer in the Seventh Soviet Press in Odessa, a reporter in Petersburg, Tiflis etc." (Babel's *Autobiography*). Gorky wanted this gifted stray from the Odessa ghetto to become the literary exemplum of revolutionary literature. He wonderfully and terribly did.

The 1920 diary exhibits the transformation of the brilliant, bookish Babel into a half-reluctant, half-enchanted Cossack, an outsider turned inside-out. It charts his ever-deeper, ever-more-horrified and ironic view of the war. A hapless pleader for decent restraint, he turned into an infuriated, then exhausted hater of inhumanity. Through the spring and summer of 1920, as he wrote his elliptic notes, he kept telling himself, "Remember," "Describe," "Mustn't forget." The observer is stocking up for the writer; Babel is becoming Babel.

What has survived of the diary—there are seventy-five missing pages—falls into a bell-curve pattern. The early and late entries are cryptic memoranda:

> Revolting tea in borrowed mess kits. Letters home, packets for Yug-Rosta, interview with Pollack, operation to get control of Novgorad . . . booklets of cigarette paper, matches erstwhile (Ukrainian) Jews, commisars. . . . Love in the kitchen.

As the summer goes on, the entries lengthen and sharpen, fill with descriptions, portraits, and scenes which appear nowhere else in Babel (except, perhaps, in the confiscated manuscripts).

> 31 August 1920. Czeniki
> Farmhouse. A shady clearing in the wood. Total destruction. Not even clothes left. We pinch every last speck of oats. The orchard, apiary, destruction of the hives, terrible. Bees buzzing despairingly, the men blow up the hives with gunpowder, muffle themselves up in their great coats and attack the hives, a wild orgy, they tear the frames out with their sabers, honey drips onto the ground, the bees sting them, they smoke them out with tarred rags, lighted rags. In the apiary chaos, total destruction, smoking ruins. . . .
> Budyonny says nothing, smiles, occasionally showing his dazzling white teeth.

28 August 1920. Komanów

A pogrom . . . a naked, barely breathing prophet of an old man, an old woman butchered, a child with fingers chopped off . . . stench of blood, everything turned upside down. . . . The hatred is the same, the Cossacks just the same, it's nonsense to think one army is different from another.[*] . . . There's no salvation.

By September, everyone is cracking up.

3,4,5 September 1920. Malice

. . . the Pole is slowly but surely squeezing us out . . . I'm sick, quinsy, fever, can hardly move, terrible nights in suffocating, smoke-filled cottages, on straw, my body is covered with scratches and bites, itching, bleeding, nothing I can do.

The command is passive or rather nonexistent.

6 September 1920. Budyatichi

. . . A nurse, a proud, dim-witted, beautiful nurse in tears, a doctor outraged by yells of "Smash the Yids, save Russia!" They are stunned, the quartermaster has been thrashed with a whip, the contents of the clinic tossed out. . . . I cannot see where it will end.

7 September 1920. Budyatichi

Have gone deaf in one ear . . . abrasions everywhere.

I'm losing strength.

9 September 1920. Vladimir-Volynskii

. . . Curse the soldiery, the war, the crowding together of young, tormented, wild, still healthy people.

The final entries are numb, exhausted. It's all over.

The Poles hacking us to bits. . . . Life on the train. . . . Smoking, gorging Muscovites . . . all bad-tempered, all have stomach trouble. . . . Long

---

* "'Cover me,' a 9-year-old boy, Ngudjolo Bulo, asked his mother. . . . The boy's left hand was chopped off completely, along with most of the right, apparently as he tried to shield himself from his [Lendu] attackers. . . . Bandages cover deep machete gashes on his face." *New York Times*, 24 January 2001.

wait in the station. The usual tedium. We borrow books from the club, read voraciously. . . . Conversation about our air force, non-existent, all the machines damaged, the airmen haven't learnt to fly. . . . The Red Army man . . . pokes his finger in to scratch the mucus from his throat.

In 1854, Babel's literary idol, Leo Tolstoy, age twenty-six, arrived in besieged Sebastopol to fight the battles which he would record in *The Sebastopol Sketches,* the work which convinced him that he was a writer. Like Babel, he had written before; unlike Babel, he had fought before (in 1852, against the Chechens). Sixty-six years later, Babel underwent a similar personal and literary transfiguration. To see his diary notes become the spare epiphanic stories of *Red Cavalry* is to see the difference between documentary and artistic truth. Babel once said that the difference between an early and a late draft was like that between a "greasy paper bag and Botticelli's *Primavera.*" Compared to *Red Cavalry,* the 1920 diary may be a greasy bag, but it is Babel's bag, and, therefore, precious, a few more words from that—as he called himself once—"master of the genre of silence."

# Benjamin's Way

"Dear Gerhard," the thirty-two-year-old Berlin-born intellectual Walter Benjamin wrote his most faithful correspondent, Gershom Scholem, in 1924, "Mussolini set foot on this island [Capri] at noon today. He does not look like the lady-killer the postcards make him out to be: corrupt, indolent, and as arrogant as if he had been generously anointed with rancid oil. His body is as plump and unarticulated as the fist of a fat shopkeeper."

This description of the canny bully (two thousand of whose political descendants recently gave the Fascist salute in the Piazza del Popolo) may serve to show Benjamin's literary talent. It was, I think, this more than his theoretical ability which transformed him from an academic wind tunnel into an observer, recorder, and commentator on the streets, arcades, placards, furniture, toys, knick-knacks, goods, and services which serve technological man in place of good and service. ("The eternal is in every case far more the ruffle on a dress than an idea" [Benjamin, *Passagen-Work.*]) The turnabout turned Benjamin into one of the intellectual divinities of humanist studies around the world. It's happened years after Scholem, Mr. and Mrs. Adorno, Hannah Arendt (once married to Benjamin's cousin), and others found, edited, and wrote about his published and unpublished work (much of it left behind in Paris's Bibliothèque Nationale en route to what he'd hoped would be publication in America).

The collected letters, published in German sixteen years ago, were available in 1966 when Hannah Arendt published the *New Yorker* essay which introduced Benjamin to most English-language readers. That beautiful essay seems to me as much off as on the mark. It made Benjamin out to be a brilliant, fatally unlucky klutz, not the way I see him.

Benjamin managed to lead much of his life more or less as he wanted.

Even its final days—ending in suicide near the Spanish border—had been somewhere on his agenda, at least since the protest-suicide of his young friends, Fritz Heinle and Rika Seligson, at the outbreak of World War I.

Benjamin grew up overwhelmed by the furniture of a wealthy German-Jewish household. "Wherever I looked I saw myself surrounded by screens, cushions, pedestals which lusted for my blood like the shades of Hades for the blood of the sacrificial animal" *(Berlin Childhood)*. He described his five-year-old self in an Alpine outfit posing for a Berlin photographer, then carrying "a mighty sombrero" and a staff whose "end is hidden in a bundle of ostrich plumes." The oddity here is that the boy holding the sombrero and staff is not young Walter Benjamin but five-year-old Franz Kafka staring with suspicious puzzlement into the lens of a Prague photographer four years before Benjamin's birth. The literary graft is a sign of Benjamin's shifty self-doubt, which he countered by intellectual deference. For years, he wished to compose a work made up entirely of quotations (lifted from context to reenergize them). It also has something to do with his desire to understand the ready-made world of commodities, here the over-furnished apartments of such middle-class Jews as his own and Kafka's parents. Benjamin's father sold *objets d'art* for Lepke's dealership on Berlin's Koch Street. (What would Benjamin have made of these names had he lived to read about the contract murderers Louis Lepke of Murder, Inc. and the "bitch of Buchenwald," Ilse Koch, who converted human skin into lampshades?)

The Marxist Benjamin understood the bliss as well as the alienating anonymity of industrial culture and he spent his last years in Paris studying it. The unfinished work about it, *Arcades, or Paris, Capital of the Nineteenth Century,* may have been in the heavy briefcase—"more important than my life"—which he lugged up and down the Pyrenees the last two days of his life.

The German inflation of the 1920s—whose finest relic may be Thomas Mann's story "Disorder and Early Sorrow"—forced Benjamin's father to reduce, then eliminate the allowance which supported his thirty-year-old married son and his son. Benjamin thought of the professoriat, but the University of Frankfurt did not accept his postdoctoral *Habilitationsschrift* on the *Trauerspiel* (German melodrama). Sensing the coming rejection (in which the young Max Horkheimer had a hand), Benjamin wrote Scholem that he didn't want an academic career but wanted to "become the best critic of German literature."

In 1924, on the island of Capri, this ambition altered. He met Asja Lacis, "a Bolshevist Latvian woman from Riga who performs in the theater and directs, a Christian," who turned him toward social criticism, toward changing the world. She dissuaded him from emigrating to Palestine, where Scholem had settled and where he attempted to create a professorial job for Benjamin. Benjamin promised him that he'd learn Hebrew and come, but, although he used the university funds Scholem got for him, he stayed in Europe.

In 1930 Benjamin divorced his wife, Dora, repaying her dowry with his inheritance. On his own at last, he supported himself writing reviews, essays, translations (including two volumes of Proust's novel), radio plays (the last about a Mississippi flood, a sort of capsule *Wild Palms*), and even graphological analyses. Poor when writers could still afford to be poor, Benjamin flourished. His existence was rich and passionate: books, ideas, projects, walking the streets and arcades of Europe, writing notes, reviews, and letters (on the fine writing paper he loved), gambling, swimming, flirting, thinking.

In 1928 he published two books, his *Habilitationsschrift* and an organized collection of lapidary paragraphs, *One-Way Street*, "named Asja-Lacis-Street after the engineer who broke it open within the author." He began the experiments with hashish, which, I think, deepened his suicidal bent. Asja had gone to Moscow, his mother had died, he was alone, and the Nazi darkness had descended on Germany.

There were another eight years, exile years in which one publishing outlet after another closed down. Intellectual life died in Germany, then in the rest of Europe. Friends and relatives were murdered. Benjamin kept working, desperately. He lived on a tiny stipend from Horkheimer and Adorno's Institute for Social Research (which had moved to New York). The war broke out. He fled south to Lourdes and Marseilles. Detained there, he met a man who said that his wife, Lisa Fittko, had come over to run an escape route through the Pyrenees. On September 25, 1940, she helped the asthmatic, awkward man, lugging his manuscript-heavy satchel, over the mountains to the Spanish border.* For want of

---

* After an earlier version of this was published in the *Chicago Tribune*, I received a letter from Lisa Fittko. For decades, she had lived a few blocks away from me in Hyde Park, Chicago. A year or two earlier, she'd published *Solidarity and Treason: Resistance and Exile, 1933–40* (Northwestern University Press), in which I learned that Benjamin was the first person she'd escorted to the border.

exit visas, the Spanish guard refused him and two others entry. They made it down to Port Bou, a French fishing village. That night, in the hotel, he wrote the last letter of his life (to Adorno) and injected himself with a fatal dose of morphine. Neither his grave nor the manuscript he carried over the Pyrenees has been found.

# *Almonds*

Everything was implicit, as the nut in its husk, the future and the present, and the harbor. C A L V I N O

Es steht das Nichts in der Mandel.
[There's nothing in the almond.] C E L A N

## 1.

I hadn't been avoiding Frankfurt. Far from it. I'd wanted to come back, and, a couple of times came close. A few years ago, I drove by it on the autobahn, so astonished at the skyline—which hadn't existed when I'd lived there with Jean and Billy in 1951–52—that I nearly went off the road. This time, though, I had a reason to come, at least bits of different reasons.

My life isn't orderly. Half the year, I'm away from New York. A freelancer makes his lance, then finds things to stick it in. I never had trouble finding them, which led me to discipline myself by accepting almost every assignment. How else become more than you'd been?

This becoming life was for Jean and her first successor, Rowena, unbecoming. "Who needs life in airplanes? I'm not accumulating frequent flier miles." (Jean) "You live the exterior life. I live internally. And I get airsick." (Rowena) Sarah, to whom I've been married since 1980, is in tune with my—what?—shifty drift. Before her pots made her wellknown and very busy, she'd take off with me at the drop of a hat. As for Jean, after our two German years, she spent a lot of time alone with Billy and discovered that I was superfluous. Rowena? Her airsickness had less to do with interiority than extramarital flight. We were married for ten months.

## 2.

OK, Frankfurt.

I was in L.A. doing a piece on movie interest in the artistic and intellectual figures of the century. Hemingway, Fitzgerald, Picasso, and Stein were as familiar to movie audiences as the Eiffel Tower, but after Beatty made *Reds*, Hollywood wanted to drag up odder fish. Old Burt Lancaster wanted to make a film about old Ezra Pound; Barbara Streisand optioned a book about Jackson Pollock; T. S. Eliot's widow had closed him off (though not to the astonishing royalties brought in by the musical *Cats*), but Lawrence, Joyce, Rilke, Valéry, and God knows who else were floating properties.

At the Beverly Wilshire, I had a call from Lyon Benjamin, assistant to the director, Floyd Harmel.

I do much work by phone and deduce more than I probably should from voices. Benjamin's was a staccato tenor. Phrases sounded as if they were painfully selected and more painfully joined to their predecessors and successors. The voice itself wasn't reedy or breathy, but exceptionally tense. "I'm interested," it said. "In a man—who may be—a cousin of mine. Dead in 1940—sixteen years before I came on—the scene. Suicide. French-Spanish border—trying to escape—Vichy *miliciens*. Heart trouble—carried a manuscript—over the Pyrenees. Wouldn't give it up—more precious than his life. Had an American visa—but—" the pause here was theatrical, not laryngeal. I've received assignments from types who use so few words you're suspended in their silence, and from others who need ten calls to let you know what they're after. Usually they don't know themselves, until they pick up your response to their fumbling. Lyon Benjamin knew. "That day, the Spanish required—a French exit visa. Benjamin—my perhaps cousin—didn't have one. He returned to the French harbor village—Port Bou—injected himself with morphine—and croaked."

"That it?"

"The man was—Walter Benjamin."

"Yes?"

"The great literary critic."

"I don't work much in that area."

I heard the intake and expulsion of breath; the living Benjamin was disappointed, or pretended to be. I don't embarrass, I don't get humiliated, I don't mind being seen as a naif. Benjamin sensed the score. (He did a lot of telephonic work himself.) He started from scratch, even spoke with ease, legato. "I think there's a film in his life. The last intellectual. Maybe that's hyperbole. Still, the man was at the center of European thought. Lived by it, died for it. And no anchorite. Lots of chicklets. Movies haven't handled intellectuals well."

"Zola."

"Different. The Dreyfus Case. Before my time. The film."

"Before mine. The Case."

"You've done film work. I have your bio."

"Very little."

"But not bad."

In my four-decade writing life, I've done three scenarios and six treatments which got nowhere. Not my line. I tend to see lives at their crests, in crisis. The reportorial knack is seeing the gestures, locating the key words, then spelling out what you've seen and heard. Movies go up and down. My two films made no waves, but I appreciated Benjamin's spare appreciation of them. (More, and I would have discounted it.)

None of my work gets much appreciation. I publish articles, not books. Now and then, one causes a stir. There is next to no fan or hate mail. I don't hear about my skill except from editors, and little from them. New assignments are my reviews. I like it this way. Skill hides itself, and the "skiller." Invisibility makes my work easier. The better known the writer, the more he becomes the story. Throwing your mug around is a career in itself, a nerve-wrackingly contingent one. The more time you spend on the career, the shorter it is. (And the longer the credo, the less credence.)

"*The End of His Rope*'s a classy film. And a fair money-maker."

"I didn't have a piece of it."

"You'd have a piece—of this."

"This being a film about your cousin."

"Exactly. Mr. Harmel has—a certain amount—of seed money. We cast it out—selectively—if you can cast selectively. One seed in fifty takes. When it does—you have—a Harmel film. An event. Cultural. Popular."

I'm not a movie fan. Films run through me. I might be able to name ten staying films. *The Godfather. Citizen Kane. Ambersons. City Lights. La Strada. My Darling Clementine*, a Bergman or two. Do even these stack up with the top two hundred novels? I don't think so. They're too diverting, you don't have a chance to sink into them. Bodies, beauties, endangered vehicles, guns, Astaire and Rogers. Floods of temptation. Still, in this world of erotic, visual rat-a-tat-tat, Floyd Harmel holds up, makes pictures you think about.

I finished my assigment, did another in Bogotà, then holed up for a week and read at, in, and around Walter Benjamin. His writing was full of the heavy formulations which, decades ago, turned me off academic life, but there were also sensuous, pleasantly perverse, and surprising observations; he was a writer. More, he'd lived more or less as I have, on his wits (at least after his father stopped supporting him, his wife and son).

There were other similarities. He'd had three important women in his life, although he'd married only one of them. Like me, he'd had one child, a son, whom he saw as seldom as I see Billy. We even look somewhat alike, burly, heavy in the belly, thin-nosed, brown eyes, black hair. His was thicker and rode more fiercely from the scalp. He also had a thick black mustache and thick eyeglasses. Unlike Lyon Benjamin, who turned out to be a self-hugging little fellow, pigeon-toed, knock-kneed, cross-eyed, and bald, I could have passed for Walter Benjamin's cousin.

I decided my scenario would center about Benjamin's love affair with a remarkable, beautiful, promiscuous—does this word still make sense?— young woman, Asja Lacis, whom he met on Capri in 1924. Asja, a Latvian Bolshevik, was an actress, director, and pioneer in children's theater.

In the next month, I wrote Cousin Lyon an outline, then a treatment, got my twelve thousand dollars and a go-ahead to do a scenario.

3.

In March 1994 I had an assignment for a piece on the Italian election (the one which brought in Berlusconi). I went to Rome, then spent a day looking over Capri. I flew Lufthansa to Rome so that I could stop over in Frankfurt. Benjamin's postdoctoral dissertation—*Habilitationsschrift*— had been rejected in 1924 by the Goethe University there, and it was in Frankfurt that he'd decided—as, twenty-eight years later, I would—to live as a literary free-lancer. He wrote for the *Frankfurter Zeitung* and other newspapers, for magazines, for the radio; he even did graphological analyses. In any case, under a Benjamin tax-cover, I stopped in Frankfurt.

I had other Frankfurters on my plate, a couple I'd met at a European political conference in Bellagio. There, on a tennis court set in a grove of aspen and cypress, Jochen, a law professor, and I played tennis every late afternoon for the five days of the conference. His companion, Cristina—for whom he'd left his American wife—twice fished my copy out of the—to me—alien Word Perfect waters.

En route to Rome, in the two-hour Frankfurt stopover, I left a message on their answering machine saying I'd be coming back in a week, would they please get me a hotel room, close to their place, if possible.

4.

From September 1950 to March 1951, I'd worked in Heidelberg. My main job was teaching two courses in American literature at the university. As an assistant, I received only auditor's fees *(Ohrgeld)*, which amounted to less than three hundred marks a semester, so I also worked for the U.S. Occupation Army as a GS-3 in the Staff Message Control. This paid enough to support Jean and me in a room across the Neckar from the castle (in whose chapel, under tourists' eyes, we'd been married by a U.S Army chaplain). When Billy was born the next winter, we needed more space and money. I got a job in Frankfurt as a GS-7 teaching illiterate American soldiers (those who hadn't reached sixth grade and had thus been illicitly recruited).

In March 1951 I took the train up to Frankfurt to find an apartment there. Stepping out of the beautiful, battered iron-and-glass station, I saw a fifteen-foot cardboard cut-out of Charlie Chaplin, mustache, derby, battered shoes, cane. An advertisement for *City Lights,* a movie I'd been trying to see for years. I did my business at army offices in the old I. G. Farben Building, got the apartment keys, signed for dishes and linen, and filled out a form for Frau Gortart, the maid who'd helped us with Billy in Heidelberg and for whom the army would now pay. Earning $3,500 a year, GS-7s still lived well in occupied Germany. That evening, I trolleyed downtown to see the film.

I remember feeling set apart from the audience. We'd lived a year in Heidelberg but weren't used to being part of a German movie audience. (We saw films at an American army theater.) German opera audiences were different: there wasn't the same passive gawking in the dark, more a—not always—restrained passion, rare license for the severely injured, slowly recuperating Germans of those days.

Near the end of *City Lights,* the tramp gets out of jail. Back walking city streets, he's mocked by a couple of urchins. He takes off after them, missing a kick or two. The audience—including this member of it—roared. Through the window of a flower shop, the tramp sees the formerly blind girl for whose successful eye operation he'd gotten the money (for which he'd been imprisoned). He stares at her lovingly. Noticing the odd little man, she comes out and gives him a flower. He keeps looking at her. She touches his hand and realizes that her savior was not the princely millionaire she'd imagined but this tramp. Her shock and recognition are beautiful, and Charlie's answering expression, a fusion of love, pride, and comprehension, is the close-up to end all close-ups, the expression on which I'd like to close my eyes in this world and to see as—if—they open in another.

When the lights went up in the theater, I stayed in my seat, overcome. The German audience, in overcoats, hats, and scarves, rushed up the aisles, faces frozen, even angry. Something had happened to them in the film's final sequence. Until then, they'd laughed as I had. Why weren't they moved by the beautiful conclusion? Was it un-Germanic? Frankfurt was still squatting in wartime rubble. Around the half-skeletal cathedral were ex-blocks of stony nothing. Were the feelings of its citizens also in the rubble? Had they been decimated by bombs and a dozen years of man-handling by another little mustached man?

5.

Nostalgia makes everyone a poet. I was in Frankfurt for poetry. There are eighty-six thousand, four hundred seconds in a day. Perhaps fewer than two thousand of my daily seconds have been turned into assigned words, although in most of my conscious seconds, there is a pressure in me, so familiar it's as natural as the circulation of my blood. Interrupted, it bleeds. Yes, I wanted to see where I'd been, wanted to feel what I believed I'd feel, but part of this want was the awareness of literary gold in the feeling.

In 1952 I wasn't a writer. I was vaguely preparing to be a professor. The teaching job I had was tedious, seven hours a day teaching soldiers to read, add, and subtract, but the money—free rent and maid, plus three hundred percent profit on four weekly cartons of American cigarettes (which the German mailman picked up and paid for once a week)—was princely. In two years, I saved three thousand dollars, enough to support Jean and Billy if I went on for a doctorate.

If the job was tedious, life wasn't. I came home to wife and baby in an apartment heavy with mahogany tables and sideboards and to Frau Gortat, who cooked and served our sauerbraten and chops. At twenty-three, I felt like a manly provider. Nights, I read, enormously and with tremendous joy. Once a week, I traded Italian for English lessons with a

Neapolitan barber at the Frankfurt military post, and twice a month I studied the *Aeneid* with a German Latin student from the university. Somewhere in there, I wrote my first article, a survey of German cultural and political affairs, modeled on Genêt's *New Yorker* pieces on France. The *New Yorker* rejected the piece, but on one of the great days of my life, a *Partisan Review* editor, Catherine Carver, wrote that they'd accepted it. I was going to be in a magazine that published Sartre, Eliot, Orwell, Silone, Camus, Auden. The company was intoxicating, although I stayed sober enough to know I didn't belong to it. I thought I might be a little closer to Genêt. If I had a gift, it was for a kind of verbal photography. I could report what was going on. I wasn't much of an interpreter or theorist. The interpretations in my *Partisan* article were quoted from the *Frankfurter Zeitung.*

Still, I'd felt a door open; I was a journalist. Even before the article was accepted, I'd sensed that was the way for me to go. I did not want to stand in front of students, dropping stale information and opinions into their mouths or wiping up the misinformation and opinions they spat back.

Back then, our German friends worked for the U.S. Army and HICOG (the High Commissioner of Germany) in the I. G. Farben Building. They'd been schooled, and a few had killed, as Nazis, but, as far as Jean and I could tell, they now thought and felt as we did. They were starting over; we were starting out, and were in spiritual step.

Now and then, we brought them cigarettes from the P X or American gasoline coupons for trips up the Rhine and to the Taunus Hills. This was not the source of their affection for us. If it were, even such naive enthusiasts as we would have spotted curds in it. We trusted our antenna. After all, we were Jews, we should be able to sense racial antagonism.

Our parents, back in America, were less trusting. Jean's father went on about the school battles he'd fought with "Krauts and micks who called me 'sheeny.'" He wrote us, "Anti-Semitism is the daisy in the German lawn. Pluck it out, wake up the next morning, it's there again. Hating Jews is their avocation. They take it up when there's nothing else to do. Keep your eyes open."

"He's from another time," said Jean. "He doesn't understand what's going on." The most we conceded was that for our German friends our Jewishness was a sort of amulet they could touch to cure their old racial scrofula. "Take Götz," said Jean. "Who could be more decent, tolerant, and gentle?"

Götz had been an aide to Admiral Raeder. He'd spent six months in an English prison camp, where, he told us, he'd read Hölderlin and "was turned inside out." He had one of these top-heavy philosopher heads you sometimes see in German university towns, forehead for much of the face, with a strip of hair like an afterthought. His eyes, very light blue, sat deep in sockets. He went over a Hölderlin poem with me line by line, "written," he said, "in 1804, as madness was sinking into him."

> Why did you spread night over my eyes
> so that I couldn't see the earth?

Thinking of Götz and Germany rather than Hölderlin, I was moved. (Although my insides stayed where they were.)

One winter evening, walking home to Neuhaußtrasse from the Far-ben building, I realized that I felt at home in Frankfurt. My feelings had leapt over the rubble of hatred to the days when my German great-grandparents lived here. Two nights earlier, Jean and I had gone to a concert. The young Fischer-Dieskau and the older Tiana Lemnitz had appeared with a wonderful pianist (name forgotten) to sing Schumann's *Liederkreis* and a bunch of Schubert songs. The songs were beautiful, not beyond words but through them. Simple, even simple-minded lyrics full of clouds and streams, love and lost love, they were, in their musical outfits, heart-rending. Outside, in the chill air, waiting for the trolley on Eschersheimer Landstrasse, I said, "Why should we let those Nazi murderers stand for Germany? This is Germany."

Jean said, "The murderers came out of this *Schwärmerei*. All this moping and melancholy. I know it's beautiful, but it's a veil for the other."

"Maybe so." I'd read about Germanic vagueness, the lack of legal clarity, the forest spirits, brutality, superstition, arrogance, and xenophobia which, since Tacitus wrote about them, have defined Germany and Germans. I knew a little about the other Germans, Goethe, Kant, Nietzsche, Rilke, and Kafka (the last two Czechs, but writing German), the mathematicians, physicists, chemists, and then the 150 years of music, Bach through Schumann. That was also Germany. Every castle has latrines. OK, if the German latrines were horrible, most of the castle was glorious.

My grandparents had passed down a Germanic credo to my parents: cleanliness, neatness, punctuality, obedience, hard work, doing your duty.

My parents had nagged me with these virtues, and I'd mocked them, but they were in me, they governed my habits, my values, the way I dressed, the way I lived. I thought they might be the reason I'd discovered my vocation in Germany.

## 6.

Jochen and Cristina gave me a map and pointed out the route between their apartment and the Farben Building. I went up Bockenheimer Landstrasse to Opern Platz. The morning was cold, sunny, full of crystal flash off the stone, steel, glass, and concrete. Frankfurt was a hard, proud city. It had elected the Holy Roman emperors and was, until after the Franco-Prussian War, a free city. Now it dominated with money. The new towers were banks. Yet the city was *gemütlich* as well as proud, a cozily horizontal city in which the skyscrapers looked embarrassed, out-of-place. The low, solid, grey-and-chocolate stone snubbed the bemetalled glass of the presumptuous banks. This was Goethe's city, poetic in its burgher heart. And it was my city. Wasn't my assignment here to understand that? The feeling I had for it was a form of love, one I wanted and was pushing myself to get. You were supposed to feel this way. Nostalgia was an emotional pension earned by living long enough to return.

I crossed Eschersheimer Landstrasse, and there was Neuhaußtrasse. Fantastic joy filled me. I floated down its hundred yards of umber six-flats rising from tiny lawns. Here and there were basements newly whitewashed, roofs and chimneys newly tuckpointed, but otherwise it was unchanged. Number 7. Our house. I could see the back garden where Frau Gortat had married Herr Willy. (Jean and I were their witnesses.) Here was the bay window by whose light I'd read *Clarissa* and the *Aeneid, I promessi sposi* and Heine. Here my parents had come to visit us. I saw them, at least saw the photograph we'd taken of them in the garden holding Billy. A dozen years younger than I was now, my mother's curls were brown, her smile lovely.

Forty-three years ago. They'd been dead twenty years, and Billy was an angry forty-year-old who hardly spoke to me, and, when he did, told me how wrong I was about everything I wrote, said, and was. "I love you," went his last postcard, "but I can't have anything to do with you. You're out of touch."

I walked back to Eschersheimer Landstrasse. The English bookstore where I bought Everyman and Penguin novels was gone—a pang—but much else wasn't. The medieval watchtower, fat and confident as a sausage, had been repainted and stood where it had stood for five hundred years. The Hauptwache, which Goethe thought Frankfurt's most beautiful house, was as it had been. One day, forty-three years ago, classes at the army school were suspended so that Americans could redeem their scrip-money for new scrip. Germans stuck with old scrip were out of luck. American soldiers came down to the Hauptwache to trade scrip for German marks at a terrific rate. One of my first grade students, Private Hoover, an enormous black man with a mouth full of gold teeth and a constitutional resistance to the printed word, was dealing marks and scrip with a banker's aplomb. The week before I'd said to him, "Private Hoover, I'm afraid you're not going to make it to second grade." The teeth gleamed. "Thass all right, Mr. Dortmund, don't you worry none bout't. 'Sno blame on you." After Money Change Day, they gleamed again. "Made me four hunnert thirty-one dollar, Mr. Dortmun'." "You're a financial genius, Hoover." Gleam.

I walked through a crescent of half-timbered houses to the cathedral. In 1952, the houses were sheared in half, the rooms agape like mouths. Porcelain toilet bowls shone in the rubble. One-legged and one-armed men were everywhere, as were midgets and hunchbacks. By the station was a poster for *Snow White and the Seven Dwarfs: Schneewitschen und die Siebener Zwerge.* Jean and I decided to see it, but instead spent the evening with our landlord—I don't remember how we found the room—Graf Posadowski, a soft-voiced, soft-faced aristocrat who took in our thirty marks and what we were and offered us schnapps in his book-lined study. He sat in the dark in an embroidered armchair. His English was elegant, the phrases treasured and surrendered with regal grace. "I am required to fill out a questionnaire, a *Fragebogen.* Since I am, unfortunately, of noble birth, I am required to put down the names of all the people I know who are equally unfortunate. I have been writing names of dead people for four days." He told us of one such noble cousin. "His plan was to assassinate Hitler. He made an appointment to demonstrate a piece of equipment for him. He strapped an explosive device under his tunic. His plan was to embrace the Führer, pull a cord, and explode. Hitler broke the appointment. Axel made another. That too was broken. Then Axel was sent to the Russian Front and perished." The count walked over and poured schnapps into our glasses. "May I request a favor?"

"Of course," said Jean.

"Our German cigarettes are frightfully expensive and the tobacco is

suspect. Could you buy for me from your PX a few boxes of Chester-
fields?"

Said Jean, "Of course, your Excellency. We'll find a soldier and give
him some dollars."

"No 'Excellency,' please," said the count gently. "Only the cigarettes."

7.

I crossed the Main on an iron bridge and walked up Museum Row to the
German Film Museum. For Benjamin, film was the exemplary art of the
age of mechanical reproduction. A collaboration of humans and machines, its making differed from that of the older, religion-based art. The
film artist performed for no audience but the camera, so there was no
"aura," no felt look exchanged between painter and viewer. Yes, the
painting looked too, as in that Rilke poem about the headless marble
torso, when the viewer realizes, "There is no place that doesn't see you.
You've got to change your life."

That was going a bit far for me, but I was looking for a Frankfurt
aura.

Oddly enough, four days earlier, in Rome, I'd had an aura-like experience with a work of art. I'd taxied over to the Vatican Museum at 8:15
A.M. and was first in line to see the Sistine Chapel. When the guard raised
the bar, I'd hoofed it like a maniac up and down stairways, through the
marble labyrinth, finally into the chapel itself. Except for three guards
gabbing in front of the white curtain behind which restorers worked on
*The Last Judgment*, I had the place to myself. I walked from one side to
the other, then up and down, taking in the ceiling frescoes, the creation of
Adam, of Eve, their expulsion, the flood, then the surrounding prophets
and sibyls reading—it seemed to me—the stories depicted above their
heads. I felt Michelangelo's intellect touching mine. I knew that the ceiling was about making something out of nothing, about illusion, volume,
space, destiny, about the human imitation and betrayal of creation.

When the tour crowds came in, I took off. I bought a couple of books
on Michelangelo, walked past the crowds swelling each other, then along
the high brick wall to the Bernini Colonnade, down Conciliation Walk,
around Castel Sant'Angelo, and across the Tiber. When I got to the
Campo dei Fiori, I drank a cappuccino in front of the hooded bronze
head of Giordano Bruno and read the books. They didn't put words to
what I'd seen and thought, but they knew when Michelangelo had painted

what, when he'd fired an assistant, how he lived—miserably—what he wrote to his spoiled brothers and father back in Florence. One book included a sonnet he'd written about painting the chapel. With my pocket dictionary, I worked out a version of it. It went something like "I've grown a goiter in this den . . . which drives my belly to my chin, my beard to heaven, my nape upon my spine. . . . My breast bone's a harp, the brush-drops dripping on my face turn it into pavement. My loins are in my paunch, my ass [*cul'*] its counterweight. . . . I'm taut as a Syrian bow . . . my perceptions are crazy, false: a twisted gun can't fire straight. [He calls to his friend Giovanni da Pistoia.] Johnny, stick up for my dead pictures and my honor because I'm in a bad way. And I'm no painter."

I worked up a lot of fellow feeling for the fellow. Young, early thirties, he thought himself old, ruined, dying. Full of common and business sense as well as genius, full of feeling for which he never found anyone worthy, except, late in his life, the young marchese Vittoria Colonna. He poured everything into marble. Considerate, tender, erotically, fraternally, and filially passionate, it was only the precious marble from Cararra which responded to him. The aura.

The encounter with Michelangelo was why I went not to the art but the film museum. After caviar, I wasn't up—or down—to hot dogs. (The museum was crammed with apparatus and diagrams about human attempts to preserve what had been seen.)

## 8.

At one o'clock I sat with Jochen in the café of the Literatur Haus on Bockenheimer Landstrasse, waiting for Cornelia Snapper, a friend who was writing her *Habilitationsschrift* on Walter Benjamin and who worked mornings as an archivist for the Deutsche Bank.

The café consists of a few black tables served by two casual waiters. I was the oldest person there, although there were a couple of gray or graying beards and heads, one of which was Jochen's. (He is twenty years my junior.) Since he had only come to introduce me to Cornelia and had an afternoon seminar, we ordered (beer and goulash). We were also expecting Cornelia's companion, Eberhard Kurst.

Jochen seemed edgy. "What's *los*, Jochen? Worried about the seminar?"

"My wife." She'd called about their twelve-year-old daughter. "She says Peggy's made a date, she doesn't know what to do. She lets her watch *Beverly Hills 90210*. What does she expect?"

"Is having a date so awful?"

"She should have space for herself now. Some kid could ruin her for years."

"Nothing will ruin a daughter of yours."

"Her mother thinks that's a recipe for disaster. Disaster is spelled C-r-i-s-t-i-n-a."

"I was a pretty good father, and my son's a bitter, middle-aged bachelor who regards me as what's keeping him from doing anything useful."

"Sons are competitive. You've had three wives, so he'll have none. That'll show you." Jochen's bearded face contracted. "I love this little girl. I can't bear what I may have done to her—but I can't exist without Cristina."

"We live one life after another. Our kids resent it, resent us. When are they going to live?"

A girl in a blue denim jacket headed our way. Extremely pretty, short blonde hair, blue eyes, a smile in every pore. I got up. "Cornelia?"

"How did you know?"

"Jochen said you worked for the Deutsche Bank. I was looking for a banker."

She kissed Jochen and shook hands with me. "So I look like a banker?"

"Exactly."

"Good. I like to look important."

There is, I think, a Boyle's Law of Emotional Diffusion. In time, people feel more or less the same about one another. If one cools, the other cools. Cornelia Snapper didn't immediately feel charmed by me, as I was by her, but she felt that I was charmed, and this pleased her. We joked, and this pleased both of us. We liked each other.

I am poorly constructed inside; my emotional mortar has never set properly. Sometimes I think that Sarah is its fixative, but then I pass someone in the street, even see someone in a movie, and I feel the mortar crumbling.

Not that I often fall, an antique word that rings true to my antique psyche, although half or more of me believes the encounter is a triumph. In any case, it's never simply casual, insignificant. Even when a connection is made, there is seldom any follow-up, letters, phone calls, even memory. Basically I've married my Sistine Chapels.

Eberhard, a bespectacled, pleasant man in his mid-thirties, showed up, and Jochen left. The three of us talked CDU, FDP, the break-up of dominant parties in Mexico, Japan, Italy, and Germany, nationalism, fundamentalism, the political manipulation of skin hue, ethnicity, chauvinism and ideology in Serbia, India, Sri Lanka, East Africa, and— Eberhard's phrase—"the Soviet Dis-union." Their persistent note was national self-indictment: Germans were "humorless," "myopic," "grandiose," "fascists-in-the-egg."

"I must know the wrong ones."

"You're passing through," said Eberhard. "We put on Sunday clothes for you." He touched Cornelia's shoulder, shook my hand. "I'm off to train more of us. Cornelia will take care of you. 'Til tonight." We were all going to see a movie called *In the Name of the Father*.

"What can I show you?" asked Cornelia. "Museums? The Goethehaus? Or would you rather be on your own?"

"I've seen all the museums I want to, and if you have the time—"

"Come to my place. I'll give you tea and a view of the city from our roof."

Bless the amalgam of beauty and niceness. I had to fight dazzlement. "Whither thou, thither I."

"?"

"To your place. Is it far?"

"Ten minutes. Up Reuterweg."

"It wasn't Reuterweg in '52." It was against the erotic tide that I mentioned a year before her birth. "He was mayor of West Berlin. Every letter had to have a two-pfennig Berlin-rebuilding stamp attached."

"You must give me German history lessons."

She walked her bicycle, I behind, gauging hers in the blue jeans. Her walk was flat-footed, toes pointing out, a confident walk.

The house too looked confident, a five-story limestone on a street of its cousins. Cornelia lived on the top floor. No elevator and no concession from her to any difficulty in the ascent. Flattery? The door opened into a small kitchen with a table, oven, fridge, and chair. Versailles it wasn't. The other room featured an unmade bed, a quilt thrown back like an invitation. "Sorry about the bed," she said. "Tea first, or view?"

I sat facing the open quilt, repressing post-staircase huffing and newer excitement. "Perhaps tea."

She filled the kettle. "Jochen said you were writing a movie about Benjamin."

"His affair with Asja Lacis."

She filled mugs and sat within two feet of me, tea steam touching her face, whose every pore glistened with receptivity, amusability; she was the friendliest beauty. "I don't think of him as a person, only an idea-machine. Germanic. That's why it takes me so long to write."

"I'm the opposite. Ideas fly right past me. I don't know what Benjamin's talking about, or what others mean when they analyze him. This man Adorno says that he was 'in flight from the trance-like captivity of bourgeois immanence.' For an hour I failed to understand what that meant."

"Pure professorial German. Anything to do with innerness makes us think we're getting the truth of things. If it's *innig*, it can't be bad."

"For us, 'inner' means someone's putting something over on someone. Inner circle. Or it's dangerous. Inner city."

The pores and blue eyes lit up. "*Bei uns*, 'inner city' means historic, old, the Altstadt, the true center. Want to see?"

We went up to the roof. It was windy, cold, glittery. Cornelia brushed hair from her eyes. She pointed to the cathedral, the bridges, the towers, the Farben building spread below us like a great orange gun turret. "The city's fighting itself," I said. "The present and past don't fit."

"This is all I've known. I don't see what you see. Want to see where I get my name? Look, beyond that small domed church, to the right of the Dom." She hoisted my arm and pointed it. Her hand on my arm roused me. "A little more to the right. There, Goethe's house."

"On Cornelia Street?"

"*Nein*, Hirschgraben. Not even my parents would name me Hirschgraben Snapper. Cornelia was his sister." She dropped our arms, brushed hair from her face. Where do the mistresses of beauty learn their enchanting gestures? "It's so windy. I'll show you her picture downstairs."

There she handed me a postcard of a long-faced, long-nosed woman, hair pulled back over a powerful forehead, eyes closed, the slightest smile on her full lips. "She looks unhappy."

"Post-partum depression. She died at twenty-seven. Two years younger than I."

"And your parents named you after this sad person?"

"The great genius's sister; his only real companion."

"The secret sister."

"Yes. The new archetype, the sister of the great man, history's trash."

Tea and sympathy, as the popular play of the fifties had it. It was about age-and-youth, a headmaster's wife, a lonely student. I can't remember if she loved him. I too was on a double track, ageless inside except for the knowledge that I wasn't. Bolder and even older seniors than I would have led Cornelia to the open quilt, but fixed in my burly self, I stayed where I was. No risk, no gain, yes, but no loss either. And I had something to lose, the amiable feeling that this genial, arm-touching beauty had for me. Who knows, if I restrained myself, there'd be something more another time. Other times were getting rarer, but I hadn't thrown in the towel. In any case, to advance only to be pushed off, even as gently as Cornelia would have done it, would be unbearable. Need I could bear.

I told her my life, my wives, my interviews, travels, famous and odd friends. A Desdemonish glint lit her face, but I was no Othello. I interviewed Othellos.

9.

*Setting: Capri, Summer 1924.*
*A small grocery store, wooden bins of fruit and vegetables, shelves of old-fashioned cartons, cans, and jars. Male store-keeper in apron, mustache. Making purchases is* WALTER BENJAMIN, *short, solid, thick black hair, eyeglasses catching and throwing off sunlight from the windows, narrow nose, dressed in suit, necktie.*

B E N J A M I N *(pointing at tomatoes and holding up three fingers):* Tre pomodori, signore. *(Enter Asja Lacis in white dress, carrying packages. She is Benjamin's height, dark gray eyes, dimpled chin, pretty, her Italian is almost non-existent.)*

A S J A: Buon giorno. Io—I wish—je voudrais—ich möchte gern. *(Shrugs, dropping two packages, which Benjamin picks up. To Benjamin):* Sank you, sank you. Merci. *(To store-keeper, as she looks around for what she wants):* Mandeln. *(Store-keeper shrugs.)* Mindahl. Almonds. Amandes *(waving hands, shaking head, dropping packages).*

B E N J A M I N *(smiling, picking them up. To her):* Entschuldigen sie. *(To store-keeper):* La signora desidera delle mandorle. *(Store-keeper fetches a bag of almonds, scoops out a long spoonful, looks questioningly at Lacis. She nods happily. He pours them into a smaller bag and wraps them up.)*

A S J A: Grazie, signore. *(To Benjamin):* Vielen dank', Mein Herr. *(Close-up on Benjamin's serious but delighted face. Cut to sunlit street. Benjamin is carrying all the packages but the sack of nuts. Now and then he drops one, they both stop to pick it up, faces close to each other, smiling. Cut to Asja's apartment. You can see her twelve-year-old daughter, Daga, reading on a small balcony which overlooks the Bay of Naples. Benjamin is seated at a small table set for three with glasses of red wine, silverware. Asja brings plate of spaghetti to table and, while they talk, serves it. They drink, eat, talk.)*

B E N J A M I N: I've seen you and your daughter for days now. You seem to float in your white dresses. Lovely sight. She has such long legs.

A S J A: She's thirteen. She's acted with me twice, once in Brecht. He said she was very good. We go to Moscow in a few weeks to work with Piscator. There are exciting things happening in the theater there. In everything. Why don't you come? Palestine is the past, Moscow the future.

B E N J A M I N *(close-up, smiling):* I do see some future there.

A S J A *(close-up, smiling, touching his cheek, then calling):* Daga! There's spaghetti and wine for you.

D A G A *(looking up, craning her head to see them at the table, going back to her book):* Save some. I'll eat later.

1 0.
Waiting for Jochen and Cristina, I read the literature section of the *Ef Ah Zed* (the *Frankfurter Algemeine Zeitung*). A momentary shock: there, in an aquarium, nose to nose with a moronic-looking dogfish, was a photograph of Billy.

Not Billy, of course, but, said the article, "the bard of the Fallen-Wall epoch of German literature," one Durs Grünbein of East Berlin. Not really, when I got down to it, a Billy clone, but with a similar bell of brown hair and large-eyed innocence.

My recognition system had been shunted onto the strange double track of these Frankfurt hours. So I saw the younger, softer Billy, the one who was still, somehow, mine.

Reading German, my spirit eases when I see the indented, italicized lines of poetry set in the solid blocks of prose. Even the clearest German prose worries me, if only because I know that waiting somewhere on the next page is a construction which will ambush me. I'll have to look up five words I don't know, and by the fifth, the meaning will have been derailed.

Line by line, poetry may be harder, but there's less of it, and that less—like a photograph—goes a long way, and you feel you've penetrated essential German-ness. I like reading about German poets. Here was not only the bard of the Fallen-Wall but "his ancestors, Brecht, Celan, Rilke and Trakl," good German company, the suppliers of neatly packaged profundity. And once you opened the package, there was often something special just for you, a sort of high-grade astrology. It was better reading about the poet, for you didn't have to bother with the whole poem, only the lines the critic selected and interpreted. This critic offered a neat line of Brecht, *"Mit kalten Spruchen innen tapeziert"* ("Tapestried inside with chilly maxims"—appropriate enough) and three lines of Celan so clear I thought I was missing something.

> und zuweilen, wenn
> nur das Nichts zwischen uns stand, fanden
> wir ganz zueinander.

I didn't have to look up a word and came out with the following:

> and sometimes, when
> only Nothing stood between us, we found
> ourselves completely beside each other.

Completely beside each other. Billy and I. Cornelia and I. Billy was hung up on the old "I," an "I" I did not want to revisit. The history of that "I" was streaked with feelings another poet had called "savage, extreme, rude, cruel, not to trust." With his therapist's "help," Billy remembered the noise of paternal rumbles with visiting ladies while Mom was off at Grandma's, and a backyard where he dodged a terrifying bulldog while Daddy diddled its mistress within. Grünbein's Wall had fallen in 1989. Would my death crumble Billy's?

There were three other items in the *Ef Ah Zed* that magnetized me. (Odd that focus on a subject magnetizes a field and exposes what bears on it.) My magnets were Benjamin and Billy, Frankfurt, poetry and almonds. So there on Grünbein's page were four lines of Rilke on, magnetically, the almond *(Mandel)*:

> Mitte aller Mitten, Kern der Kerne,
> Mandel, die sich einschliesst und versuesst,—

> dieses alles bis an alle Sterne
> ist dein Fruchtfleisch: Sei gegruesst.

This too I could work up without my pocket dictionary:

> Center of centers, kernel of kernels.
> Almond, which encloses and sweetens itself—
> all this to all stars
> is your fruitmeat: Hello there.

This, I thought, could be worked into Benjamin's courtship scene. The idea was that Asja, guided by that occasional scenario writer, Nature, had shopped for this most amorous of nuts. Something like that.

The second item magnetized from the *Ef Ah Zed* came from an account of recent brain research which described a neural shortcut for emotions through the amygdala (Greek for almond: *amygdalon*) before another neural pathway—from stimuli to the cerebrum—worked them into the complexity called feeling. So what passed between Asja and Walter on Capri went from almonds to passion through the cerebral almond. Something like that.

The third item was dissonant Frankfurt history. It came from a new book on the first Rothschild banker, Meyer Amschel, Goethe's fellow Frankfurter. Not, however, one he was likely to know. Frankfurt's Jews were crammed into the filthy Judengasse, from which they could see the bridge—perhaps the one I'd crossed over the Main. On it was carved a sow whose shit-clogged asshole was being offered to the long, dripping tongue of a hook-nosed gentleman wearing a yarmulke.

I I.

*In the Name of the Father* turned out to be less a story of brutal injustice than the transformed relationship of a father and son imprisoned in the same cell. Most unsettling to this father sitting in the dark beside Cornelia, into whose ear I whispered English versions of the actors' rapid Irish-English.

Afterwards, we went across the street to a café, loud with the rock music I cannot discriminate or bear. The four of us—Cristina had gone home to write a paper—drank beer and managed a few sentences of post-film critique in the musical intermissions. Time for goodbyes.

In the street, I realized I'd forgotten my cap and went back to the café.

Our waiter, seeing me, twirled it on his forefinger, an expression on his amused young face which I read as mockery. Was it my age which amused him? (What was an old codger doing in such a place, forgetting his hat and who he was?) Or was it another daisy in the German lawn?

Another uneasy undercurrent in this Frankfurt day. On the dark street, I shook hands with Eberhard and then, as Cornelia leaned toward me, I kissed her mouth.

I 2.

*Setting: Moscow, December, 1926.*
*Scene 31: Asja and Benjamin are in her small apartment. Outside, glimpses of the Kremlin. They've been arguing.*

A S J A: If he weren't as stupid as the general, he'd have thrown you into the street. I wouldn't care. We're not each other's property.

B E N J A M I N: You get pleasure from these morons.

A S J A: Pleasure's pleasure. It doesn't destroy the pleasure I have with you. Pleasure's not something you deposit in the bank.

B E N J A M I N *(shakes his head, goes to the window, stares):* I used to think snow so beautiful. I must have had a warmer coat.

*Scene 35: We follow Benjamin to a baker's. Medium shot through glass window as he buys cake and carries it out. We follow him through the snowy streets, back to his small hotel. In the lobby, to his amazement, sits Asja.*

B E N J A M I N: Why didn't you go to my room? The key is there.

A S J A *(looks at him with uneasy affection):* No.

B E N J A M I N *(opens the box with the cake and shows it to her):* For you. *(Asja touches his arm, shakes her head. They look at each other puzzled.)*

*Scene 39: We follow Benjamin out of the lobby of the hotel in his overcoat and fedora. He's carrying a large suitcase. Asja is waiting in the street An old taxi pulls up in front.*

A S J A: Perhaps I'll come to Berlin in the spring.

B E N J A M I N: Let me know. *(They look at each other. She kisses him on both cheeks. He gets in the taxi. As it takes off, he looks around and sees her staring at the taxi. It's dusk, the suitcase is on his knees. He puts his head down on it.)*


13.

> From: Lyon D. Benjamin
> To: Edwin Dortmund
> Date: April 30, 1994
> In re. Scenario: Almonds. Fulfillment of Section III.b. Agreement entered into February 9, 1994. 678-A-985-439

> Benjamin fever cooled around here. Apparently need higher gradient fuel for the fin de siècle. Another decade perhaps. Regrets.
>
> LB


14.

> Frankfurt / Main, May 12, 1994.
> Dear Edwin,
> Thank you for sending this fascinating script.
> Will the movie have a performance in Frankfurt? If you invite me, I will buy a new dress.
> I wish my work went so well. Perhaps like Benjamin and you, I was not created to be a professor. I follow him into the labyrinth but cannot find the way out.
> Eberhard suggests we go to Capri in June. Maybe I'll find the way out in the Blue Grotto. It would be much fun to run into you there.
> Cornelia


15.

"Dear Cornelia," I wrote in my head.

"Capri! Isle of goats. This old one can't see himself gliding through blue grottos munching almonds in your boat." Letting myself go is always easier when my fingers don't have to type letters on a sheet or monitor.

"Something odd. Three months back from Frankfurt, I can't remember your face. I confuse it with the melancholy one of Goethe's sister. Your body, though—which I never saw—breasts, bottom, groin, is something else. *Fruchtfleisch*. Now and then I lay it over my bed-partner's familiar, still loved, flesh.

"Frankfurt poetry."

The capitalism of memory: what I deposited in 1952, I cashed in 1994 with the accumulated interest of forty-two years.

A twisted gun can't fire straight.

"This Father's Day, Billy, out of his incalculable blue—or mind—telephoned. I told him about seeing the house in which he'd spent his first two years. His response: 'I hate the past.'

"Cornelia, untouched-by-me darling, better luck with your Benjamin than I had with mine. And better luck with your Germany than Benjamin had with his among the daisies."

# IV

# MISCELLANEOUS COMMENTARIES
## AND OPINIONS

How these curiosities would be quite forgott, did not such idle fellowes as I am putt them downe! J O H N  A U B R E Y, *Brief Lives*

Where there is much desire to learn, there of necessity will be much arguing, much writing, many opinions; for opinion in good men is but knowledge in the making. J O H N  M I L T O N, *Areopagitica*

*Within the miscellany, this is a miscellany, churned up on one hand by more or less aimless curiosity and on the other by feelings (anger, hope, the quiver of an idea) about current events some of which come in new books, some in the day's news, a few in the rare public occasions in a quiet life (see the "Statement for the Meeting of the University of Chicago Senate"). In any case, the hope is that however transient the news or the occasion, the words found appropriate then are not just mortar for chinks in the implied autobiography but themselves amusing and instructive.*

# Warriors of the Open, 1996

1.

The U.S. Open is over. Steffi beat Monica, Pete walloped Andre. The winners took in more than a half million dollars, the losers nearly three hundred grand. And why not? They fight our battles as well as their own, draw out, transform, and cleanse our frustration, our anger, our incapacity.

The network motormouths—only John McEnroe's was bearable—told us that the big story was Monica's comeback. Except for a warm-up tournament in Toronto the week before, she'd had no match-play since a deranged fan of Steffi Graf had stabbed her in the back more than two years ago. Now she was not only on the circuit again, she was playing almost as well and fiercely as ever. She was taller, stronger, had a better serve, and, twenty-one now, babbled faster and giggled more than ever. The word she used most was "fun." Playing tennis was fun. New York was fun. At night, while Steffi hid in her rented apartment and watched television, Monica was *on* television presenting an MTV award, or at Broadway shows, or signing autographs and getting photographed, smiling, giggling, laughing; *having fun.*

Except on the court. When she tossed up the ball to serve, her soft, almost pretty face sharpened and twisted in a rage that had nothing to do with fun. When she hit her groundstrokes, particularly at crucial points, she emitted a bestial, orgasmically passionate grunt-screech that dominated every sound in the stadium.

In the stands, watching their remarkable golden goose of a daughter, sat Mr. and Mrs. Karolyi Seles. They had brought her to America years before the fires burst from the ethnic chips of the old Austrian empire. In the sunny tennis camps of America, they watched her turn into a tennis prodigy.

Then, two years ago, back on the old continent, in the country of her chief rival, the knife attack. Monica, the embodiment of controlled aggression, encountered the terror of its uncontrolled twin.

Weeks later, although the back wound healed, Monica didn't. She'd been attacked where she was most at home, where her form of rage was not only tolerated but rewarded. A few hundred miles away, her family's old neighbors were shooting, raping, torturing, and murdering each other. What was this world about? What was she herself about? Did what she felt inside as she pulverized tennis balls have anything to do with the horror out there? She said that she could not bear to watch—televised tennis.

Her rivals visited and telephoned. Sponsors tempted her, her family nursed, consoled, listened, and advised. After a time, she'd worked it out. What she felt and did on the courts was not aggression, rage, and hatred, it was *fun*. She was not beating her opponents' brains out, just their tennis games, games played with fluffy golden balls on lined courts in the comfortable precincts of the world's nicest towns.

In the women's final of the U.S. Open, she faced her old German rival. Steffi had not been knifed in the back, but her father, Peter, who'd handled her fortune as he'd once handled her tennis life, had done her in. He was arraigned, then imprisoned for tax fraud. And something even more intimate was doing her in: her beautiful, powerful tennis body. Bone spurs were brushing nerves in her back and cutting into her feet.

It was not at all clear what would happen when these two wounded young veterans met. The first set was so close that Monica thought she'd won it with an ace and did a little joyous jig. But no, the serve had been a fault, and when she served again, Steffi won the point and then the set. In the second set, Steffi rested, and Monica took it at love. In the third set, Steffi beat her cleanly with great forehands and service aces. Games before the end, Monica knew what was happening and started smiling, laughing, telling herself to remember that it was, after all, fun.

When it was over, she was at the net congratulating Steffi, embracing and kissing her. For us, viewers, customers, couch potatoes, tennis hackers, passive combatants, it was beautiful. These two *belles laides* were our champions, our girls.


2.

The next day, it was Pete and Andre, not Hungarian Croat and German but American Greek and American Persian. Sampras and Agassi, monolingual multimillionaires, self-tutored, self-absorbed, their faces, bodies, words, and deeds the stuff of ten thousand stories in a hundred languages.

The World's Best, yet there is modesty as well as confidence in them. Winners, they have also had much experience with losing, especially, losing to each other. (Each had won and lost eight matches.) In their mid-twenties, they have the won-and-lost veneer of grizzled vets, and maybe something else, the warrior genes of the ancestors whose wars Herodotus chronicled.

From them came no Selesian giggling or babble. They were *professional*, businesslike, untalkative, although both have developed an amusing, charming fluency. A media darling whose breakouts from tennis prison have been extrapolated by ad agencies into Declarations of Punk and Rebellion, Agassi has accepted, challenged, and, more recently, mocked such depictions. What he is is an original tennis genius whose special gift is amazing eyesight, body coordination, and the court sense built from them. For all recent opponents but Sampras, he has the self-assurance of the hole card ace.

Sampras is bigger, stronger, a better athlete, a better tennis player (which doesn't always mean a greater winner). Still, Agassi, tutored by the shrewd Brad Gilbert, his version of the Persian king Xerxes' wise uncle Artabanus (Herodotus, VII), knows that Sampras's moodiness can lead to slippage and collapse. He is far more attentive to Sampras than Sampras to him.

They walked on court, Sampras's dark, wire-curled head low on his slouching—as if unwilling—body, Agassi rapid, pigeon-toed, somewhere between rooster and last-minute plane-catcher. They warmed up, then started, slowly, feeling each other out, not extending themselves, as if points didn't count, as if to show that they could win them when they needed to. They traded services until the break point of the ninth game, an exchange of eighteen marvelous ground strokes capped by the nineteenth, a Sampras backhand that won the game and broke Agassi's spirit. After that, Sampras coupled power with shrewdness. He used the swirling, curling wind, looping wobbly parabolas which disrupted Agassi's timing. When Agassi adjusted, Sampras blasted backhands and running forehands down the line. His serve got stronger and sager. Agassi's shaven, balding, earringed head sweated and sank lower and lower.

The only turnabout came in the third set: Sampras slumped. Still, you felt even that was controlled, as if some shrewd Hellenic gene were telling him, "Don't humiliate him with a straight set loss or it'll rouse an unstoppable fury in the next Slam."

The match over, the twin stars shook hands and exchanged intimate, amiable words at the net. We, the Vegetable Viewers of the World, wanted to hear these also. Not content with riding behind our warriors in the battle they'd fought—our own battles mostly dodged, and, when not, mostly lost—we wanted their private words, their innermost beings.

No luck this time, but perhaps, a few Opens hence, microphones will be in their pockets or on their rackets, and we will share not only their tennis genius but their human poetry.*

---

* How pleasing for us tennis fans in 2001 that Andre is now accompanied to tournaments by his wife, the retired Steffi Graf. (Some of us imagine the tennis product of such genes, ambition and intensity.) Another pleasure—somewhat compensating for Steffi's absence on the circuit—is that her retirement was as fine as that of Michael Jordan, Wayne Gretzky, and Ted Williams, that is, it came after brilliant performances, first at the French Open (which she won), then at Wimbledon (where she lost in three sets to Lindsay Davenport).

# Tears, Idle Tears, I Now Know What They Mean

Stories create or describe situations which arouse feelings. Since there's an almost infinite number of situations and since the language of storytellers is almost infinitely varied, it might be assumed that feelings too are infinite in number.

No student of feeling believes this. Indeed, the learned consensus seems to be that there are either four, six, or ten basic feelings, and that's that. Perhaps culture and society depend on emotional simplicity, since recognition of other people's feelings is a crucial ingredient of both. The expression of feeling can be as complex as Proust's great novel or Beethoven's late sonatas and quartets, but not every reader or listener can follow such complexity. Nonetheless, the feelings underlying the complexity are common and understandable to almost all.

The most complex classification of feeling known to me—since reading Tom Lutz's fascinating book*—was made by Charles Fourier in *The Passions of the Human Soul and Their Influence on Society and Civilization* (1851): 12 orders of passion broken into 33 genera, 135 species, and 405 varieties. If this abundance did not doom Fourier's taxonomy to ridicule and oblivion, then his association of each order with "specific notes in the musical scale (love is mi or a major third) and specific alcoholic beverages (love is a thick white wine)" did.

Unlike Fourier, Lutz works toward as much simplicity as this complex subject allows. And complex it is. Crying is one of those world-in-a-grain-of-sand phenomena. It touches almost everything human (no other animal cries) and is treated in almost every art and science. Yet, Lutz tells us, there is still no science of tears, "no lamentology or lac-

* Tom Lutz, *Crying: The Natural and Cultural History of Tears* (New York: Norton, 1999).

rimology," only "a medical subfield of dacryology . . . the study of the lacrimal system."

Lutz describes the anatomy, chemistry, psychology, anthropology, and sociology of weeping, the history of theories about and fine descriptions of it in poetry, fiction, and drama. The reader learns and learns and learns from this book: the three types of tears (emotional, reflex— the poke-in-the-eye tear—and basal—the constant liquefaction of the cornea); their enzymatic stimulation by prolactin, the stimulant of breast milk (an element in women's greater tear production?); the 4,000 tearful episodes of the first two years (except in societies and families which punish infant weepers); the C–C$\sharp$ range of the first cries; the puncta through which, unseen, most of our tears drain; the parasympathetic nervous system—maintainer of somatic equilibrium—the regulator of tears which can thus be seen as restorative, that is, cathartic; Aristotle's use of this medical term in his analysis of tragedy; Van Haeringen's 1981 discovery that "tears have 30 times the amount of manganese than is found in the blood," which suggests that tears "stave off depression" since depressive brains are manganese-rich; the evolution of tearing linked (by Paul MacLean) to the development of the cerebrum after the discovery of fire: "the smoke that got in those early human eyes" during cremation rituals may have led to the association of tears with loss.

There is also considerable exposition of the culture of mourning: who weeps and why, the changing roles of crying in American politics and gender—candidate Edmund Muskie mocked for wet eyes then, many men (candidates and athletes more than poets) denounced for dry eyes now. Some of the best pages here are Lutz's analysis of grief and tears in literature and life—he is a professor of English at the University of Iowa—in movies and songs, Homer and Hemingway, Dostoievski and Dickens.

A famous tear-provoker, Dickens could also work up healthy tear-mockery: "Tears were not the things to find their way to Mr. Bumble's soul; his heart was waterproof. Like washable beaver hats that improve with rain, his nerves were rendered stouter and more vigorous by showers of tears, which, being tokens of weakness, and so far tacit admissions of his own power, pleased and exalted him."

Cry away, he tells Mrs. Bumble. Weeping, he says, "opens the lungs, washes the countenance, exercises the eyes, and softens down the temper." She, who "had tried the tears because they were less troublesome than a manual assault," proceeds to grab him by the throat with one hand

and inflict "a shower of blows (dealt with singular vigour and dexterity)" with the other.

In Lutz's shower of lacrimal information, such Dickensian delights are like the pergola in *Top Hat* to which Fred Astaire escorts Ginger Rogers out of the storm to sing and dance "Isn't It a Lovely Day to Be Caught in the Rain?"

# King of a Rainy Country

Je suis comme le roi d'un pays pluvieux. B A U D E L A I R E, *Spleen*

Sartre's wrong, says Jeff Smith: "Hell isn't other people. Hell is me." Me is "the inadequate self," the one "no promotion or praise will" help for long.

At this millennial turn, there are nineteen million such Me's in prosperous, Prozac-soaked America. Indeed, a sliver of the prosperity is due to Prozac and other antidepressants whose sales account for 80 percent of the profits of the great pharmaceutical firms.

This is not the sole contribution melancholia makes to prosperity. Twenty-four hundred years ago a somewhat hyperbolic Aristotle asked: "Why is it that all those who have become eminent in philosophy or politics or poetry or the arts are clearly of the atrabilious temperament?"

Why indeed? Judging by this book, part medical, part cultural, but—at its best—autobiographical, the answer may have to do with the need of many depressives to first understand and then end their internal civil war.* For such an effort, concentration, knowledge, analytic power, and tenacity are needed.

Walking the streets of Missoula, Montana, where he worked in a community mental health clinic, Jeff Smith was gripped by the inner enemy he called *Mr. Shoulder*. Back in the Appalachian hollow in which he grew up, his eighty-one-year-old grandmother told him that the dark companion was a family curse. Smith set out to discover what he could about it. He learned that one in four American women, one in eight American

---

* Jeffrey Smith, *Where the Roots Reach for Water. A Personal and Natural History of Melancholia* (New York: North Point Press, 1999).

men—the number gets larger every decade—suffer severe depression. People of different backgrounds suffer it in different ways: Latinos complain of nerves and headaches, Chinese of back pain, Middle Easterners of stomach aches. Male depressives are often flat-footed and bald, their blood denser with the "fight or flight" hormone, cortisol, and lower levels of certain fatty and amino acids; their neurotransmitters are relatively inactive.

There is more biochemical information here, much too about the history and theory of depression, but *Where the Roots Reach for Water* is more than a pharmaceutical companion to Robert Burton's seventeenth-century compendium, *The Anatomy of Melancholy.* The more is Jeff's story, which begins with the end of an affair with Barbara and gets into high gear with his Missoula meeting in a music store with and love for Lisa Werner, a German teacher. Their subsequent marriage comes close to shattering on the rocks of his jealousy, narcissism, and fantasy.

Almost as absorbing is the author's account of his lifelong flight from the narrowness of his upbringing (by loving, divorced parents, step-parents, and grandparents), in which the joy of his mother and himself for the books brought by the once-a-week bookmobile plays a large part. The books transport them over the solitude of the Appalachians and lead him to become the first college student in his family. Books, jazz, country and classical music, walks, friends, gardening—there's a fine account of his garden—clinical work with the depressed and shattered compose a life whose intermittent destruction makes a sad, noble story.

When Lisa brings him home the first time, she reads him her translation of a Rilke elegy:

> That my streaming countenance makes me more radiant.
> That the hidden weeping should then bloom.
> How you will be dear to me then, oh nights of despair . . .
>
> We who squander our sorrows.
> How we look beyond them into the mournful passage of time to see
> whether they might end.
>
> But they are seasons of us, yes, our winter:
> Abiding leafage, meadows, ponds, landscapes we are born into . . .

Smith has not squandered his sorrows but has described without sanctifying them or his struggle against them. "I had conquered nothing, mastered nothing, transcended nothing."

His book ends with ten pages of bibliography and five of thanks to his friends, family, doctors, Lisa, and the Creator "for everything, even melancholia."

# Logging Expiation

That a thoughtful, witty, scrupulously written book about the operation
and failure of a small Vermont sawmill can be published and distributed
is as good a witness as anything else to the variety of contemporary culture. That there are individuals running intense little enterprises and others chronicling them reinvigorates what much else suggests is sagging or
edematous, American individuality.

Timothy Lewontin is, as he says, a child of privilege. The son of a
distinguished scientist,* raised in comfort and well-schooled, he wished
to "prove to myself and those who cared about me that I was capable of
working long and hard at distasteful tasks for dubious reward." What he
was after was "a simple expiation of the guilt that all privileged people
feel." The way to do that was to at least "understand what it is to live
without those privileges." No matter that such Orwellian expiation is
rarer than he thinks. No matter that, as he says, he fails: "One cannot escape what one is." By working long and hard hours in Parsons' mill
alongside the unprivileged, by describing the work they all do and the
fate of the enterprise,† Lewontin surmounts the privilege he expiates.
Here is the grit of social equality and fraternity, the bitterness as well as
the strength of the melting pot.

Parsons' mill is worked by alcoholics and workaholics, lunkheads,
drifters, boasters, and those whose "loquacity" is largely muscular. Over
it presides a septuagenarian tyrant, Henry Parsons, half-loony with suspicion, pride, and misanthropy. He is also a shrewd, brilliantly ingenious
entrepreneur, the sort of man whom a great novelist would resolve by
simplifying. Lewontin records just enough of his ornery power and con-

* His father is my old friend Richard Lewontin.

† Timothy Lewtontin, *Parsons Mill* (Hanover: University Press of New England, 1989).

trariety to stir fascinated wonderment. A landowner, ex-publisher of a small newspaper, this laconic, furious driver of himself and others runs the sawmill less for profit than for personal expression. "On" it, he plays with the power romantic poets imagined was in the winds which drew from them their soul music. It is what he does with young Lewontin and the other men who work under his furious direction. He exposes their essential character, the timorous deference of some, the steely resistance of others. He animates them as he animates the mill and Lewontin's account of it.

There are lots of books now about workers and their work. Oral historians such as Studs Terkel have recorded the complex relation of a person's being to his job. Such books detail the complexity of what would otherwise seem banal activity. So here, there is much pleasure learning about the ins and outs of turning logs into dowels to serve as rungs of wooden ladders or thin strips into the laminations of wooden tennis rackets; the running of great boilers; the rapid appraisal of the grain and straightness of ash boards; the disposal of sawdust, even techniques for binding and stacking wood for shipment. So much difficult activity underwrites the ease, beauty, and security of burgher life. The relation of mess to order is a governing ratio of such activity, just as the ratio of property to achievement is the crucial social ratio.

The core of Lewontin's book is the complex relationship of the author to Henry Parsons. Timothy Lewontin was a modest, sensitive, independent man of twenty-six. He had taught school, managed a movie theater, sold ice cream from a truck, and worked as a mill hand and carpenter.

He is, above all, a thoughtful observer and judge of his surroundings. Parsons is something new in his experience. Humped over an old tube radio every lunchtime, he listens to the world news, but the rest of his long day he's making powerful news of his own. His temperament is that of the corncob fanatics celebrated by Melville, Twain, Hawthorne, Faulkner, Bellow. These Ahabs, Einhorns, and Snopeses, like Satan, can tolerate no one. Everyone and everything constitutes an obstacle to their almost Platonic idea of perfection, and their formula is always the same, the one described by Santayana, *the redoubling of effort after forgetting the aim*. Parsons succeeds by failing: all the workers are fired and the mill closes.

Within this story, calmly, quietly, and untragically told, is both the grandeur and failure of the country, as within its scrupulous narration, is, somehow, the country's salvation.

# Montaigne in Illinois

"I go out of my way," wrote Essayist Number One, "but by license not carelessness. . . . I want the material to make its own divisions . . . without my interlacing them with words, with links and seams put in for the benefit of . . . inattentive readers." As to style, "I love a simple, natural speech, the same on paper as in the mouth . . . succulent and sinewy, brief but compressed . . . better difficult than boring . . . irregular, disconnected and bold."

Montaigne's four-hundred-year-old prescription describes these wonderful essays by David Foster Wallace.* The best essays—blends of fact, scene, observation, analysis, portraiture, and commentary—Wallace says, are often written by fiction writers, "oglers" who "watch over other humans sort of the way gapers slow down for car wrecks: they covet a vision of themselves as *witnesses.*"

It's this ogler's greatest charm that, like Montaigne, he creates a piecemeal but consistent self-portrait that runs through the book. Wallace's portrait is of a precocious, physically timid, endlessly self-conscious, endlessly curious, naïve sophisticate, a great shower and explainer, a loved and loving son, neurotic, brilliant, good-hearted, and self-deprecating ("extremely sensitive: carsick, airsick, heightsick; my sister likes to say I'm 'lifesick'").

In the best of these essays, he shows up as a fledgling journalist, one who forgets to bring a notebook, is astonished at his press perks, and is puzzled by journalistic requirements ("how many examples [do] I need to list in order to communicate the atmosphere?").

It is the self-portrait, as much as the constraints of Wallace's jour-

---

* David Foster Wallace, *A Supposedly Fun Thing I'll Never Do Again: Essays and Arguments* (Boston: Little, Brown, 1997).

nalistic assignments, that saves the essays from what old-fashioned novel-readers like me thought the narrative-killing excess of his thousand-plus-page novel, *Infinite Jest*. Some of that mastodon meat is in the essays—tennis, teens, television—and some of its manner, too—footnotery, abbreviations, acronymania. But only here and there, say, in the tribute to director David Lynch (*Eraserhead, Twin Peaks, Lost Highways*), does the *IJ*-shy reader want to call for halter, bit, reins, and whip.

The title—and longest—essay is a blow-by-blow account of an expense-paid, week-long luxury cruise in the Caribbean, a counter to a "polished, powerful, impressive . . . best that money can buy" essaymercial by a writer Wallace admires, Frank Conroy (who tells Wallace that he's ashamed of having written it). No one will mistake Wallace's uproarious demolition of the "sybaritic and nearly insanity-producing indulgence and pampering" on board the *Nadir* (his rechristening of the cruise ship *Zenith*) for an essaymercial. It has more interesting characters than most novels, as much solid information as a technical brochure, and its genial depiction of the commerce of "Managed Fun" is as devastating as Henry James's analysis of the economic significance of the skyscraper in *The American Scene* (1907). Fifty times more amusing—and five hundred times times cheaper—than the cruise itself, Wallace's account of it may lose him a hundred perks for every hundred new readers.

There are two essays on tennis, one about becoming a teenage tennis whiz by learning to play the winds and cracked surfaces of central Illinois courts and the second, one of the best essays I've read about professional tennis, focused on the world's seventy-ninth-ranked player, Michael Joyce, as he competes in a Canadian Open. It's full of tennis lore, wisdom, and thumbnail portraiture: Michael Chang, with his "expression of deep and intractable unhappiness," and his mother, who "may have something to do with the staggering woe of Chang's mien"; Jim Courier, who "can hit winners only at obtuse angles, from the center out"; Petr Korda, who "has the body of an upright greyhound . . . plus soulless eyes that reflect no light and seem to 'see' only in the way that fish's and birds' eyes 'see.'" (There is even a lethally seductive sentence about Du Maurier cigarettes. If Wallace loses his journalistic assignments, he can moonlight as a copywriter.)

Perhaps the gem of the book's four gems is a fifty-four-page essay on the 1993 Illinois State Fair. There is more about the look, sounds, smell (Wallace is a great smeller), feel, and meaning of rural Illinois here than I've seen in such small space since Bellow's 1957 ten-pager for *Holiday* magazine: "Miles and miles of prairie slowly rising and falling . . . a sense that something is in the process of becoming or that the liberation of a great force is imminent, some power like Michelangelo's slave only half-released from the block of stone." Wallace's lyrics are more staccato, his assessments swifter and less powerful than Bellow's, but he has lots more space and covers much more: not just the fair but its visitors, officials, reporters, Governor Jim Edgar ("impressive") and his wife (whose "tragic flaw" is her voice), the prize horses, cattle, and swine, the auto races (although "What I know about auto racing could be inscribed with a dry Magic Marker on the lip of a Coke bottle"), baton-twirling, clogging, ag people, Kmart people, message-bearing T-shirts, the flatness, the space, the loneliness of the Midwest where Wallace grew up and from which, years ago, he fled.

Perhaps the highlight of the state fair essay is this great scene: Wallace has invited Native Companion, his old Philo High prom date, to go around the fairgrounds with him. N.C., who "teaches water-aerobics to the obese and infirm," is now married, has three children, and bungee jumps. She accepts a carny's offer to try out The Zipper, the wildest of the near-death-experience rides. Our "air-sick, heightsick" author manages, with "an act of enormous personal courage," to watch as she's strapped into a cage and spun, hurled, and tumbled "like stuff in a dryer" in a horrifying ellipse. A long scream, "wobbled by Doppler," comes from the cage. "Then the operator stops the ride abruptly with Native C.'s car at the top, so she's hanging upside down inside the cage," with her dress hanging over her head. The operator and a colleague ogle her. After another scream from the cage, "as if Native C.'s getting slow roasted," Wallace, outraged, almost summons enough saliva to "say something stern." At this point, the two carnies, "laughing and slapping their knee," start bringing her down. N.C. bounds out of the cage and, in a burst of expletives, tells them "'that was . . . great.'" Wallace is furious. "'They were looking up your *dress*. . . . I saw the whole thing.'" N.C. looks at him. Her color is high. "'You're so . . . *innocent*, Slug,'" she says.

Four hundred years ago, dear old Montaigne described falling off his horse and "dying." For four hundred years, readers have loved him for his account of it. Perhaps four hundred years from now, readers will love Not So Intrepid and Not So Innocent Slug Wallace.

# O*i*ck on Ka*f*ka, Frank, and O*i*ck

Music can mimic, deepen, and even transfigure the rise and fall of feeling, painting can subtilize, refine, and enchant vision, but it is verbal analysis and narrative synthesis which transform human existence into comedy, pathos, heroism, degradation, tragedy, and ten million variations and extensions of them. "Kafka had taught us how to read the world differently," Cynthia Ozick writes in her essay on the difficulty of being and of translating Kafka. (A beckettian letter of his leads her to call her piece "The Impossibility of Being Kafka," which is either cliché or hyperbole.) In this new collection of essays,* Ozick broadens the spectrum of American criminality by seeing in the murderer-by-mail, Theodore Kaczynski (the Unabomber) Dostoievski's Raskolnikov, and goes on to see in Raskolnikov's creator a genius twisted by Unabomber-like "obscurantist venom" and ideologism.

In other essays she draws on Lyndall Gordon's studies of T. S. Eliot and Henry James to describe the anguish, desolation, egocentricity, selfishness, and suffering behind their dismissal of the artist's personality as a critical tool. In the most celebrated of her polemical essays, she attacks those who have "washed away into do-gooder abstraction the explicit urge to rage that had devoured" the young literary genius Anne Frank (born in 1929, one year after Ozick).

It is a part of Ozick's complexity that she prefers the unpolemical part of her own work, what she calls "memory's mooning and maundering," to the feisty, learned attacks which have stirred literary and other pots and created her modest celebrity. She understands how making a case reduces the "oceanic proliferating complexity of things." (She praises this formulation of Saul Bellow's.) So Anne Frank—demeaned as "do-

---

* Cynthia Ozick, *Quarrel & Quandary* (New York: Knopf, 2000).

gooder"—contains not only rage but the touching, youthful optimism which has made her an iconic saint of the Holocaust. Ozick knows well how much more there is to Eliot, James, Dostoievski, and even Kaczynski than what she's polemically written about them.

Narrative, like polemics, sacrifices "proliferating complexity," but that is because the story can bring "oceanic possibilities" to a controlled boil. A fine narrator herself, Ozick understands that well. (See her four-page story "The Shawl.") Perhaps it is the comprehensiveness of her comprehensions which creates the carapace—or stigmata—of her essays and stories.

Five of Ozick's twelve books have alliterative titles: *Fame & Folly, Metaphor & Memory, Art & Ardor,* and the newest essay collection. (The title of the collection of stories about the messy, magical charmer, Puttermesser, lacks the ampersand.) Like other poetic devices—rhyme, meter, stanzaic form—alliteration sometimes propels the writer toward useful invention. So here, Kafka is called one of "those writers who have no literary progeny, who are *sui generis* and cannot be echoed or envied." "Envied" is the alliterative bonus, surprising enough so that we are more conscious of it than of the alliterative vehicle which delivered it. (Only a masochistic writer would buy his ambition at the price of being the tormented Kafka.) More often, though, Ozick's alliterative tic italicizes the chief drawback of her work, a hyperbolic inflation of style and statement which, like flashy clothes, diverts from what counts most. (Witness "memory's mooning and maundering.") Intoxicated by the power of poetry (see "What Is Poetry About?"), Ozick sometimes strains to attain it: "He sprinkles his poem, cannily and profusely." Wouldn't a different verb do the work of the second adverb? Kafka's "fables are too entangled in concrete everydayness, and in caricature, to allow for incandescent certainties." Does one get entangled in concrete? What does "incandescent" contribute?

Ozick understands the dangers of poeticizing. "Too much metaphor overloads us with softness," she writes in her essay on an overwritten Swedish novel. Like alliteration, metaphor is part of what she calls the "furious flow" of verbal and mental energy. In what I think is the best of her book's twenty essays, "A Drug Store Eden," there are few metaphors, and there is very little alliteration. Ozick's spare, tender, finely detailed account of her parent's Bronx pharmacy (behind which her Uncle Ruby started what became the garden in which young Cynthia read, dreamed, and thought) is a small masterwork. Ozick knows that world so well, there is no need to elaborate or advertise it.

There is another wonderful essay in the book. It is also about something the author knows long and well, New York City. It's called "The Synthetic Sublime." ("Sublime" is one of Ozick's signature words. The nouns "surround"—meaning surroundings plus ambiance—and "conundrum" are two others.) The essay exhibits Ozick's unshowy learning—she's a wonderful detail forager—her summary power, her magical accuracy: "New York in July is out of synch, not quite itself, hoping for ransom, kidnapped by midsummer frolicking." It also has the heart of all Ozick's fine work, which—damn James and Eliot—is Ozick herself.

> Now and then, heartstruck, I pass the crenellated, quasi-Gothic building that once housed my high school, where latecomers, myself among them, would tremble before its great arched doorway, fearing reprimand; but the reprimanders are all dead.

Bless that "heartstruck," that "myself among them," and bless Ozick.

# Jane Jacobs's Ideas

I write this review a couple of hours after pushing a metal stylus through holes by the names of presidential, senatorial, and local candidates in the uncurtained puppet-theater voting booths among my neighbors in Hyde Park. Home, after coffee and the newspaper, I read a few pages of De Tocqueville's great book of 1840, *Democracy in America*. The pages deal with the early debate over elections. If elections "recur only at long intervals, the state is exposed to violent agitations every time they take place." If they occur frequently, "their recurrence keeps society in a feverish excitement, and gives a continual instability to public affairs,"* a consequence of which is "the promulgation of bad laws." De Tocqueville quotes Hamilton in *Federalist* 73 on this "blemish in the character and genius of our government" and a 1787 Jefferson letter to Madison suggesting that a year "be allowed to elapse between the bringing in of a bill and the final passing of it." I also read a letter of Abigail Adams to her husband John in 1776 in which she writes that "although your sex lay almost an exclusive claim" to the "art of Government," she will cite a passage "in favor of a Republic" in an essay about Alexander Pope. It deals with the arts and sciences' need for "unlimited freedom to raise them to their full Vigor and Growth."

It's good to know that what brought me and my neighbors to Kenwood Avenue in the early morning had to do with the intelligent men and

---

* In the hectic weeks of uncertainty and fury following the Bush-Gore presidential election of November 2000, the controlling thermostat was not the constant reminder of the country being one of laws not impassioned people, but the barrage of more or less witty commentary about such novel phenomena as ballot dimples and chads. Less amusing was a U.S. Supreme Court whose marmoreal impartiality and equanimity dissolved in the ideological heat felt by almost every citizen-voter.

women who, two hundred years ago, worked out the ways our desires could be translated into action.

In the late eighteenth century, despite the claim of Abigail Adams that men claimed special expertise in the "art of Government," there were no professional experts, only people who thought hard and acted more or less in accord with what they thought. Today, the discussion of the issues in this election—work and wealth—has been dominated by professionals who examine them with refined statistical tools. Jane Jacobs is more like an eighteenth-century amateur, a Hamilton or Abigail Adams, thoughtful, widely read, but "unqualified" in the "professional" sense. So, only a couple of economists are alluded to in her new book. Her examples come from the *Wall Street Journal,* the *Toronto Globe and Mail,* and the popular books of historians, anthropologists, and scientists. She has worked out her notions about the moral foundations of commerce and politics more or less on her own, as, three decades ago, she did in her famous book on urban life, *The Death and Life of Great American Cities.* She was censured then as she will be now by those who feel that analyses not backed by precise, thorough, usually quantified studies are largely smoke and mirrors. Yet there was a vividness, energy, and eccentric freshness about Jacobs's city book, and these virtues distinguish this one.*

Its basic notion is that the two activities human beings share with all animals, foraging for food and protecting territory, are governed by one group of attitudes, whereas the uniquely human activity, commerce, derives from a totally different one. Jacobs call these groups "moral syndromes." The "commercial moral syndrome" includes optimism, industriousness, efficiency, thrift, the shunning of force, easy collaboration with strangers and aliens, respect for contracts, openness to inventiveness and novelty, and the promotion of comfort and convenience. The syndrome of the "hunting fathers" (an Auden phrase Jacobs would approve: she uses "guardians") who protect our territory and its citizens includes obedience, discipline, loyalty, ostentation (as in the grandeur of public buildings), the dispensing of largesse (as in aid to hurricane victims), fortitude, fatalism (as in the concession speeches of defeated guardians), the exertion of prowess, and the avoidance of trading. Guardians

---

* Jane Jacobs, *Systems of Survival: A Dialogue on the Moral Foundations of Commerce and Politics* (New York: Random House, 1992).

must not trade state secrets or government contracts. When guardians become traders (as in a corrupt government or in such "hybrid monsters" as the Mafia), or when traders adopt guardian habits (contracts awarded to friendly or corrupting interests), their systems collapse. Almost every political election dredges up the debris of such syndromic crossovers.

Jacobs also discusses what she calls "syndrome-friendly inventions." These come from people who, say, advance commerce by making microloans to micro-enterprises too small to be underwritten by banks. An example is the Grameen Bank in Bangladesh, which was started by an economist named Mohammed Yunus after a street vendor told him his problems. Sometimes inventors are in governments. Jacobs discusses the "extraordinary ingenuity" by which Taiwan industrialized itself, creating a tax system which forced money from real estate transactions into industrial investment.

Examples invigorate this book. When Jacobs discusses the Oregon conifers infected by truffle spores excreted by animals which are the food of the northern spotted owl, or the commercial implications of Deuteronomy, or the tragic consequence of converting the happy hunter Iks into idle, destructive farmers,* the text bubbles. She is better at mining particulars than in intricate analyses of her notions. Still there are pleasant surprises there as well. So after discussing the security measures of "commercial people"—collateral, letters of credit, bills of lading, security deposits—she writes,

> Offhand, you'd expect obsession with security to be associated with pessimism, withdrawal, and fear of the future, maybe chronic, bitter suspicion of it. . . . But look at it this way. People who take practical steps to forestall surprise misfortunes are, by definition, optimists.

(Ross Perot would have been better served by this counter to the charge of paranoia than by hoofing it around a Dallas stage to the tune "Crazy.")

---

* Colin Turnbull's thesis about the Iks has been exploded by such genuine investigators as the linguist Bernd Heine. See "The Mountain People: Some Notes on the Ik of North-Eastern Uganda," *Africa* 55 (1) (1985). The interplay between anthropological observer and the humans observed is one of the standard topics of the discipline. Clifford Geertz speculates finely about its "uncertainty principle" and complementarity notions (my, not his, equivalences) in his *Available Light* (Princeton: Princeton University Press, 2000).

The form of Jacobs's book allows for, even invites disagreement. It's cast into dialogues conducted by persons of differing interests. In fact, two of her disputants get engaged—matrimonially—at the end of the book, an arrangement which suggests the affectionate relationship between the book's intelligence and its readers.

# Our Regenstein

When, twenty-five years ago, I took my first squint at the corrugated flanks of the new University of Chicago library, I said, "When are they going to take it out of the box?"

I didn't like the library, didn't like its lunar plainness—where were the Gothic curlicues, fretwork, gargoyles?—didn't, in fact, like its existence. My office is in Wieboldt. To get the books I needed, I only had to walk down two flights of stairs, use my faculty key to get into Harper and walk the dark, book-laden corridors in splendid, if miserly, isolation. It was like being in an old spiderwebbed wine cellar, my cellar. Unbearable to lose it.

But lose it I did. The books were carted off to the new monster, and one had to make the long, three-minute trek through the quadrangles to find them.

Slowly, the monster became familiar. He even looked OK, different but OK. His desert-colored flanks were not unhandsome, his clean oblong boxes had a sort of amiable grandeur. In a few weeks, he no longer seemed a stranger in our Gothic village. Not only did his flanks fit in with our Indiana limestone, he even consorted with the strange tomato brilliance of Henry Moore's atomic energy sculpture, visible from his northwestern windows.

Then there was the brightness, the spaciousness, the sheer democratic generosity of the place, the books all out there, the carrels, the desks, the space, the deep leathery chairs. Yes, by God, this was a very nice library, a very nice place to be.

So years have passed in happy, mostly happy, coexistence. Like thousands of others, I have spent thousands of hours in this special space-time place, this treasury of the past and launching pad of the future. Past, future, the ever-transient present have magically interflowed here.

Regenstein.

Our Regenstein. We name it as we name a family pet; but this is a pet that will not die, or will not if we care for it as we have its first quarter century.

Bless you, Regenstein, bless those who gave and built you, bless those who take care of you, bless those who use you, and bless those all over the world and the long future who will be transfigured by what happens in your bright space.

*In 1999–2000, I was a fellow at the Stanford-based Center for Advanced*
*Studies in the Behavioral Sciences. Every Wednesday evening, a fellow pre-*
*sented a synopsis of his or her work in progress. As the only non–behavioral*
*scientist among the fellows, I tried to compensate by sending out a memoran-*
*dum of my reactions the next day. The one sent after Larry Cuban's presenta-*
*tion was slightly revised for submission to an op-ed page.*

## Chipping at the Schools

I.

"Chipping" is etymologically related to "cheap," but Stanford professor
Larry Cuban's research into the adoption and use of computers in Silicon Valley schools—pre- and primary through university (Stanford)—
makes clear that the expenditures have been anything but cheap. They
are, let's say, large, although, as Princeton professor Alan Krueger (a fellow Fellow, and my year's tennis partner)* points out, they are not a large
percentage of the enormous school expenditures (let's say, about 10 percent of them) and may be worth it.[†]

Cuban's research makes clear that although the availability of computers in the heart of Computer Country, Silicon Valley (Santa Clara
and San Mateo Counties plus a slice of San Francisco) grows and grows,
their use by students and teachers doesn't. Ways of teaching and student
test scores are practically unaffected by them. Cuban's research into the
effect of such technologies as radio, film, and television on school performance in other days reveals a similar pattern: large claims for more or
less revolutionary transformation, minimal change in practice and result.

The large claims are made by politicians, school boards, and adminis-

---

* My racket must have an affinity for economists. My Chicago partner for twenty-odd
years has been Gary Becker.

[†] He mentions the availability of jobs for computer-trained people. I wonder if a similar
argument could be made for school investment in yo-yos or even rifles since the more that
were needed for schools, the more workers would be required to manufacture them.

trators and by the manufacturers and sales force of the new technology and by others who profit from investment of one sort or another in it. The public schools are an ideal testing—that is, dumping—ground for such proclamations and expenditure. Populated by the underaged and the underpaid, they are the obvious social location for everyone's interests, political or emotional, vested or "disinterested," wild, mild, or mad.

My own sense is that Cuban's research should persuade policy makers and school boards to at least pause before making further large expenditures on computers even though such pause might mean the loss of the lucrative temptations dangled before them by vested interests. There are plenty of other uses for the money: the repair of rotting schools, the construction of new ones, the raising of teachers' salaries, and the cautious hiring of new teachers.

## 2.

Cuban's forthcoming study raises general questions about schools, teachers, technology, and social transformation.* He has investigated the use of computers by engineers and physicians and found results comparable to his school findings: the practitioners make next to no use of the new tools.

He asks "Why?"

Here are answers which come to my mind.

1. *Inertia.* People are reluctant to change habits—that's the meaning of "habits." They are even slower to change when they sense that their jobs may be undercut or eliminated by adoption of new tools or techniques.

2. *Mental Torpor.* To invent ways computers can be used in preschool, high school, and college requires an intellectual energy few are able, willing, or trained to exert. The most rapid and inventive employment of new technology is related to the intensity of the interest: so (a) life-and-death experiences of patients—and their enlightened physicians, (b) money-making or -saving, (c) diversion for the sportive—often mischief-making—adolescent and post-adolescent (usually male), and (d) the interest of trend-setters and the fashionable. This last may lead to investing in tulips (compare the tulipmania in seventeenth-cen-

* Larry Cuban, *Oversold and Underused: Computers in the Classroom* (Cambridge: Harvard University Press, 2001). The book contains much that is unmentioned in this brief response to Cuban's fifty-minute presentation.

tury Holland), raising dummy antennas on televisionless houses (1950s America), or buying the very latest equipment—stereo in the 1980s, software in the 1990s—by people not all that interested in music or information.

Eventually—meaning a time frame longer than the two-year-span Cuban's research uses—the most important—or, perhaps, lucky—technology not only catches on but transforms society. So the children of the '50s who made little use of television in class are, twenty years later, largely dependent on it for entertainment and information. Computers are taking less time to catch on than technology used to take and already are "indispensable" to people who'd never touched one years, months, or even days earlier.

One can envision their increasing use in classes: correspondence with children in other places; research projects deepened by the extraordinary availability of information and illustrative spectacles (paintings, architectural masterpieces, performances of *Hamlet*); model-making and "testing"; electronic contact with exceptional minds, extraordinary people.

At this point, though, one might examine what elements of the school experience are computer-resistant.

3.

People are in schools not just to learn how to think or to learn about what has been and might be, or to learn what they have not learned at home or in the playgrounds of their pre-pre-school years, but to be physically, *actually*, with other children under the supervision of an adult who is not their parent. Being with other people, amorously, athletically (competitively), and in intellectual or emotional fellowship is a good. Every diminution of that good must make a large claim to be successful.

Solitude is another human good, although, like socializing, it can become problematic, even dangerous.*

The technologies of which we've been speaking—radio, television, and computers—are fusions of socializing and solitude. Most computer use is done by oneself in solitude but always involves communicating with others, even if the others are represented by banks of information (data) or games which they've created. (One can watch television by

---

* For the rare few, it can be a spur to extraordinary invention. Thus Beethoven, who in 1802 was driven to solitude and almost suicide by his deafness—see the so-called *Heiligenstadt Testament*—within it created revolutionary sound forms which have brought unheard-of pleasure to millions and millions of hearing people.

oneself, but the "vision" is of other people. It's why not a few who live alone turn on the television set—as others turn on the radio or stereo—as soon as they get home. It relieves the solitude. Telephone answering machines and email also supply "company.")

The relevance to Cuban's work is that a large portion of schooling can't be affected by computers. Theoretically, a computer could instruct and interact with the student to a degree that would make teachers irrelevant or obviously inferior conveyors of material or techniques of investigation. (The courses offered by computerized educational systems use this as a sales pitch.) With computers, a student might find companionship in remote places that would be more exciting and challenging—users might pick up each other's languages—than he could find in his local school, but the computers—of today, at any rate—cannot supply the physical presence, the spontaneity, the offhand humor, the affection, even the aggressiveness and meanness of *actual* contact with others. The sheer fallibility of others, the clash of even third-rate and ninth-hand opinions may be as important to the school experience as the disciplined, selective, rarified, *perfected* offerings of the computer.


4.

One day technology may supply, say, most of the excitement of an NBA game by *simulation;* it may even offer the sort of mental and physical data lovers experience. Humans, perhaps then created by purified fusions of genetic matter, might conceivably spend rich happy *lives* in a solitude they might not even recognize as solitude (because there is no alternative), but this projection à la Huxley's *Brave New World* would not be welcomed by anyone who reads this. In traditional reaction to dystopian creation, it would be regarded as an infernal conclusion to the human experience.

In short, the human reaction to technological and much other change is to *make haste slowly (festina lente)*. Larry Cuban's research might not have been aimed to support this conclusion, but I think it does.

# From Van Meegeren to Van Blederen

Dutch art. Sure, Vermeer, Rembrandt, Van Gogh, de Kooning, but then there's the brilliance of recent Dutch art criticism. We're thinking of the two great Vans, Meegeren and Blederen.

Fifty years ago, it was Van Meegeren. Arrested by Dutch authorities for selling a precious part of the national heritage—canvasses by Jan Vermeer—to Hermann Goering, Van Meegeren said that he'd painted the Vermeers himself. Put into a cell with paints and canvas, he proved it by painting yet another.

A genius? In a way, yes, but his genius was that of critic and scholar, not painter. As painter, he was a competent, unimaginative journeyman. As critic and scholar of Vermeer's technique and development, he was, however, first-rate. He understood the brushwork, the use of light and space, the preferred expressions, the arrangement of figures, tables, sky. Actually painting "the Vermeer" was not much harder than tracing an existent one.

Now, fifty years later, there's Van Blederen, another critical genius, another more or less failed artist. On Friday, November 21, 1997, he entered Amsterdam's Stedelijk Museum and headed for Barnett Newman's abstract canvas *Red, Yellow, and Blue*. Eleven years earlier, he'd made what he thought was a definitive criticism of this painting: he'd slashed it repeatedly with a sharp knife. More than the usual dull criticism, this was interactive art, collaboration. He had "added" to the painting.

His addition had not been well taken; he'd spent five months in jail for it. Worse than that, the government had paid a New York conservator $300,000 to override his critique and restore Newman's original abomination. Now Van Blederen intended to restore his addition to it.

Alas, the best laid plans . . . En route to *Red, Yellow, and Blue*, Van Blederen came upon another Newman monstrosity, *Cathedral*, a

96 inch × 213 inch dark-blue painting with the narrow pale-blue vertical stripe Newman called a zip. Zip indeed. Van Blederen raised his knife and improved *Cathedral* with five long and two small slashes. Then, fulfilled, he leaned against the wall to admire his work and await the philistine minions to take him into custody. The wages of genius.

Can cultural collaboration go further? Van Blederen's makes even the superb U.S. congressional critiques of Mapplethorpe and Serrano take a back seat.

*Traditional philosophic questions first took some form in my head in 1943 when I read Will Durant's genial introduction to them in his* Story of Philosophy. *Two years later, the excitement of early twentieth-century physics opened a small franchise in my unnumerical head when Anatol Broyard, a physics student in my dormitory at Chapel Hill, gave me Sir Arthur Eddington's* The Nature of the Physical Universe *for my seventeenth birthday. Fifty-six years later, I am still trying to understand the evermore mysterious Everything. I read science columns, magazines, and books which try to clarify the cosmos for us curious innumerates, and continue to bother friends and acquaintances who work in these fields with poorly phrased questions. Most have been exceptionally patient. In the summer of 1963, after he'd brought over a letter that had been misdelivered to his house across the street in Cambridge (England), Paul Dirac introduced himself, took a cup of tea, and began a series of morning talks which often included responses to such questions as, Did he ever visualize what lay in back of the equations he formulated? (Yes, he said, he sometimes did.). At the University of Chicago, my respondents have been David Malament, a distinguished philosopher of physics, Jim Cronin, whose Nobel Prize was received for devising one of the key experiments of twentieth-century physics, and S. Chandrasekar, who refused to discuss some matters in nonmathematical terms but who could also be a peerless expositor. The following report on the cosmic revelations of April 2001 shows that the wonderful collegiality of the University of Chicago is alive and kicking.*

# Dark Energy, Dark Matter, and the Waves of Genesis

Great tidings this second April of the third Christian millenium. "We are living in the most exciting time ever in cosmology." This from Michael Turner, the University of Chicago cosmologist, after the discovery of "minute patterns in a glow from primordial gases, possible traces of the cosmic match that ignited the Big Bang and led to the creation of the universe 14 billion years ago." (*New York Times,* April 30, 2001, p. 1).

Twenty-eight days earlier, the cosmological news was the photograph of an *event* which had occurred eleven thousand million years ago.

The *event*—a word as distant from its enormous actuality as the happening itself—was the "explosion"—another verbal inadequacy—of a star. The interpreters of the exploded star were astonished to find it much brighter than expected, comparatively undimmed by cosmic dust. Their explanation of the brightness revived a theory conceived and then abandoned as "my biggest mistake" by Albert Einstein, the "cosmological constant." This constant, a countergravitational force, slowed the expansion of the universe and thus accounted for the unusual brightness. Our cosmologists prefer to use the term "dark energy," perhaps because it links to another mysterious phenomenon, the so-called dark matter which they believe accounts for 96 percent of everything in the universe, everything, that is, which does not compose all that we earthlings see, feel, taste, measure, and are.* Like every star and ray, every atom and quark, we are composed of ordinary, undark matter.† The cosmologists don't assess which is the right and which the wrong stuff. What they do care about is that 4 percent of ordinary matter is the amount which assures a flat universe in which light travels in straight lines.

Like many who are not deterred by mathematical innumeracy from wondering about the *rerum natura*, I brooded about the significance of the news. Unlike my glorious predecessor in wonderment, T. Lucretius Carus, I did not invoke *alma Venus* for guidance but Turner, a University of Chicago colleague whom I'd neither met nor even—as far as I know—seen. I emailed the following question to him across the cyberian campus:

> If gravity is the Einsteinian expression of the curvature of the universe, might dark energy mean that the universe is not a closed multi-dimensional ball but a sort of multi-dimensional sack open to, well, something or other?

* Jim Cronin, May 8, 2001: "We have no idea at all what it is." In response to a draft of this paper, Professor Cronin wrote, "'We have no idea at all what it is' is my own opinion. There are hoards of speculation that the dark matter is super-symmetric particles, axions, neutrinos. But the simple fact is that while the indirect effects of this dark matter are indisputable we have no direct detection of it and as a consequence there are surely possibilities that go beyond the three speculations that I mention."

† The measurements and estimates were made by the late David Schramm, who died in 1998 after he piloted his plane not into the dark but into the ordinary matter of a Colorado mountain.

A few hours later, in the collegial spirit which so often lightens the spirit here, Turner replied:

Hi, Richard

The SPATIAL CURVATURE of the universe (shape) is determined by the amount of stuff in the universe (matter, photons, dark energy, etc). Recent measurements of the cosmic microwave background and direct inventory indicate that we live in a critical density universe, which by Einstein's equations must be flat. The actual nature of the stuff that makes up the Universe determines the SPACE-TIME CURVATURE which you should read as the expansion history of the Universe. A matter-only critical universe would expand at an ever slowing rate; however, our universe, with its dark energy, has a different history: the expansion rate is increasing (the universe is accelerating).

So yes, there is a sense in which your intuition is correct: the nature of the stuff of the universe affects the space-time curvature (read expansion history); however, it does not affect the shape.

Cheers,
Michael

Cheers, indeed. There are many levels of understanding, and I stand on one of the lowest, incapable of understanding any numerically expressed version of what Professor Turner wrote, yet, thanks to his generous words, I now had a sense of the difference between the universe's rate of expansion ("expansion history") and its shape.

APRIL 30, 2001

Twenty-eight days later, Turner's colleague, John Carlstrom, leader of the team operating the "daisy," the Degree Angular Scale Interferometer (DASI) at the South Pole, reported its detection of the patterned glow of quantum fluctuations. (Their instruments had to be very alert: the glow lasted one octillionth of a second, a decimal point followed by thirty-two zeros and a one.) The fluctuations first "rattled," then inflated the fist-size ball of Everything That Is ("infinite riches in a little room") into the enormous expanding universe.

Reports from the "Boomerang" team of Cal Tech and the "Maxima" team from Minnesota and Berkeley confirmed DASI's conclusions about the sound-like waves of this genesis of everything. The quantum fluctuations "that rattled the universe . . . resonated like a vast organ pipe, with one main tone, or wavelength, and a series of overtones or harmonics" (*New York Times,* April 30).

A year earlier, the Boomerangers had detected the fundamental but had found or heard no evidence of the overtones. That absence raised the possibility that the generally accepted theory of creation, Alan Guth's "inflation" theory, might be wrong. The new results, while not "absolute proof," were almost "uncannily" in agreement with it. The discovery confirmed what Guth called "the ultimate free lunch": the creation of everything out of nothing.

To have these enormous events described not by the poetic genius of Genesis or *De Rerum Natura* but by these brilliant mathematicians and physicists makes one think of the enlighteners whose return to our dark cave Plato's master praised two millennia so long ago. Does it affect or alter my feelings about the ultimate metaphysical and religious questions I have put to myself almost all my thinking life? In a way, yes. Unlike Lucretius's master Epicurus, I do not see "man's life foully grovelling upon the ground, crushed beneath the weight of religion"* but feel a kind of wondering, even sympathizing, though slightly contemptuous pity for every single thinker, prophet, philosopher, saint, or sage among my fellows who has tried to explain the unimaginable, counterintuitive tidings delivered by these extraordinary instruments and mathematical models in—often gorgeous—stories which go under the rubric of myth, religion, legend, faith, and metaphysics. I subscribe to the modest philosophers who say that humans are incapable of conceiving what would answer the questions raised by the theories derived from the physicists' instruments. This is the closest I can come to the sense of triumph Lucretius described: "Ergo vivida vis anima pervicit" (Thus the vivid power of his mind prevailed, 1. 72).†

---

* "Humana ante oculos foede cum vita iaceret / in terris oppressa gravi sub religione." *De Rerum Natura* 1.62–63.

† Princeton's distinguished cosmologist, Dr. John Wheeler, writes, "The past is theory. It has no existence except in the records of the present. We are participators, at the microscopic level, in making that past, as well as the present and the future."

*In the 1992 presidential election, the spunky, clever, egomaniacal Ross Perot erupted not only as a Naderian giant killer but as one of the planks with which he walloped Bush the First and Clinton (the First?), the voice of the national debt. No economist, politician, voter, or talking head known to me predicted that the debt would be whittled down by the clintonian prosperity of the '90s. Back then my somewhat spoofing suggestion appeared in the L.A. Times (The numbers were my own, an example of what Bush II might legitimately call "fuzzy math.")*

## Eliminating the National Debt

Ross Perot has directed his expensive searchlight on the four-trillion-dollar national debt and its menace to the nation's well-being. He proposes to deal with the menace by instituting various taxes, spending cuts, and entitlement caps. He calls for patriotic sacrifice equivalent to his own intermittent willingness to sacrifice the serenity of private life for public—presidential—service. He invokes the spirit of his beloved mother, whose charity extended to every beggar who came to the Perot door.

Such high-mindedness has led to the following proposal.

Perot is said to have a fortune in excess of three billion dollars. Let's say that he could live comfortably on five hundred million (which would still provide a nest egg of seventy million dollars for each of his seven principal heirs). He could then transfer two and a half billion dollars to the U.S. Treasury. (The complexities of conversion and transfer could be worked out; the model might be the billion-dollar "transfer" made by Michael Milken in less serendipitous circumstances.)

Perot's contribution would not end here. He might be willing to persuade the rest of us to follow his sacrificial path. Suppose twenty-five of the nation's thirty-odd billion and multi-billion dollar families would make equivalent contributions. The Walton family of Arkansas is said to be worth about twelve billion dollars. If they could manage to subsist on, say, a mere billion, that would mean eleven billion for the Treasury.

We're beginning to talk about what the late Senator Dirksen called "real money."

There are about one million families with a net worth of anywhere from a million to nine hundred million dollars. Persuaded by the sacrifice and patriotism of Perot—or perhaps by statutory fiat—they could contribute by themselves almost enough to eliminate the debt. (My rudimentary calculation pegs a simple millionaire's contribution at $38,000.)

The debt would be entirely eliminated if everyone participated in the great venture. (Perot's proposals call for sacrifice from everyone.) Middle-class adolescents might surrender the price of a CD; indeed, a welfare mother could offer forty or fifty cents to this national cause. Not only would the debt be eliminated, there would be enough left over to supply Medals of Fiscal Honor to every contributing citizen. Every American chest would swell with pride (except for those too poor and otherwise degraded to respond to the perotian call).

Ross Perot speaks often about moving from words to deeds. Here is his moment. With a single signature, he enters the Pantheon of the country we know he loves so well.

*The following was written during the Senate Judiciary Committee hearings on the nomination of Clarence Thomas by President Bush I to the U.S. Supreme Court, which, nine years later, more or less legitimately brought about the electoral victory of his son, President Bush II. Thomas's verbal outburst in 1991 was matched by his loud silence during the oral arguments of* Bush v. Gore *in December 2000. Talking the next day at a Virginia high school, he explained his silence, telling the students that at their age he spoke with a Geeky (Gullah) accent which reinforced the strangeness he felt as the only black student in his class. When he did speak, he was mocked. Keeping silent, he learned that any question he wanted to ask would eventually be asked by others. He said that the habit of silence continued in college and law school. On this occasion, he spoke fluently and movingly, which reinforced my view of the gulf in Justice Thomas's being. It contrasted back then with the serene integrity which radiated from Anita Hill, the University of Oklahoma Law School professor called out of obscurity to testify about the sexual moves a younger Thomas had made on her when she'd worked for him in Washington. This piece appeared as an op-ed in the* Chicago Tribune *on October 15, 1991.*

## His Good Name

As a small contribution to the Thomas-Hill debate, let me offer what Albert Einstein called a "thought experiment."

Imagine that by dint of hard work, intelligence, courage, and self-discipline, you have risen to the heights. At the pinnacle of your well-merited success, you are unjustly accused by a former protégé with whom you believed that you were on excellent terms. She accuses you of having stolen from her.

How do you react to this untrue charge, a charge which endangers much of what you've worked and struggled for your entire life? You react first with astonishment and horror. How and why has this terrible mistake been made? You try to contact your protégé, to ask for an explanation and a retraction of her charge. Something must have happened to her. Has she suffered some sort of psychopathic episode? Has such a fine person somehow been twisted by your enemies? Or could you have so badly misjudged her?

You fail to reach her. Anger takes over. Secure in the knowledge of your innocence, you prepare to fight the mendacious charge. You prepare to sue her for slander, you issue an open challenge to take a lie-detector test, and offer to take one yourself, although you know that delusional personalities can "pass" such tests and truthful persons, in the hands of unskilled operators, can "flunk" them.

Although you feel demoralized at this accusation and suffer some very bad nights, your inner conviction of innocence steels you. You have fought other battles, have prevailed against other enemies. Marshaling your forces, you are actually reinvigorated. The worst that can happen is that you lose in the short run but will eventually prevail.

Now let us try a variation of this "thought experiment."

You are the same person, one who, with immense effort and discipline, has fought his way to the top. You have done much good and are highly respected for it, although you have bucked certain dominant trends and made many enemies. However, you once did do something quite wrong. You did take some money from your protégé.

At the time you were needy and believed that she did not really need what you took, although to your surprise, she did refuse your request for a loan. Perhaps you asked her the wrong way. Perhaps she didn't understand how needy you were, how much it would help you, and since you would be grateful, how much it would eventually help her.

After the theft, you did manage to make up to her. You paid her back, partly by helping her at every stage of her career. You maintained cordial relations with her. You were convinced that if she hadn't forgotten the theft, she had at least forgiven it. In any case, as far as you know, she never revealed it to anyone.

What should you do?

Should you confess that like all men you're a mixture of bad and good, and that one time in your life you slipped because of a desperate need and because you believed that you weren't seriously harming your protégé? If you apologize and ask forgiveness, you may lose a great position, but so be it. At least you have purged yourself and can sleep at night, cleaner and in a way freer.

But no, your old enemies are waiting to devour you. They will eat you alive. Why should you let your reputation, your carefully constructed life, and great opportunity be sacrificed to one person whom you've helped far more than injured? So you do not contact her, you do not confront her; intelligently you do not attack her, at least not directly. You shut off avenues to a path which might lead others to the discovery of your mistake. You absolutely deny her accusation. When you learn that she has taken a lie-detector test, you denounce the validity of such tests, for, of course, you cannot afford the risk of taking one.

This is a difficult choice. Your life will always hang by a thread. You can't sleep, can't eat. You curse the outrageous system which lets a man's whole life be undercut by a single mistake. It is the ugly justice of lynch mobs.* In a way, you've been lynched.

This is the "thought experiment." I end, though, by looking at the Shakespearean speech which was read with an actor's brilliance over the microphones and to the nation's cameras by one of Judge Thomas's most passionate supporters, Senator Alan Simpson. The speech from the tragedy *Othello* concerns the difference between stealing a man's money and his reputation. Its heart is:

> Who steals my purse steals trash . . .
> But he that filches from me my good name
> robs me of that which not enriches him
> and makes me poor indeed.
> *Othello*, III.3

Senator Simpson did not say, nor did anyone else that I know trouble to point out, that the character who makes this brilliant speech is a man of very high reputation, a man who is called "Honest" again and again, an able and brave man, but a deceitful, hypocritical, and villainous one. The speaker is Iago.

---

* In Thomas's passionate outburst, he claimed that this hearing was a form of lynching.

*Over the years, I've sent 20 or 30 letters and 10 or 15 unsolicited op-ed pieces to the New York Times which has printed about 4 of the letters and 1 op-ed piece. Here is one of the rejects.*

## *Letter to the Editor,* New York Times

April 6, 1995
To: The Editor

Mickey Kaus's analysis of the "cunning" which masks the ineptitude of Republican welfare legislation (*Times,* April 6) isn't harsh enough. Thirty-something legislators prattle about "unburdening our [!] grandchildren" and congressional millionaires slogan on about "ending the cycles of dependency" while grabbing ever larger slices of the pie for themselves and their monied ilk.

A finer note is sounded in Pope John Paul II's encyclical, "Gospel of Life," which describes "the war of the powerful against the weak," those whose very existence "compromises the well-being or lifestyle of those who are most favored" and who, therefore, "tend to be looked upon as an enemy to be registered or eliminated."

(signed)

## To Go with an Old Necklace

From Egyptian sand
They fetched Nefertum,
Old bit of gold strand,
A god of perfume.

Two millennia and more
Since this slim chance,
A gentleman of two score
Found romance

With a demoiselle of one
(Advent was the season),
Saw in that stiffened gold redone
In plate, a reason

For presentation.
(Was it too lame?)
Invitation
Turned claim.

And now, gold clutch of space,
Junction of Then and Far,
Hangs on a new face,
The old, ajar.

*Meetings of the entire faculty of the University of Chicago are rare events. I recall one I attended during the Vietnam War which debated what to do about the contributions of university scientists to the government's Institute of Defense Analysis. The second one, held in the spring of 1986, concerned the so-called divestiture of university investments in South African firms. Nelson Mandela was still in jail, apartheid was still burning the soul of the state. The resolution devised by some of my colleagues was phrased in the inflammatory diction I disliked, but I agreed with it rather than with the opinion of respected colleagues including the new president of the university, Hanna Gray, and my friend, the provost, Gerhard Casper (who, a few years later, became the president of Stanford). I read the following statement—one of twenty-five or so made by faculty members—to the assembly.*

## Statement for the Meeting of the
## University of Chicago Senate on April 29, 1986

Although I'm not pleased with the hectoring tone of Resolution One,
   although I have doubts about the efficacy of divestiture,
   although I believe that the university is more a theater for opposed viewpoints than a mouthpiece for one,
   although I believe that there are many terrible regimes and institutions in the world (not a few of which are in Africa), and
   although I believe that I do not have the right to interfere with the monetary or personal disposition of any other colleague except as it interferes with my own,
I am going to vote for Resolution One [the resolution to divest].
   I do this because the university guidelines, as defined by the Kalven Committee Report, say that it is an "obligation of the University as an institution to oppose" measures which "threaten the . . . mission of the University and its values of free inquiry" and to take a stand in "situations involving University ownership of property . . . receipt of funds . . . awarding of honors . . . and membership in other organizations."
   This obligation in mind, I realize that were this not 1986 but 1936 and

were the resolution to read not "Republic of South Africa" but "The Third Reich," there would be very little question in the minds of most of us that we could not endure the university investing in firms which operated in such a way as to support that state.

I vote for the resolution because the Republic of South Africa seems to me about as wicked in its racial policies and in the official mendacity, hypocrisy, and violence which compound them as was the Third Reich.

Despite the doubts expressed above, I will vote for the resolution because I believe that to refuse to make a significant gesture of fraternity with the persecuted is to risk a charge of collective moral cowardice and spiritual vacuity, the charge leveled at the *universities* of the Third Reich.

Finally, I support this resolution because this university, which I love, not only occupies a sacred precinct in time, but in space. Its position is in a city a majority of whose citizens, by the fact of their skin color and parentage, would suffer immediate degradation were they to find themselves in South Africa. To offer high-minded and prudential reasons against the resolution, would, therefore, seem to me to constitute not only a rationalization of my own disposition to accept a status quo in which I have been exceptionally comfortable, but an open insult to my university's neighbors, to this city, and indeed to those members of the university who would endure a like degradation. Although my own preference would be for a resolution calling upon every trustee to examine his duties and conscience and come to the conclusion to which I've come, I opt for my present course because this world seldom offers ideal choices, only a choice of different imperfections. I choose the least imperfect, which is the support of Resolution One.

*I seldom respond to requests for "a paragraph on the meaning of life" or "your favorite Cajun recipe," but, for a reason I can't remember, I typed out the following within minutes of receiving a request from Karen and Lawrence Katz for a book called* Words to Live By *(Two Rivers Press, 1996).*

## A Few Words from Someone
## Who's Written a Few Too Many

The words I've written these past forty-five years are, I suppose, "words to live by." At least, I meant them to amuse, deepen, and even instruct readers. Most of them come from the mouths of invented characters or from viewpoints which I don't call my own and are meant to depict and express some of the trillion human situations, comic, tragic, exciting, ordinary, difficult, and felicitous which make up that precious intermission in the void which humans call their lives. They are not scripture, at least in the sense that scripture is mythic and prescriptive. In the sense that scripture is full of story, they are scripture—but can others live by them?

Yes and no. If people see and feel in the words the expression of what they'd left unexpressed, sometimes painfully, then perhaps the words will count as a sort of *vade mecum*. For me, there are and have been certain words which, in difficult moments, I've recited to myself, and some moments have been eased by the recital. It's good to have such *vade mecums*.

Deeds and words. *How to be, how to act.* Words are crucial for understanding and, now and then, transcendence, but finally, I don't know how many of my words are useful for others or, indeed, for myself.

## ❧ V ❧

## ON FICTION

*Most of the following short pieces were commissioned and written as reviews of novels assigned by the book editors of the* Chicago Tribune. *When I came to Chicago in 1955, I decided to write now and then for the city's newspapers. It was not just that I could use the extra money—I could—but I thought it part of the job of a citizen-writer-professor. Much of what I knew had to do with books so that's what I usually wrote about. My first reviews were done for the* Chicago Sun-Times. *I shifted to the* Chicago Daily News *(and its fine book editor, Bill Newman) when the* Sun-Times *editor, Hoke Norris, left and, when the* Daily News *died, shifted to the* Tribune *(and its good editors, John Blades, Larry Kart, Diane Donovan, and Elizabeth Taylor). I reviewed for other publications, as well, much longer ones for literary quarterlies, medium-sized ones for weeklies like the* Nation *or the* Spectator, *shorter ones for the Sunday* New York Times Book Review. *Every assigned review is limited in length and thus in scope. Writers adjust their thinking as well as their style to certain lengths, and although very few reviews as brief as most of those here will endure as long as a summer snow, assembled they may spell out an interesting way of looking at things. No general reviews anywhere today approach the length, historical interest, or, for that matter, analytic and comic brilliance of those Macauley did for the* Edinburgh Review *from 1825 to 1844, so it's a bit disconcerting to read his modest disclaimer of them beside one's own. (One's dollar in the collection plate doesn't look very large next to the billionaire's foundation check, although both are called charitable contributions.)*

*In the review of Mary Morris's novel, I compared the narrative power of movies and literature. It occurred to me after seeing Oliver Stone's film* Platoon. *I walked home wondering if any novel could come close to matching the power of its war scenes. At home, I read the battle scenes in* War and Peace. *How very different their power. In Tolstoy, the point of view shifted from paragraph to paragraph. You saw and to a degree felt what it was like to be Prince Andrey, then Boris, then Boris's horse. Dramatic exchanges fused with interior ruminations and then with brilliantly sensuous evocations of sights, sounds, smells, tastes, and feelings. The mind wasn't bombarded, it was in a whirl of apprehension and comprehension. So again, I felt at ease with my métier, but I also want to acknowledge here the power and splendor of movies. The beauty of a film like Billy Bob Thornton's* Slingblade *is matched by very few novels: the conception is deep and perfect in its detail, the narrative is powerful, the characters rich and complex, and the protagonist one of the finest characters in American art. Few recent works are as funny and moving as this one. There may be more really good recent films (I think offhand of* Fargo, Pulp Fiction, The Godfather *I and II and* L'hiver au coeur) *than there are very good novels, but I think there are far more run-of-the-mill good novels than there are run-of-the-mill good films. (I differ here from the reporter protagonist of "Almonds.") More recently, though, in the past ten or twelve years, the quality of the average good film may have altered more than that of the average good novel. It has in part to do with the availability of inexpensive video and other digital equipment, in part with the greater numbers of people who know movies well and want to make them. The average good movie has become faster, more and more allusive (and, usually a sign of every sort of sophistication, self-reflexive); the subject matter is bolder, franker, and has subtler ways—in censorship countries—of being yet more bold, more frank, as well as more influential. So the new Chinese and Iranian films and the African ones shown at Fespaco—the annual Pan-African festival held in Ouagadougou, Burkina Faso—contain more of the genius and liberating possibility within those countries than their prose fiction or poetry, if only because a far greater portion of their population sees and perhaps lives by and for them. Recent American films such as* Three Kings *and* Traffic *or English ones such as* Secrets and Lies *deal powerfully—if only rapidly and sensationally—and artfully with great public events or conditions (the Gulf War, the war on drugs, racism) and serve their spectators in similar ways, exciting, reforming, moving, influencing. (A "drug" novel like Richard Price's* Clockers *was more powerful as novel than film because the novelist-*

*scenarist apparently spent his inventive energy on the novel, and the director was unable to reenergize the material. This was the book-to-movie paradigm for most of cinematic history.) In any event, although I think that the civic-cultural relation between movie and fiction is altering, I don't have either the knowledge or the insight to spell it out further, let alone predict what will happen in the next decade.*

*I've wondered if I were starting out today, if I'd do better trying to make movies—perhaps documentary movies about subjects which bedeviled me—than write novels, but decided that the interdependence and contingency of movie-making would sacrifice much of what's most precious about writing fiction: its almost total independence not only from everyone else but from much of one's own life.*

## A Few Things American Fiction Says

I.

Much of what Americans know or think we know about Japan comes to us through newspaper, magazine, or television accounts of its economy and politics. So we know something about the post-World War II triumphs of its industry, the discipline of its work force, the quality of its manufactured goods, the intricate relation between its Ministry of Trade and business leaders, and, more recently, the collapse of its real estate market. What does all this tell us about the quality of Japanese life, the feelings of Japanese individuals? How much does the Nikkei index tell us about—if I can use such a word—the Japanese soul?

Part of my own family knows much more about Japan than I do. My daughter and her husband have spent four of the past eight years living in Japan. He studied Japanese language and culture for ten years. My grandson was born in Japan. When my granddaughter first returned to this country after two years in Japan, she missed her Japanese friends so much that for several weeks she would speak only Japanese, leaving this grandfather totally in the dark about what she was saying. Before they went to Japan the first time, they talked to a distinguished American, head of a Japanese American society whose purpose is to promote understanding between the two nations. This gentleman told my daughter that she would never understand Japan or really get to know a Japanese person. She was upset by this prediction but sensed that what this man told her couldn't be entirely correct, if it was correct at all. She thought—though she was too courteous to say it to him—"I've read Japanese novels and stories in what are supposed to be good English translations. Who knows better what people are like and what they're really thinking and feeling than novelists, story writers, and poets? Even if they don't understand other people, they have some understanding of themselves. So when they write about it, their readers share this understanding."

Of course, understanding is complicated. In some ways, we cannot understand anybody else, no matter how close we are to them. We cannot enter each others' minds. Indeed, the great psychologists and novelists of this century have shown us that, in many important ways, we don't even understand ourselves; old fears and new desires prevent us from understanding the reasons we feel, think, and act.

Of course, here, my interest is in misunderstanding based on cultural difference rather than psychological limitation. Anthropologists have made such differences the center of their concern. They examine the ways people raised in one culture differ in belief, behavior, speech, and thought from people in another. Consider the well-known debate between Marshall Sahlins and Gananath Obeyesekere about the killing of Captain James Cook by Hawaiian islanders two hundred and seventeen years ago. Sahlins dealt with Cook's death in the context of Hawaiian beliefs about gods and men; Obeyesekere claimed that Sahlins's "understanding" of the event demeaned the Hawaiians whose myths, he said, played no role whatsoever in the killing. Obeyesekere said that Sahlins's interpretation was itself a European-derived myth "of conquest, imperialism, and civilisation." I mention this quarrel because it occurred to me that if the Hawaiian islanders of the seventeenth and eighteenth centuries had composed and published a body of novels, stories, and poems, there might not have been one.

Luckily for people interested in the United States, there is a great body of literature on which to draw. It is a newer literary body than Japan's, but nonetheless rich and varied. All sorts of gifted Americans have described lives, feelings thoughts, families, work, games, love, and death so that others can not only understand, but feel with them.

2.

Many Americans and Europeans collaborate in what I understand is the common Japanese notion that only a Japanese can understand Japan. This notion is often explained by the long isolation of Japan from Western countries, by the Shinto belief that Japan is a country singled out by the solar spirit of the universe incarnate in the Japanese emperor, and by what is said to be the special difficulty of the Japanese language, the language Saint Francis Xavier said was invented by the devil to make trouble for him and his fellow missionaries.

If this belief in the inaccessibility of Japan and the Japanese is as much myth as fact, then the equivalent American myth-fact is its opposite. We Americans are supposed to be very easy to understand, because we are supposedly open to all who wish to know us. Our myth-fact may stem from the fact that our country began as a rebellion against a hierarchical society and was founded on the presumption of its citizens' political equality. As for our chief—if not official—language, it was grown on English soil, and though now clearly American, it is also still clearly English. Most Americans arrived speaking a different language. In a way, then, we are a country of foreigners or, at least, of emigrants and refugees.

A recent American slogan, "What you see is what you get," expresses our supposed transparency. "Just look at us, and you'll see what we are, and what we have. We hide nothing. We're not mysterious." So, for instance, we are supposed to have no class system covertly manipulating our one-on-one competitions. Hah. You don't have to be a novelist to sniff out class distinctions in every phoneme, every shoelace, every gesture. Sure, our society is far more fluid and interchangeable than that of seventeenth-century Spain—although *Don Quixote* shakes this presumption—but an enormous amount of energy is spent by our upper class trying to dress, dance, act, and run for political office as if it were from a lower class. (Not that George Bush [I] didn't get to like pork rinds and country music.) Story writers, novelists, and commentators help abolish the falsity of myth-facts. So, in his 1994 Nobel Prize lecture, Kenzaburo Oë said that much of what had shaped his view of the unknowability of truth came not from Japanese writers but from William Blake and that he'd learned about Blake through his true literary godfather, Yeats. Such Japanese writers as Tanizaki, Mishima, Kaiko, and, more recently, Haruki Murakami have acknowledged the influence of Western life and literature on their work and life. Writers who are considered overly Westernized are called by their milk-shunning compatriots *Batakusai*, "Butter-stinking." (Would so popular and "Japanese" a poet as Shuntaro Tanikawa be *Batakusai* because he celebrates John Coltrane and makes fun of Oscar Hammerstein's lyrics?)

3.

Literary influence is almost as complicated a matter as national character. I believe that, owing to the post–World War II translations made by former American soldiers who studied Japanese during the war, modern

Japanese writing has influenced postwar American writing. (One of them, Harold Strauss, an editor for Knopf, published many of them.) What their effect on American life and sensibility has been is difficult to assess, but I think that some of the ease of modem Japanese-American relations is due to them. It is also due in part to such writers as Faulkner and Mishima, who cross the Pacific and then tell their countrymen what they found. (A few younger American writers—Jay McInerny and Brad Leithauser, for instance—have recently written novels about their Japanese experience.) Certain qualities I take to be Japanese, obliquity, suggestiveness, stylistic restraint, and economy, have figured in the work of the American Minimalists, whose subtle, bare, often bleak, often comic stories sound as if they might have listened to Tanizaki's sixty-year-old admonition to his contemporaries: "Do not try to be too clear. We Japanese scorn the bare fact, and we consider it good form to keep a sheet of paper between the fact and the words that give expression to it." Raymond Carver, Ann Beattie, Mary Robison, Tobias Wolff, Amy Hempel, Bette Pesetsky, and other Minimalists do not so much conceal facts as conceal the way their characters react to them. The indirection or unsentimentality of their stories has, to my taste, a Japanese flavor.

American Minimalists are better at stories than novels. It takes a Tanizaki, writing in and out of the tradition of Japanese literature, to succeed in a long work which is continually allusive and indirect (although, judging only from a translation, his *Makioka Sisters* limps in its middlemarchian legweights). The appetite of even sophisticated American readers who enjoy subtle literary hors d'oeuvres is, in the long haul, only satisfied by the meat and potatoes of strong character transformation and knockdown confrontation. Even within the elaborate, syntactic mesh of Henry James, the hungry American reader finds and devours dramatic conflicts and developments. Our best Minimalists do not succeed with novels, or, like Raymond Carver, do not write them.

It took the director Robert Altman to make Carver a novelist. His fine film, *Short Cuts,* based on several Carver stories, transformed Carver's bleak obliquity into a sensuous, technicolored, quasi-Tolstoian novel-film. Carver's stories are quieter, subtler, and deeper. One can see a bit about what they say by comparing one of them with one on a similar subject by D. H. Lawrence. The differences don't illuminate only those between two different writers, but between two different times and English-language cultures.

Carver's story "Cathedral" is about a blind man who visits a youngish, thirtyish American couple. After dinner, he and the husband, partly to cover the uneasiness which is the social weather of so much American fiction, smoke some dope, and, instead of talking, listen first to the radio, then to a television program about cathedrals. The blind man asks the husband to describe cathedrals. The husband tells him that they're very tall, have devils carved on them, and need supports called buttresses. The blind man doesn't make much sense of this. He suggests that they get pen and paper and draw a cathedral. The story, told by the husband, continues:

> So I began. First I drew a box that looked like a house . . . then I put a roof on it. At either end of the roof, I drew spires. Crazy.
> "Swell," he said. "Terrific. You're doing fine," he said. "Keep it up."

The blind man tells the narrator to close his eyes but keep on drawing.

> His fingers rode my fingers as my hand went over the paper. It was like nothing else in my life up to now.
> Then he said, "I think that's it. I think you got it," he said. "Take a look; what do you think?"
> But I had my eyes closed. I thought I'd keep them that way for a little longer. I thought it was something I ought to do.
> "Well," he said. "Are you looking?"
> My eyes were still closed. I was in my house. I knew that. But I didn't feel like I was inside anything.
> "It's really something," I said.

That is the end of the story. The blind man now understands what a cathedral is, the narrator understands what blindness is, and perhaps something more. It is quiet, intimate, simple, suggestive, and I think, somewhat Japanese.

Lawrence's story "The Blind Man" is heavier, denser, more pointed. Pervin has been blinded in World War I. Married and living in the country, he is happy as long as he can feel the "sheer immediacy of blood contact with the substantiated world." (The word "blood" would never show up this way in a Carver story.) One day Bertie Reid, a young lawyer friend of Pervin's wife, comes to visit. Pervin somehow hates him, even as he knows the hatred is a foolish product of his own weakness. Alone with Bertie, Pervin asks if he can touch hin. Reluctantly, Bertie says he can. Pervin feels his skull, his closed eyes, his mustache, mouth, chin, shoulders, arms, hands. Bertie shivers with revulsion; he feels annihilated. "Yet he was under the power of the blind man as if hypnotized." Pervin tells Bertie to touch him, his eyes, his scar. He presses Bertie's fingers "upon his disfigured eyesockets, trembling in every fiber . . . while Bertie stood as if in a swoon." Pervin says, "Oh, my god. . . . We shall know each other now, shan't we?" He tells his wife, "We've become friends," but she knows better, for she can see the terror and revulsion on Bertie's face. Bertie was "like a mollusk whose shell is broken."

This is the last line of the Lawrence story, one of misunderstanding and irreconcilability, as Carver's was of understanding and inarticulate reconciliation. Every line of the Lawrence story bears the weight of his authorial voice and power; Carver's style is almost invisible. All the "he saids" in it proclaim an almost childish awkwardness, yet it is as artistic a construction as Lawrence's. The writer, though, disappears, which suggests both a modesty and a confidence in the audience that is not present in Lawrence. Lawrence's almost patronizing authority hammers his sensibility into the reader. You sense that Lawrence feels you, the reader, should consider yourself lucky, whereas Carver seems to say, "Look at this odd situation. Maybe you'll find it as puzzling and touching as I did, though I'm not sure I understand it." If one generalizes about the cultures which spawned these two writers, one could guess that Lawrence's was a hierarchical one full of patronizing authority, whereas Carver's was full of technological affluence—the radio, the television— but puzzled and full of gaps, eager, though, to cross them. Perhaps contemporary America, for all its power, speaks at times with a Carver-like awkwardness, even crudity, but also with a deferential modesty about imposing itself or its convictions on others.

4.

Asked to say something about recent American fiction to a Japanese audience, I began by putting down the names of writers who published good work in the past twenty-five or thirty years. After I wrote down a hundred names, I stopped. If nothing else made it clear, the list showed me that this has been, and is, a very rich time in American fiction. Never before have we had so many good writers.

How deal with such a range of excellence?

Literary classification spots recurrent themes, patterns, styles, and conventions; it bunches writers by subject matter, region, sexual preference, ethnic origin. Japanese writers, I understand, are often classified by the cities from which they come or write about. Much is made of the differences between, say, Osaka and Tokyo. In Mishima's *Thirst for Love (Ai No Kawaki)*, we read about the Tokyo woman, Etsuko, who is frightened by Osaka, a city of "merchant princes, tramps, industrialists, peddlers, white-collar workers, idlers, bankers, city officials, Gidayu reciters, kept women, pennypinching wives, bar girls, shoeshine boys." Etsuko fears the city, and Mishima makes clear that this means that she fears life. Much of Tanizaki's marvelous *Some Prefer Nettles (Tade Kuu Mushi)* is a contrast of the harsh, Westernized modernity of the Tokyo style and that of the older, traditional Japan found in corners of Osaka and the puppet theater of Awaji. (One could compare this novel with its American contemporary, F. Scott Fitzgerald's *Tender Is the Night*, a book which also deals with the divorce of sophisticated, well-off people. There is even a parallel temptation in the form of beauties manufactured and distributed to the world by the new film industry in Hollywood.)

Some American writers are good at writing varieties of English which convey the ethnic or regional flavor of customs, ways of acting and thinking. For a time such regional varieties were scorned; a national style and accent concealed them. More recently, there's been another burst of interest in accents and styles, at least in the arts, crafts, couture, cuisine, and comedy. When ethnic or class differences are expertly rendered on the screen or the page, most native readers or observers are as delighted as most foreigners are baffled by them. I don't know how many Americans who think themselves fluent in Japanese can, say, distinguish the speech differences of Osaka, Kyoto, Kobe, and Tokyo. How many English-speaking foreigners can differentiate a Boston streetcar conductor's speech from that of a Georgia farmer?

Of the leading American fiction writers, only Poe, Hawthorne, Henry James, Hemingway, and Fitzgerald did not make speech difference a crucial part of their novels and stories, although Hemingway and James could transcribe off-center speech, and Fitzgerald occasionally, as in the portrait of Wolfsheim in *The Great Gatsby*, helped create characters with distinctive syntax and diction.

I want to mention one other form of classification and indicate the sorts of generality that can be drawn from it. A recurrent story in American literature is the pursuit of a wild animal by a boy or man: Melville's *Moby Dick*, Faulkner's "The Bear," part of Hemingway's *The Garden of Eden*, and, most recently, Cormac McCarthy's *The Crossing*. Literary archaeologists might deduce that such stories reflect the two-century-long conquest of the North American continent with its brutal elimination of the native people and animals. The conquest left behind a tremendous longing, part regret, part guilt, for the vanished, vanquished wild world. The longing shows up not only in the stories but in the form and dress of American recreation, the moccasins, flannel shirts, jeans, and soft hats we favor on weekends and vacations. This is the so-called alternative life-style to the one of buying and selling, prosperity and power. The stories express and explain this pursuit of the wild in ways which define American self-conceptions as, say, Homer's epics defined those of the Hellenic world.

## 5.

I want to end by discussing four works of recent American fiction (all published in 1995). The books, chosen not quite at random, are *In the Cut*, a short novel by Susanna Moore, *The Point*, a book of stories by a newly published young writer, Charles D'Ambrosio, *Sabbath's Theater*, a novel by one of the best and best-known American writers, Philip Roth, and finally, *Telling Time*, a novel by the excellent but little-known older novelist Austin Wright.

*In the Cut* is about a thirty-four-year-old woman named Franny who lives in lower Manhattan, where she teaches creative writing to intelligent underachievers, mostly black and Chicano teenagers. She is a scholar of speech and language and writes articles about them. She has been married at least once but now lives by herself and likes it, although it increases the danger of living in her dangerous neighborhood. She prides herself on living as if without fear: courage is as important to her as her fine critical intelligence. The book's other chief characters are a gifted black student who wants special attention and who shows up at all sorts of hours and places; Franny's best friend, Pauline, an intrepid, flamboyant woman whom Franny has known since her days in London (which hardly figure in the book's action); Malloy, a detective, whom she meets because he's investigating the murder of a woman Franny has seen fellating the probable killer; and Malloy's partner, a detective who turns out to be the killer, and who, at the end, is about to torture and kill Franny. Franny narrates the story in clear, unemotive prose which remains unemotive even when it describes exciting, terrible things. The sexual descriptions, which have none of the weary, catalogued frenzy of the Marquis de Sade's, are as intimate and detailed as any ever written by a serious woman writer. Franny's sexual life is crucial to her and to the novel, but there is a horrible connection between it and murder, as if women's sexual freedom has aroused certain twisted men to terrorize, maim, disarticulate—to use one of the police terms Franny studies— and murder them. If literary archaeologists were left only with this book, they would say that the New York City of the 1990s was a terrible place for brave, independent women. The fine tolerance of the exotic and bizarre, the ease of life, and the variety and richness of its possibilities are compromised if not annihilated by the madness such tolerance and variety arouse. At the same time, the clarity and confidence of the author's style proclaim a new, unchained independence.

The stories in D'Ambrosio's *The Point* are full of the unhappy events on which fiction centers, but they are lyrical, comic, unsentimental, wise. and clear-headed. The thirteen-year-old boy in "American Bullfrog" gets drunk and sick, loses his virginity in a messy way, gets annoyed by his parents, runs away from home—to the next door neighbor's house— and ends up enjoying a talk and a drink with his father. The boy is as charming, awkward, manly, and decent as Huck Finn or Holden Caulfield. Such boys are one of the staples of American fiction and, I think, American reality. (Now there's a growing literature of charming, energetic, and moving young girls as well.) Many D'Ambrosio characters are in "dysfunctional" families, those in which there is divorce, violence, alcoholism, and even suicide, but the basic tone is optimism. Even when the loopy, charming girl in "Her Name" dies of cancer, and the young man who's been driving her cross-country dumps her body into the waters of a marina, the feel of the story is lyrical. "It seemed a paltry ritual—the dirt, the light—but he was determined to observe the ceremony. . . . Down she swirled, a trail of light spinning through a sea that showed green in the weakening beam and then went black." The seven stories are mostly set in the northwest part of the country around Seattle, an area associated with new freedoms, new music, frontier messiness and excitement, a California less worked-over and expensive, less crazy, and less menaced by fires and earthquakes. D'Ambrosio may be the bard of this unparadisal land of promise with its knots of meanness, dysfunction, and casualty understood as if part of one of the great trees growing in its forests.

The other books deal with dying and its other face, erotic love.

Roth's *Sabbath's Theater* is about an old puppeteer, Mickey Sabbath, whose fingers are curled by arthritis. He's lived in the Massachusetts countryside for thirty years supported by his despised second wife but enthralled by his longtime mistress, whose sexual brio has gratified not only him but many other men about whom she, at his urging, tells him. She dies, and his misery and loneliness, disgust for his wife and contempt for most others, send him down to New York for what he thinks will be his death trip. But Sabbath is too powerful, energetic, sexually vital, furious, and charged up with hatred for the hypocrisy, phoniness, do-goodism, and civic virtue of the world to slip away passively. In the luxurious apartment of an old friend who gives him food, shelter, money, comfort, and what might for someone else be ease of mind, he ransacks drawers, masturbates on the man's daughter's panties, attempts to seduce his wife, and steals money with the terrible connivance of a Chicana maid whom he mesmerizes with terror. Meanwhile, he's remembering his two marriages, his life as a merchant mariner in the whorehouses of South America, his career as a puppeteer, which has led to public dis-grace, and his seduction of a young student, which does likewise. He drives to his childhood home on the Jersey shore to pick out his burial site and discovers there a hundred-year-old cousin who lives by himself in a fog which doesn't exclude vitality, if not happiness. In this cousin's house, Sabbath finds and takes the things of his beloved brother whose death in World War II combat broke his mother's spirit and his own heart. He drives back to his house in the country, spies on—and terri-fies—his wife and her new lesbian lover, then goes to the grave of his mistress, on which he urinates. There he's surprised by her son, a police-man, who almost shoots him. Sabbath thinks he is ready to die, but then, in the book's last line, declares that no, he has reason to live, because, af-ter all, "everything he hated was here."

Sabbath is a marvelous, new, if somewhat repellent character, a sort of Dostoievskian force of nature, American style. He exults in Ameri-cana, the flag which he finds with his brother's things and which he wraps about himself, his ancient, fog-bound cousin, the thieves, coke-heads, and weirdos in the New York streets, and above all, the women every-where who make life a permanent erotic adventure. The book's narrative energy itself is near the heart of the best of the American spirit, unfet-tered by preconceptions, something to be constantly reinvented and refelt, a theater of tremendous emotional possibilities, comic and tragic, farcical and sentimental. This world is heaven and hell now, and in it one celebrates Sabbath, the holy day, every day.

In Austin Wright's *Telling Time,* Thomas Westerly, a geologist and college president, dies on the New England island where he and his wife have retired. His adult children go through his papers and discover that his life was a misery of self-disgust. Westerly was unfaithful to his wife—with next to none of Sabbath's nihilistic joy—vengeful and careless—he'd failed to tell the police that he'd accidentally killed a jogger. The complex plots are interwoven by different narrators. No American writer manipulates such intricacies as well as Wright. What counts for our purpose here, though, is his depiction of the dissolution of upperclass American tranquillity. The only structure which seems to survive is that of the novel itself, its intricate art and expressive power. So the great note of modernism is sounded again amidst the flood of minimalism, impressionism, psycho-physical violence, and spiritual commodification. What Thomas Hobbes called "the short vehemence . . . of carnal pleasure" is sunk into the muck of the characters' ironic self-contempt. *Telling Time* is a closer relative of *The Scarlet Letter* than of *Sabbath's Theater.*

6.

Even this fraction of recent American fiction reveals its extraordinary range, technical brilliance, and—indirectly—revelatory power, which alone says more about the country than the Dow Jones Industrial Index.

# Malamud's Stories

The essential Malamud story wastes no time. "Marcus was a tailor, long before the war, a buoyant man with a bushy head of graying hair, fine fragile brows, and benevolent hands, who comparatively late in life had become a clothier." So begins "The Death of Me," and in the same first paragraph we know that the successful tailor has to hire an assistant for alterations and then a presser. The assistant is a Sicilian, the presser is a Pole, and they hate each other, no reason given. This hatred will be the death of Marcus. The story is focused, intense, unrelenting, yet, because of the almost madly narrow intensity, comic. The presser, Josip, gets letters. As he slices his salami, he reads them through cracked eyeglasses. Before he'd "dipped two sentences into the letter, his face dissolved and he cried, tears smearing his cheeks and chin so that it looked as though he had been sprayed with something to kill flies. At the end he fell into a roar of sobbing, a terrible thing to behold, which incapacitated him for hours and wasted the morning."

I said that a Malamud story wastes no time, but what about those "fragile brows" and "benevolent hands," what about the fly-spray look of Josip's face and the enormity of the grief which wastes the morning? Are they necessary? Not of course for the anecdotal bones of the story, but for what really counts, the Malamudic essence, of course they are. The surprising qualifiers break into the essential character, Marcus's decency and fragility; the excess of Josip's grief lets us know that the doings in this little shop are set amidst terrible human pressures, ultimate suffering. The inextricability of the absurd, the excessive, and the ferocious laid out there—"a terrible thing to behold"—yet somehow within you is what make Bernard Malamud's *Complete Stories* one of the essential American books.*

---

* Bernard Malamud, *The Complete Stories*, ed. Robert Giroux (New York: Farrar, Straus and Giroux, 1997).

More than six hundred pages, fifty-five stories, beginning with "Armistice" (1949) and finishing with bare factual accounts of Virginia Woolf and Alma Mahler (published shortly before the author's death in 1986), these are the pith of a fine and finely spare, if not parsimonious, writer's life. True, there are also eight novels, one of which, *The Assistant*, is a little masterpiece, and another of which, *The Natural*, is a fantastic paean to baseball and mythic heroism, but in my view, Malamud, like such writers as Maupassant, Chekhov, Babel, and Frank and Flannery O'Connor, did his best, his essential work in the short story.

The stories center around single encounters, basic situations; the stitchwork (the "fragile brows" and "benevolent hands") alters the texture and pace, diversifies the intensity, transfigures and sublimates the anecdotes in such a way that more would become less. That is, extend this intensity of application, and the responsive emotions would run out, as one can only bear so much of another's suffering or, for that matter, amusement. As I see it, the prize-winning novel, *The Fixer*, goes on too long and too monotonally, and so weakens reader empathy and sympathy. (I prefer the generally ignored *Tenants*.) Even the long story "Man in the Drawer" (about an unpublished Russian who begs a visiting American to take his manuscripts to the States) saps the peculiar tension of classic Malamud.

It is no accident that this intensified brevity makes Malamud the poet of the American Depression. The harsh, tedious, sordid, soul-ripping effects of marginal existence become in Malamud's stories the poetry of desperate and often comic relief, momentary escape, wrenching, almost insane confession, or, as in "The Death of Me," lethal hatred. Despite their promise to Marcus not to fight anymore when he leaves, Josip the presser and Emilio the assistant "locked themselves together and choked necks." Marcus rushes in and has a heart attack. In Malamudese, "his heart, like a fragile pitcher, toppled from the shelf and bump bumped down the stairs, cracking at the bottom, the shards flying everywhere" (perhaps one phrase too much). The two "assassins" read in his glazed eyes the terrible consequences of their irrational hatred.

Several of these Depression stories are set—like *The Assistant*—in a small grocery store which, even before a supermarket moves in down the block, can barely support the couple who spend every waking minute tending to it. Malamud's parents, Max and Bertha Fidelman Malamud, ran such a store, and his writing life began late because "as the son of a poor man, a poor grocer, I could not stand the thought of living off him, a generous and self-denying person." Dedicating *The Assistant* to his father, Malamud wrote, "What does a writer need most? When I ask this question, I think of my father." The life of unremitting, scarcely rewarded labor, the life which under such pressure preserves humanity, is the source of Malamud's genius.

That genius was to be advanced and enriched by Italy, where he went with his Italian American wife, Ann de Chiara, and their two children in 1956. The struggling Jewish shopkeepers are replaced by struggling, second-rate artists and scholars like Arthur Fidelman. Fidelman encounters beautiful, obsessive Italian women (some of them Jewesses) and Italian schnorrers (occasionally Jews). His artistic and sexual hungers fuse and become confused by fanatic Catholic women and Boccaccian con men. The stories lengthen, the resolutions become wilder: "Pumping slowly, he nailed her to the cross" ("Still Life"). Fidelman's affair with a Venetian glass blower's wife turns into a semi-marriage to the glass blower ("The Glass Blower of Venice"). And Malamud's prose—a terse Yinglish with omitted prepositions and inverted word order—is studded with Italian proverbs ("A hunchback's straight only in the grave"), diction, and superstition ("she insisted that Fidelman touch his testicles three times").

The best of these Italian stories certify Malamud as a bard of the century's second postwar wave of Americans abroad; Fitzgerald *redivivus*.

The *Complete Stories* contains stories set in different places with different sorts of characters, told in different ways—"So?" I hear the author say—but it is the stories written in the fifties and sixties for which Malamud will, I think, be treasured as long as people treasure the short story art.

Thanks are due to Malamud's old editor and friend, Robert Giroux, who, in his eighty-third year, assembled this collection and introduced it with grace.

# His Other Life

## I.

Only once in his long poem does the greatest of all poets allow his own name to appear. In the thirtieth canto of *Purgatory,* his beloved guide, Vergil, is about to leave him. Trembling in fright, he sees a woman in a mantle of flaming green whose first words to him are "Dante, don't cry because Vergil's going away. Save your tears for a sharper sword." A few lines later, the poet apologizes for mentioning his name. "I had to write it," he says, because like all good reporters, he respected what he heard and saw.

In this fading century of almost compulsory self-revelation, a century of literature about literature and its making written by its makers, there is, still, in the best, a vestige of Dantean shame at making oneself the subject of one's time and skill. In *My Other Life,* the new book "of fiction" by the very talented Paul Theroux, the vestige appears in an author's note whose mugginess displays discomfort in the enterprise:

> The fact that there are limits to serious travesty and that memory matters means that even an imagined life resembles one that was lived. . . . These characters do not exist outside this intentionally tall story . . . and the action of the narrative is vagrant in every sense. . . . It is the writer's privilege to keep some facades intact and to use his own face in the masquerade. . . . The man is fiction but the mask is real.

This silver foil may be thrown to divert critical flack or even legal action, but I think it's there because this maker of many well-organized novels knows that overall this book of self-revelation is a hodgepodge, a magpie "vagrant" work. Its scenes and stories seldom build on, connect with, or interweave with each other. Its chief, if subordinate, characters—such as the author's wife and sons—are left stranded (as is the curious reader by their disappearance). It is as if this author of such famous travel books as *The Great Railway Bazaar* and *The Old Patagonian Express* is accompanying his readers through the landscape of his life— "See this and then this and that over there"—without letting them settle down and make sense of things. The train itself is the organizing principle, and this train is Paul Theroux, the writer, and the experience which, for a time, derailed him from being a writer and a happy man. The experience was leaving his beloved wife and sons (here given names which are not those of the wife and two sons listed under the author's entry in *Who's Who in America*).

## 2.

The abandonment of his domestic Eden and the return to his despised Massachusetts home town engender what this reader of six or eight Theroux books thinks is his best writing. He'd been away from home for thirty-odd years, first with the Peace Corps in Malawi, then teaching in Uganda—where he married "Alison"—and Singapore. Then followed eighteen years in England living in blissful solitude with his working wife and their two sons, cooking supper, doing chores, and writing the books, articles, and reviews which bring him security and celebrity whose every ray he, a bit pathetically, notes. One suspects that this preening is a sign of the broken man who left what he loved to suffer loneliness and paralysis in snowbound Medford, Massachusetts. There he consults and falls in love with a beautiful Boston psychiatrist who helps guide him out of his ever-diminishing "half-life" and away from her.* He hangs out in bars and projects with semiliterate, semidrugged, touching teenage lesbians, then runs into a high school friend, a brilliant charmer and athlete, whose life as a black militant, drug dealer, and tortured prisoner is set down beside his own as a truly wild "other life." The book ends with an abrupt, awkward, inexplicable recovery and rededication to life and art.

Theroux's good eye and ear and clear style get most of this on the page, the touching barbarism of Bun-Bun and Weechie, the Medford project girls, who, having seen "his books," *Walden* and *Presumed Innocent*, finally gather that he is indeed a famous author, or the feckless cruelty of

---

* I suspect that the title of V. S. Naipaul's latest and feeblest novel, *Half a Life* (2001) derives from this description. (Naipaul, once Theroux's closest literary friend, is the victim of Theroux's amusing book *Sir Vidia's Shadow: A Friendship Across Five Continents*.)

English hacks and their society patrons. There's even a marvelously observed—yes, observed—private dinner for Queen Elizabeth and the Duke of Edinburgh. Theroux's version of the charming, vaguely egocentric, muffin-like queen and her detestable, snotty, loud consort will take a PR army to dislodge.

"These characters do not live?" Tall stories?

If Theroux did not encounter Elizabeth and Phillip at a private party— or know some fine observer who did—then these pages would lose their point, for they triumph only if one believes in their actuality. The fictional elements—say, a final rudeness of Phillip's and some vague, maternal counsel and a queenly touch from Elizabeth—are not hard to spot, but in essence, the events are actually, not fictionally true.

Most of the book's other fictional elements are also evident—and consistently weak. So the old German writer, Vorlaufer—forerunner— whose career has anticipated Theroux's book by book, person by person, and place by place, is clearly invented—and uninteresting. Which is not the case with Theroux's theft of an expensive pin from the wife of his Singapore tutee. Although such a theft is less likely than the royal party, I'd think that if the novelist showed up for dinner, some readers of this book might, after he leaves, count the silverware. (That author's note might be a cover for more than the book's vagrant structure.)

No, the excellence of *My Other Life* comes from the realest Paul Theroux that the realist Paul Theroux has put on paper. This Theroux works beyond the constant allusions to his celebrity, beyond the dutiful if expert reportage of exotic landscapes and characters, even beyond the excoriating portraits of broken-down London hacks and a horny London patroness (who, like many of the women he describes, pursues him).

Theroux's protestations and animadversions on the relation between poetry and truth do not improve the narrative itself. What counts in *My Other Life* is a new level of Theroux honesty which makes for some of his best-written, indeed most beautiful, pages. These compensate for the book's lumpish, "vagrant" construction and self-stroking, which, too often, substitute for authentic development and resolution.

# Austin Wright

1.

Like much else in Austin Wright's fine novel, the title, *Tony and Susan,* is deceptive.* Tony and Susan are not like most titular couples: Susan, the wife of a surgeon named Arnold, receives the manuscript of a novel written by Edward, from whom she's been divorced for more than twenty years; the novel is about a mathematics professor named Tony. More than half of *Tony and Susan* is about what happens to Tony, and what happens is, to use a word used for thrillers, "gripping." The rest of the novel is about what happens to Susan as she reads Tony's story.

Readers share some of her reactions. What happens to Tony as he drives his wife and daughter to their summer house in Maine is terrifying to readers who, like Susan, seldom, if ever, encounter violence, and, again like Susan, wonder how we'd have acted in Tony's place. More, we're bothered that Tony didn't act as Tony, in retrospect, wishes he'd acted.

As the scary events unfold, we also get involved with Susan's story, not so much her life with Arnold and their children but memories of her old life with Edward. Susan sees that life reflected in Edward's novel. Back then, Edward was in law school at Chicago but wanted to be a writer and dropped out. Susan supported him, but his writing—which he wouldn't show her because it wasn't good enough—came between them. When Edward went off to find himself, Susan took up with Arnold.

Tony, after terrible events on the road and in the woods, is coming back to life, partly through women who feel sorry about what happened to him, partly through calls from the police, who are developing leads and need him to identify the brutes who transformed his life. Slowly, he

---

* Austin Wright, *Tony and Susan* (Dallas: Baskerville, 1993).

is revitalized by hate and need for vengeance. As we lose ourselves in his story, Susan both loses and finds herself. The second climax of *Tony and Susan* is the revelation about herself which follows the climax of Tony's story.

2.

Twentieth-century physics, psychology, and even politics are, like much twentieth-century literature, marked by the interplay between observer and observation. Austin Wright has published three such novels, one of which, *Camden's Eyes,* is a masterpiece. *Tony and Susan* is another. It combines what is rare in such books: the excitement of a thriller and psychological brilliance.

3.

Austin Wright is also a fine critic. From his first book on the transformation of the American short story in the twenties* to his recent book on reading Faulkner, *Recalcitrance, Faulkner, and the Professors,* he has shown that he understands as well as anyone alive what goes on in fiction.

It would be easy to say that his critical intelligence dominates *Tony and Susan,* but Wright is a wonderful story teller, a wonderful novelist. He knows how to develop scenes and how to cut them, and he knows how to use style. So the alternation of the reflective, sensuous Susan sections and the dramatic, dialogue-filled Tony ones creates the novel's pleasurable rhythm.

There's much else to notice in *Tony and Susan,* about some of which I'm unsure. Do the many literary surnames—Ambler, Hawthorne, Macomber, Husserl, Gorman (Joyce's biographer), even Morrow (the publisher)—imply another level of narrative? If so, I didn't get it.†

*Tony and Susan* makes one want to read all of Wright's work. I have a feeling that he, like his old teacher, Norman Maclean, will be one of the rare authors who find the audience he deserves in his seventies. Better late than never.

* This work was based on a University of Chicago doctoral dissertation on which Morton Dauwen Zabel and I were advisors. Austin and I became then and have remained friends these forty-five years, although we write each other rarely and see each other even more rarely.

† After reading the review, Wright wrote me that he hadn't noticed that the names were literary—which doesn't mean that a reader-critic shouldn't see if something else isn't going on in the book.

# Vidal in Conclusion

"It is no accident that for three hundred years our people willingly, I believe—maybe even joyously—slaughtered their way across this continent, enslaved Negroes, drove out Mexicans, broke more Indian treaties than Hitler ever bothered to make. Then, for the last half century, we've made the countries of the Caribbean and Central America our property while occupying most of the islands of the Pacific including, after due incineration, our only Asian rival, Japan." This is Senator Burden Day speaking in this seventh and final volume of Gore Vidal's series on the making of the "American Empire."* The theme is taken up by many other characters, some of whom have the names and careers of well-known "real" people. How much of what, say, President Franklin Roosevelt—real—said to Caroline Sanford—fictional—was really said or thought raises the uncertainties most historical novels raise. Vidal is no professional historian, but professionals who have challenged, demeaned, or dismissed his versions of history risk powerful discomfiture, for Vidal is not only well-read but a vitriolic polemicist. His historical novels are usually underwritten by certified, if sometimes peripheral professionals and by privileged contemporaries. So some of his fascinating characterization of Lincoln (in the eponymous volume) derives from the wonderful book by Lincoln's law partner, William Herndon; and his views of American empire-building are backed by, among others, the brilliant leftist historian William Appelman Williams. (The sources are often cited in the novels.)

*The Golden Age* is set in the author's lifetime. Vidal and people he knows are both sources and "characters." Since Vidal was born into a corner of the class he deals with, that "governing class . . . whose first

* Gore Vidal, *The Golden Age* (New York: Doubleday, 2000).

principle was never to inform [those governed] of anything that might have to do with their welfare," he's been in on what—despite C-Span, the *Drudge Report*, the *National Enquirer*, and the Web—is usually denied us plebs. He was partly raised by his blind senatorial grandfather, Gore (a distant cousin of Clinton's vice president), about whom he wrote more richly and adoringly in his memoir, *Palimpsest;* his unadored mother married the man Jackie Kennedy's mother later married; and he himself made what John Updike called a "gracious offer" to California to serve as its senator. (Several such Vidalian offers have been refused. As for Updike, like many who have twitted, criticized, dismissed, or ignored Vidal, his oeuvre was treated to several thousand words of Vidalian vitriol in the *London Review of Books.*)

The literary problem of using contemporary gossip or even first-hand, inside intelligence as a source is that it tends to augment what is Vidal's chief weakness, gossip-chatter. Anyone who has read or listened to Vidal knows that he's a witty, learned man, and wit and learning fill the mouths and ears of his book's characters. Page after page is full of witty, clever, spiteful, denunciatory gossip. It's not that the talk is pointless; it always revolves around either relevant politics or the affections and liaisons of characters, real and fictional; yet its thinness is that of gossip-chatter. A Vidalian might respond that there's chatter in *War and Peace* as well, but take a closer look. Even in the book's famous opening pages—written largely in the French the Russian aristocrats speak—there is narrative interplay, everybody wanting something, hiding and revealing something, and ever-enriched description. "Le *charmant* Hippolyte was surprising by his extraordinary resemblance to his beautiful sister, but yet more by the fact that in spite of this resemblance he was exceedingly ugly." Vidal, at his best, might have managed that, but then he'd stop, whereas Tolstoy goes on for a marvelous paragraph explaining the oddity: the sister's "joyous, self-satisfied, youthful and constant smile of animation," the brother's "imbecile . . . sullen self-confidence . . . eyes, nose and mouth . . . puckered into a vacant, wearied grimace." There is hardly a page in Tolstoy which isn't loaded with insight, surprise, and narrative enrichment. There are too few pages in Vidal which have any. Yes, one "learns" that Alice Roosevelt Longworth had a child by Senator Borah, that Herbert Hoover said that what the country needed was a great poem, and that Mrs. Woodrow Wilson sat next to Mrs. Roosevelt at the brief Fourth Inaugural (Vidal knows things of this sort); one may even go along with the notion that Roosevelt not only knew about but provoked the Japanese attack on Pearl Harbor to keep his promise that the United States would only fight if attacked. This, though, is the kind of "surprise" that's debatable (which is fine) but which dies as it's revealed. Tolstoy's surprises remain surprising—there are so many of them and they're so intricately complicated by other surprises, especially as the reader sees them deepening an ever more complex story.

Tolstoy saves most of his unnovelistic historical ruminations for a second epilogue; Vidal's ruminations fill the mouths of his characters and take over the story. A few plot lines which might have thickened *The Golden Age* are raised, then starved. Perhaps the author's epic impulse— to tell the great American story more richly than it's ever been tried— makes them seem unworthy of full treatment.

A larger criticism is the papery quality of the characters, real and imaginary. Wilkie, Hopkins, Vandenberg, Stassen, Cissy Patterson, and the Roosevelts act and speak like puppets standing for notions or general class positions. Compare any scene with "real" people here to the electrifying encounter of Balashev (the emperor Alexander's representative) and Napoleon in *War and Peace*. The Tolstoy reader is stretched with tension, revelation, and sheer beauty. The question of verisimilitude isn't raised; it's beside the point. If Napoleon wasn't like this, too bad for Napoleon, he should have been; in fact, this is a "truer" Napoleon than the one whose bones disintegrate in the Invalides. In *War and Peace* something is always happening. Almost nothing happens in *The Golden Age*. In fiction, things happen only if they happen to fully created characters. It is not enough to throw the mantle of a great event on someone who's barely sketched. The bad fit is ludicrous, pathetic, unbelievable.

Is it unfair to beat the industrious, ambitious, and intelligent Vidal with such a masterpiece? I think so, particularly because the two Vidal history novels I'd earlier read (*Empire* and *Lincoln*) are far more interesting and vivid. Also, there are contemporary historical novels which stand up pretty well to Tolstoy. (Thomas Flanagan's *Year of the French* and the marvelous if less thickly historical Sartoris books of Faulkner and their lineal descendent, *Blood Meridian*, by Cormac MacCarthy, come to mind.)

*The Golden Age* succumbs to the temptation offered by its time and place. Vidal knows, knew, saw, heard, or was the person who became his characters—his grandfather, Tennessee Williams, Dawn Powell, himself. Perhaps his having known them so well is the reason he's left much of what he knows in his head instead of getting it to the page. Except for some witty speeches of Dawn Powell (in particular an attack on one of

Vidal's bêtes noirs, Hemingway) and some *Tempest*-like musing of old
Gore Vidal looking out the window of his house in Ravello in the last
paragraphs of the book, the characters and themes are diminished to
what our Prospero author reflects on in the book's very last paragraph:
"the generations of men come and go and are in eternity no more than
bacteria upon a luminous slide, and the fall of a republic or the rise of an
empire—so significant to those involved—is not detectable upon the
slide."

# Updike's Brushstroke

Updike's novel *Brazil\**—his sixteenth—came in the mail an hour after I'd read Michiko Kakutani's annihilating review of it in the *Times*.† She found it "forced," "contrived," "full of undigested information . . . racial and sexual clichés . . . ugly, repellent."

Kakutani's reviews sometimes have the fluent rigor of equations (she's a distinguished mathematician's daughter), but this one didn't add up. Although I enjoy as much as anyone seeing my literary betters skewered, a more continuous interest is in the art. Updike is a conscientious, even a noble artist. Could he have gone so far off his narrative rocker?

For a few pages, I could see what bothered Kakutani: *Brazil*'s style was "high," more than usually logy with adjectives and similes, and flecked with Portuguese and mystic stains as well.

> "This dolly, I think she was made for me," said Tristão, impulsively, out of those inner depths where his fate was being fashioned in sudden clumsy strokes that carried away, all at once whole pieces of his life. He believed in spirits, and in fate. He was nineteen, and not an *abandonado*, for he had a mother, but his mother was a whore, and even worse than a whore, for she drunkenly slept with men without money, and bred tadpole children like a human swamp of forgetfulness and casual desire.

As for the dialogue, it too was "high," a form of translationese, the sort Hemingway made notorious. "The gift I have in mind would also be a gift to myself. It is time. It is the time in my life."

---

\* John Updike, *Brazil* (New York: Alfred A. Knopf, 1996).

† In publishing this review, the editors of *The New Republic* excised these references to Kakutani, the not-quite-all-powerful chief reviewer for the not-quite-all-powerful *New York Times*.

The speaker is the rich, beautiful, "pale" Isabel, who lets the black slum-kid Tristão pick her up on Copacabana Beach and takes him home to her uncle's elegant apartment, where she forces "the gift"—her virginity—on him. "For God's sake, do it."

After a few pages, one accommodates to the style. The narrative moves teasingly in short chapters, ones that will take the reader over much of Brazil's social and topographical landscape. Isabel's Uncle Donaciano forbids her to see "this moleque"; the lovers steal his *cruzeiros* and candlesticks, head first for his mother's shanty then to São Paulo and his half-brother who betrays them to polished thugs sent by her diplomat father. Isabel goes to college in Brasilia; Tristão tightens bolts—"to a foot-pound torque of forty-three"—on a Fusca assembly line until he saves enough to escape with her to a backland gold mine, where they starve until Isabel turns tricks and has the first of the six children she will bear by other men. (The lovers' passion is too grand for children or monogamy.) Tracked down again, Tristão kills the tracker, and they're off into the Mato Grosso with her two children and a Tupi woman, Kupehaki, who shows them how to dig "succulent white worms called coró" out of the rotting bark of "the mato . . . the Brazilian pine." Indians kill Kupehaki and kidnap the children. Near death, they're discovered and enslaved by high-toned Paulist roughnecks, *bandeiros*, whose chief makes Isabel his mistress. She gets to a shaman whose magic transposes her color and Tristão's. Back at the encampment, newly black Isabel is ordered to service "the aching groin" of the *bandeirante*, José Peixoto. As she "willed herself to kneel," a "tall bearded white man" splits José's skull, then says, "You foul black whore—you were about to blow the bastard." It's Tristão. Alone again, in their new skins, they reach new sexual excitement, her "nervous network more angular than before, less rounded by perennial hopelessness." To him, "her whole body seemed leaner and knobbier, its bulges and recesses more emphatic, now that she was no longer the color of clouds and crystal but that of earth, of wet smooth wood, of glistening dung." They make their way east finding jobs in small towns until they save enough to fly back to Brasilia and her father's welcome of his rather sunburned daughter and her splendid white husband. In São Paulo, they become rich. ("The banality, the brightly masked tedium, of bourgeois life—taletellers remain balked by it.") Visiting Uncle Donaciano in Rio, Tristão wanders down to the beach where twenty-odd years ago he and Isabel met. There he's killed by thieves. Isabel finds him in the water, throws herself on his body, and tries—like her prototype, Iseult the Fair—to die with him, but "the chemicals within her continued their fathomless commerce."

A lot of ground, a grand tour of Brazil in a "tone"—the afterword says—drawn from Joseph Bédier's version of the Tristan and Iseult romance translated by Hilaire Belloc and Paul Rosenfeld. The tone goes in and out—"'Brezhnev will never permit socialism to have a human face,' argued Nestor Vilar"—not because the writer forgets, but because he both indulges and comments on it. Realism and magic are braided in his North American version of South American fiction.

⌖

Reviewing Roy Lichtenstein's recent retrospective, Updike wrote of "the multi-determination of the artistic impulse," which "can satirize and memorialize at the same time." So Lichtensten's "deconstruction of Abstract Expressionism" in *Brushstroke* exhibits "the very energy that the literalist, counter-stylistic rendering mocks."

Brazil. What do we know of it? Or, for that matter, what do we know about most of what we "know"? Most comes from books, usually translated, occasionally works of genius which are themselves products of digested views altered by the author's force and perspicacity. *Braʒil* is Updike's version of what his afterword calls "truly Brazilian fiction" (he names seven Brazilian writers), as well as "the Brazilian Bible," *Os Sertãos* (1902)* and books by such foreign observers as Lévi-Strauss, Theodore Roosevelt, and Elizabeth Bishop. The story is very roughly drawn from Bédier, whose own version is a composite of numerous medieval sources. The flora, fauna, and anthropology come largely from Lévi-Strauss and Euclides da Cunha, the author of *Os Sertão,* both of whom used the work of North American scholars. From da Cunha also come the "racial caricatures" which Gilberto Freyre (another Updike source) more moderately called "ethnic exaggerations."

Brazil's color tolerance is underscored by extraordinary sensitivity to the varied colors of its population. There are as many Brazilian terms for them—*caboclo, cafuso, mestiʒo, pardo*—as Eskimos have for varieties of snow, Masai for cattle. The emphasis on skin color which so offended Kakutani is exceptionally important to Updike, who has said that much

---

* Translated—wonderfully—by Samuel Putnam as *Rebellion in the Backlands* (Chicago: Phoenix, 1957).

of his life—his first marriage, his vocation: staining white pages with black marks—has been shaped by his skin disease. (See the wonderful section of *Self-Consciousness* on his psoriasis. He also writes about his part Afro-American grandchildren.) If anything, Updike's brilliant play with skin color should earn the same sort of political credit that the author of *Pygmalion* gets for demonstrating that a duchess consists of nothing but a few phonemes and an expensive dress. Updike has made of Brazilian sensitivity a serio-comic poem which is by no means irrelevant to our North American dilemma.

꙰꙰

Fifteen years ago, in his novel *The Coup*, Updike used the voice of an African colonel to vent—or, probably to elicit—satiric fury that his "ordinary," American characters couldn't or didn't mouth. Now in Brazil, impulses which in his realistic fiction seem extravagant, operatic, or hysterical (like the last two-thirds of *Rabbit Redux*) are controlled by his version of a Brazilian version of the Belloc-Bédier version of various medieval versions of the Tristan and Iseult romance. Updike's bifocal, or bivocal, or perhaps multi-vocal-and-focal "commentary" has the "several layers in different colors" which—as he wrote in a 1990 preface to his masterpiece, *Rabbit at Rest*—makes his "trickier novels" more interesting to him. "Plain realism has never seemed to me to be enough . . . a page of printed prose should bring to its mimesis something extra . . . a fine excess that corresponds with the intricacy and opacity of the real world."

That real world where we, compendia of other people's minds and bodies, occasionally enlarge our small uniqueness with the help of little masterpieces like *Brazil*.

# Fictionally De-Cubaed

## I.

Between Saturday, when I started reading Mary Morris's new novel, and Sunday, when I finished it, I saw the Coen brothers' movie *Fargo*. I want to say a few words about the two entertainments, but first, an account of the novel.

Thirty-six-year-old Maggie Conover, married to Todd, an architect who helps her take care of their house and five-year-old daughter, is bored with domesticity. To counter this mild form of house arrest, she usually goes abroad by herself. Todd understands her wanderlust, and not just because Maggie's job is describing exotic places for Easy Rider Travel Books. Now she's returning to *la isla*, a Caribbean island from which she'd once helped Isabel, the flamboyantly unhappy, island-confined daughter of its dictator, escape. On the trip, she is stopped at the island's airport, her passport is taken away, and she is taken under guard to a hotel, where she remembers old times with Isabel, dancing, driving through shanty towns, swimming, meeting Rosalba and Milagro, Isabel's mother and daughter, learning the history of the island and of El Caballo, its colorful, philoprogenitive tyrant. Isabel fascinates and, at one point, arouses her. It's at that point that Isabel denounces Maggie's cowardice, the refusal to help her escape, a denunciation which emboldens Maggie to "lose" her passport and ticket; that is, she gives them to Isabel.

The novel's tension is wound up in Maggie's situation: there's a good possibility she may be imprisoned. Still, between interrogations about the escaped Isabel, she wanders around, does her travel update and telephones her husband, her boss, and her father, a casual tyrant, the probable source of both her timidity and her restlessness.

Another source of tension is extraliterary. It involves the reader's translation of the nameless island into Cuba and El Caballo into Castro. Since the novel is partly travelogue, this reader kept wondering if its picturesque detail is "for real." Such wondering blurs the book's fictional authority. (Does the blur have to do with Maggie's timidity or the author's?)

Maggie is an engaging, complicated, sympathetic narrator, but beyond her own story, much of what she narrates reads like secondhand, standard exotica, the tropical flora (hibiscus, bougainvillea, papaya, tamarind), the cement-block wretchedness of shanty towns, the empty shelves and long lines, the pleasant whores, the soldiers, the Latin lovers, even the desperate, "Latin" theatrics of Isabel.

The book's style, too, is constricted by Hemingwayesque translationese, an excess of subject-predicate-object, present-tense sentences. Syntactic simplicity is coupled with psychological banality. Only occasionally do Mary Morris's authentic stylistic and observational gifts light up the book. So, imagining a letter from the escaped Isabel remembering *la isla:*

> [W]e have the smallest beasts. A frog that will rest on your fingernail. A mammal no bigger than a thimble that looks like a shrew. The pygmy owl a child can cup in its fist. . . . It is amazing that in this world of little things we are ruled by someone so big that we cannot help but feel small. As if we too have come to rest in another's palm.

Or, describing Isabel's state of mind: "You could drop pebbles down, and they would never reach the bottom of that sadness."

If only there were fifty such sentences in the novel.

## 2.

I think there is a recent turn in fiction written by such gifted American women as Anne Tyler, Susanna Moore, and now Mary Morris. The doll house door has long been opened and slammed shut, but in a number of recent books, the outside looks menacing, and the woman protagonist wants to come back home. ("Home" is the last word in *House Arrest.*) Perhaps the recent revival of interest in Jane Austen is related to it. Austen's books are about the expulsion from and happy return to domestic comfort. In her semi-jocular "Plan of a Novel" (probably written in 1816), the heroine is "hunted out of civilized Society . . . but afterward crawls back to her former Country—having at least twenty narrow escapes of falling into the hands of Anti-hero" (yes!), then, "in the nick of time . . . runs into the arms of the Hero himself."

English literature's next great woman writer began *Middlemarch* by contrasting the "epic life" of Saint Theresa with that of the "many Theresas" who found only "a life of mistakes, the offspring of a certain spiritual grandeur ill-matched with the meanness of opportunity." The contraction of epic yearning continued: Virginia Woolf's women yearn for little more than a room of their own or a day's trip to a lighthouse. In 1996, Maggie Conover just wishes to get away from home, and then, to return. Do authentic, sometimes heroic, sometimes ordinary gestures of liberation seem ambivalent to the women writers who invent or express them?

This isn't the case with the heroine of *Fargo,* the latest and finest addition to the recent film genre which juxtaposes farce and violence. Marge Gunderson, the shrewd, decent, funny-looking, pregnant police chief of snow-belted Fargo, North Dakota, is at home both at home and abroad (Minneapolis). She speaks the almost burlesque Swedenglish ("Yah" is the commonest utterance) but also knows the soft language of church and the hard obscenities of massacre. *Fargo's* minor characters, too, unlike those in *House Arrest,* are crystalline, amusing, and plot-enriching.

Nonetheless, it isn't clear that the brilliant film makes the unextraordinary novel superfluous. The novel has enough craft and artistry to supply pleasures *Fargo* doesn't: complex mixtures of recollection and immediacy, rich shifts of movement from exposition to scene, a few brilliant bits of descriptive and psychological insight, and, above all, the slow revelation of the narrator's character, less vivid, comic, and clear than *Fargo's* Marge, but in the slow intricate way of prose fiction, ultimately rounder, deeper, and more complex.

# Rupert Thompson

### 1.

An odd book.* Consciously, even conscientiously odd.

I'll explain this, but first, the plot, or, since plot doesn't count for much in Thomson's book, the situations which generate what constitute it.

A thirty-one-year-old bookstore employee named Martin Blom is accidentally shot in the head and loses his eyesight. In a clinic, he discovers that he can see in the dark.

Or can he? His doctor, Bruno Visser (the characters have peculiar names), tells him that he suffers from Anton's Syndrome, which generates the delusion that he can see. In any event, Blom, equipped with a white cane and defiant confidence in his night vision, goes into the world, a world unlike the one he left, for he's decided that new conditions require new experience. He breaks with his fiancée and moves away from his parents. (Like all the characters, even these ordinary people are peculiar: his father, a post office employee, keeps snails whom he names and whose food he sometimes shares; his mother wears an emerald necklace at dinner, although God, but not the reader, knows where it comes from.) Blom moves to a fleabag hotel in another part of the nameless city (the country too is nameless), changes his own name—although nothing in the book comes of that—and begins meeting odd people and "seeing" such odd things as couples fornicating in hotel corridors. One of the people he meets is a girl named Nina, who, after making love with him a few times, disappears. Blom seeks out and finds her mother, and then her mother's mother. One-quarter of the book is narrated not by Blom but by this grandmother, and in a more fluent, less staccato manner. The matter too is somewhat more traditional, a brief, three-generational fam-

* Rupert Thompson, *The Insult* (New York: Knopf, 1997).

ily saga whose central figure is a retarded boy/man who figures in what passes for plot. (He kills Nina and drowns when he tries to kill Blom.)

Since the author makes no attempt at suspense and invests next to nothing in plot turns, it shouldn't matter to a reader that the resolution is told here. Indeed, the reader may be relieved that a plot thread is supplied, for it is not plot but treatment which counts in *The Insult*. (The title may refer less to the wound in Blom's head than to the treatment of standard narrative process.)

2.

All fiction is involved with the relation between appearance and the form of reality preferred by the writer, as with the tension between the ordinary language which gets us through life and the similar, artistic language which creates the artistic "illusion." From Homer's time onward, writers have fiddled with illusion, exhibiting its paraphernalia or even making the exhibition the core of their work. In part 2 of *Don Quixote*, Cervantes sends his hero and Sancho Panza back to a world whose inhabitants have read his adventures in part 1. Even in the nineteenth century, that central depot of realism, whose ideal might be the title of one of its finest novels, Trollope's *The Way We Live Now*, many of the characters have been formed—or deformed—by reading novels.

In this fading century, the novelistic cottage industry is the novel about itself, the book about the writer writing it, or the novel working against the reader's expectation of what novels are and do. From *Ulysses* through the postmodern writers of France and the Americas, there has been large investment in works which play with the idea of fiction and reality, the verbal and the tactile, the conventional and the esthetic, the mad and the oneiric.

"One level of reality shedding another," as the narrator of *The Insult* says about the almost "imperceptible" shift in his world (or in his sense of it). Of his doctor's narrow view, he says, "I'd always had the feeling, talking to Visser, that reality was something there was only one of. As if it was in some way responsive to testing, as if it could be proved to be constant in all its particulars and identical for everybody." Later, he offers a historical complaint to defend his contrary view. "Our century has taken all the things we relied on. Our century has stripped us naked. Religion's gone, the family too. We're alone, among distractions, then it's over."

*The Insult* consists of fairly systematic subversions of standard fictional process. Although the dust jacket writer claims it for the noir genre of Raymond Chandler, its real home is with the Camus of *The Stranger*. Its voice is the monotone of the overwhelmed individual, the nonentity who reclaims what he can by accepting anonymity, an atom among atoms. It's as if the pavement we walked on were given voice. Such narrators are more reactors than actors, although Blom has more desires and beliefs than some. Still, there is little invested in his desires here; the novel's interest is in process itself, in the rapid, almost effortless transfiguration of "normal" characters, scenes, and developments into a sort of fictional shorthand that we might call morphing. It's as if surfing the channels were more important than what is on any or all of them: the morphing counts more than any individual morph. *The Insult* is thus an "interesting" novel but not an absorbing, let alone an exciting one.

# Call It Recall

## I.

Midsummer, 1914. Eight-year-old Ira Stigman has moved to Harlem from New York's East Side because Grandpa Zaida and Grandma Baba have come from Hungary with his Mom's nine brothers and sisters, all but terrified Genya, who will—in an unpublished section of this six-volume autobiographical novel—die in a concentration camp. Into 115th Street charge "a pair of newspaper hawkers bawling '*Malkhumah.*'" "War."

Ira's war is with his new life among the Irish and Italian goyim. In the East Side streets, he was at home, confident. Now, frightened and unsure, he grows "flabby," "morally weak." Only when he reads fairy tales or is with his high-minded, love-stifled mother is Ira happy. One day, though, "below the hill on Mt. Morris Park in autumn twilight, with the evening star in the west in limpid sky above the wooden bell tower," he's so overcome with beauty that "it set him a problem he never dreamed anyone set himself. How do you say it?" A writer is born.

This book too is born, though it appears sixty years after the author's only published novel, the famous, marvelous *Call It Sleep*. This long river of literary silence is the subject of the new novel, even though its most exuberant and delightful sections are about Ira growing up in the Harlem streets and schools and in the fine food store in which he works. The subject appears in a second typeface, usually as a dialogue with the narrator's computer, Ecclesias (the Speaker). Ecclesias is invoked with the Dantesque imploration *"or m'aiutate,"* ("help me now"). It tells the author-narrator to "salvage whatever you can" of those unwritten, unbooked years. It's to Ecclesias that the narrator relates the confusion and alienation which in the 1930s kept him from completing his second novel (about a Communist organizer), and it's to Ecclesias that the narrator talks of his blissful fifty-one-year marriage to the musician M, daughter of a Baptist minister, mother of his two sons (from one of whom he's now estranged).

For decades, Henry Roth, the "blocked writer," worked as a machinist, a forest fighter, an insane asylum attendant, a waterfowl breeder, and a schoolteacher. Ecclesias prints here one of the few stories Roth published fifty-odd years ago in the *New Yorker*. It appears as an example not of accomplishment but of estrangement from Roth's autobiographical material, the world of the Jewish boy growing up trapped by paternal incomprehension, ideological ardor, and Jewish isolation, all of which worked to cripple his vocation, his genius.

*Mercy of a Rude Stream* is, then, another novel in the twentieth-century tradition of writing about one's self writing.* Novels which deal only with this literary preening in glamorous misery before the mirror are endurable only to generic specialists and those waiting to see how they've been remembered and distorted, but novels like Proust's or the first novel of the man to whom Henry Roth compares himself, James Joyce, are among the world's greatest.

*Mercy of a Rude Stream* is not one of these, yet its author is still a terrific writer, and there are scenes in the book that have the narrative and poetic power of *Call It Sleep*.

Perhaps the five volumes yet to appear, volumes which bring the author closer to the time of writing, won't be so overshadowed by the earlier accomplishment.†

That shadow is a long one. No character in this novel comes close to the frightening father in *Call It Sleep* who tells his little David, "Shudder when I talk to you." There are no scenes here as comic as David's visit to the Metropolitan Museum with Aunt Bertha or as tense and disturbing as David's seduction by Anne, the crippled twelve-year-old. In the new book, the old narrator sets up a big scene by telling Ecclesias that he has until now suppressed it. Then, in normal typeface, the scene unrolls, but more as a brilliant tableau than a dramatic narrative. Ten-year-old Ira is sleeping in his mother's bed. His father is off in St. Louis, trying to make his fortune, his Uncle Louis, the passionate socialist, has been pressing her to sleep with him, and she is tempted. Ira is her prophylactic.

---

* Henry Roth, *Mercy of a Rude Stream*, vol. 1, *A Star Shines over Mt. Morris Park* (New York: St. Martin's, 1994).

† Those I've looked at since did not look as interesting as the one reviewed here.

He was playing bad against mom's naked legs, lying on his side and pushing, rubbing, squeezing his stiff peg between mom's thighs. She woke up.

"I didn't mean it!" Ira wailed in his shame. "I was dreaming."

She laughed indulgently, "Go back to sleep."

This is all right but not up to the wonderful pages about David, Annie, and her brother Yussie in the cellar of the East Side tenement, pages full of comic dialogue of a peerlessly gifted transcriber of accents.

Henry Roth's transcriptive power is still terrific, especially when English slides in and out of Yiddish: "Oy gevald," Mr. Klein growled, all but inaudibly. "Sit zan du khoisakh. ["There'll be chaos here."] C'mon. Take! Here is a bottle maple syrup, Oregon prunes, two pounds."

2.

Henry Roth has another gift, one of the few Joyce, like many great writers, either lacked or scorned. It's the ability to create a protagonist whose fusion of weakness and strength, clumsiness and poetry, stupidity and brilliance, make most readers want to embrace as well as read endlessly about him. If Henry Roth has not dissipated this gift in the many interviews he's given about his heroic revival and persistence in the face of crippling arthritis, literary isolation, and long estrangement from his craft, it's possible that the future volumes of *Mercy of a Rude Stream* will see such a character released from the small typeface of the dialogue with Ecclesias and take over the center of the book. Such a Lazarus, seen from inside, could be a far more complex character than the wonderful David of *Call It Sleep,* someone even richer in tragedy than the Cardinal Wolsey of Shakespeare's last play, *Henry VIII,* who, "weary and old with service," his "high-blown pride" broken, leaves himself open "to the mercy of a rude stream." Such a character might transfigure the often beautiful tableaux of these octogenarian pages into irresistible narrative and not only resurrect but redeem Henry Roth's silent decades. If this happens, this long novel will be the miracle for which all lovers of *Call It Sleep* have, against such heavy odds, hoped.

# Killing Chic

A vampire is usually supposed to be the soul of a dead man which quits the buried body by night to suck the blood of living persons. . . . The persons who turn vampire are generally wizards, witches, suicides and those who have come to a violent end or have been cursed by their parents or the church. *Encyclopedia Britannica,* 11th edition

In *The Informers* the vampire is Jamie, whose bloody death is mourned in chapter 2 but who, in chapter 10, is busy with vampiric and other activity:

I fuck her and then I play with her blood and then I rip her entire pussy out, actually detach the entire thing from her body, intact, and I suck her mouth, ropes of intestines, from the giant red-black cavity I created, wiping mounds of flesh all over myself, using it as lubricant to jack myself off with and then after that basically everything's okay.*

This is the most shocking string of words in Ellis's novel, shocking because its usual habitat is Surreal Porn. It is somewhat better written and more violent than the shock-schlock of *Hustler*. Actually, it goes against the small, if not fine, artistic grain of its author, although it may please or appease something else in him. (That may be why it's the least scary sentence in his newest West L.A. hate-poem.)

The grain of *The Informers* is the deadpan, quasi-catatonic notation of expensive tedium. Ellis described it best in his first novel, *Less Than Zero,* which too was a dribble of Camus' *Stranger* (the only book mentioned in this one). Against the backdrop of news reports (freeway accidents,

* Bret Easton Ellis, *The Informers* (New York: Knopf, 1994).

rapes, wars, murders), Ellis's beautiful, broken West L.A. teenagers consume tremendous hunks of the world's wealth. Their vampirism is chic.

I haven't read Ellis's second novel, *The Rules of Attraction*, and have read only a chapter of the one which brought him notoriety, *American Psycho*. The chapter dealt with the yuppie protagonist's encounter with a tramp whom he questions, twits, then, luxuriantly, eviscerates. It's a powerful cameo set within a lengthy inventory of labeled luxury goods. The book's most generous reviewer, Norman Mailer, wrote that its scheme was grand enough for a Dostoievski—which Ellis wasn't.

The small power of *The Informers*, like that of *Less Than Zero*, is cumulative, but its scheme is thematic, not narrational; the characters connect only lightly with each other, and their monologues don't supply interestingly different angles of the same story à la, say, *The Sound and the Fury*. The connective tissue is the similarity of the lives, the anesthetic sex, the dull gossip, and the duller activities: driving, buying, eating, tanning, bleaching. The characters search for oblivion in the precincts of booze, Valium, sleep, and hard drugs. The inventory of goods and services is so small and repetitive that it composes a sort of twelve-tone music: Betamaxes (and the portentous gloom of what's played on them), Porsches, Wayfarer sunglasses, Melrose restaurants, Perrier, salad, pools with dead rats, rooms with cockroaches, roads with tumbleweed. Southern California's austere luxe, unfelt, unexpressed, menacingly quiet, recounted in the I-see-I-say-I-do-I-am monotony of short sentences which, after pages and pages, shrivel the world and the reader's need for literature—and life.

Ellis is one of the talented post-Hemingway, post-*Stranger* minimalists whose stories spell out the sad, neurotic muck under the speed and gadgetry of American comfort (another, less fictionalized, part of which is the infuriated, terrified, demagogue-driven fundamentalism from which religious and political salesmen have profited).

When fiction sticks to its quiet guns, it's more penetrating, moving, and enlightening than the gorgeous noise of film. (I saw Mike Nichol's vampiric *Wolf* the day I finished *The Informers;* even poorer stuff. As for that other West Los Angeles tale of nocturnal blood, the O. J. Simpson trial, it, like its predecessors, the Watergate, Kefauver, and Army-McCarthy hearings, is our Dionysian Festival, our Oberammergau.)*

---

* On the *New York Times* op-ed page of February 9, 2001, I read of another station on this cultural express, *The Marshall Mathers LP,* "a masterpiece of wit and paranoia . . . filled

That Ellis did not stick to his fictional guns but sketched his tale with a
bloody pencil is the sort of sell-out his finer artistry chillingly depicts.

---

with impish, instantly hummable beats" created by the "angry blonde" rap "genius," Eminem, "whose repugnant lyrics" refer "to women and gays with the crudest of slurs" and
who "seems to regard murder and rape as recreational activities." Eminem (a.k.a. Marshall Mathers, his Christian name) "predicts that his 4-year old daughter will develop a
drinking problem" and is being sued by his mother for advocating what the commonest of
street obscenities suggests. The African driver in *Humboldt's Gift* (1976) ordered his
young American passenger out of the car when he heard him use it. (This was based on an
incident witnessed by its author.)

# VI

# ON FRIENDS, HERE AND GONE

You know these Hindoo bastards love death, but out here we don't care for it. SOL WURTZEL, Hollywood producer

*This is a section of tributes, four of them eulogies of recently dead friends, three written for occasions (birthday and other celebrations). It includes a poem written by my wife, Alane Rollings, for our dear friend, John Wallace; it follows the eulogy for him which was given in Bond Chapel at the University of Chicago in 1993. Perhaps the inclusion of such tributes is even more a self-indulgence than some of the more self-referential pieces of this book. So be it. I like these old friends in the book if only as another way of keeping them around me. I also want readers to know about them. Perhaps the few words here may stimulate some of them to learn more about these remarkable people.*

*Three of the following eulogies and tributes were delivered at University of Chicago memorial services.*

# For John Wallace

When I saw John on August 26 (1993), he'd just received two pints of blood and was revived, alert, sitting up. He wasn't, of course, the John of old, drinking coffee or gin, belly hanging over his belt, clutching the damned pipe he smoked every waking hour, bald head lit in the sun-bright living room. We'd talk over the great and small events of our lives, analyzing personnel, present and past. John freshened analysis with lines from "Lycidas" or songs from the English music hall. He had a terrific memory, was a wonderful mimic. We talked much of our families. I got to know his sisters, nephews, his dead parents, especially his conscience-stricken father agonizing over sermons in the Chesterton vicarage, yearning, as his son would yearn, for Italian hours, Italian delights. I learned about John's schools, Brownston, the small Dorsetshire public school where he met lifelong friends and where he was a long-distance runner, choir singer, walker, and bike-rider on the moors, bicycling a hundred miles a day looking for birds. He spoke a lot about Cambridge and the high-minded, inspiring petulance of F. R. Leavis, of a difficult postgraduate year in London, a failed love affair, then Florence, where he taught English to the local police and ran into an old woman at a party who advised him, since he wasn't doing anything else, to go to the United States for graduate work.

John relished stories of all sorts, true and fictional. The lives of his friends unrolled in that room, anecdotes revealing turns in their careers often marked by single sentences or even words. John's feel for language was crucial to his being; abuse of it, the willful, tragic estrangement of much scholarly prose from the beautiful texts which were supposedly its source, caused him real suffering. He was fascinated by the politics of scholarship. He knew where people were and why they were there, where they were going, why they would or wouldn't get there. He main-

tained a large correspondence which helped him follow the work of colleagues, friends, and former students with the intensity he'd once devoted
to his own research. He could summarize, criticize, and praise articles,
books, and scholarly events as well as anyone I've known.

The world, too, was in his head and conversation. He took in the news
magazines of England and America, read the *Guardian Weekly* as well as
the *TLS* and *ELH*. He followed the Chicago Bears and was as devastating a critic of their personnel as he was of the department's.

This last August 26 of his life, though, we talked of Henry James.
John said that reading James had brought him to life. "He taught me to
observe," he said. "And life opened up like a flower, a flower with a million bits." He smiled with the pleasure of remembering how he'd read
*The Aspern Papers* and—"it was only the third James I read," he said
proudly—*The Golden Bowl*.

There is, I think, an affinity between John, who'd left a class-riddled,
sense-denying England to study and live in the United States, and James,
who'd left a raw, "unexamined" United States for the dense, custom-rich
England, where he spent most of his adult life. Like James, John was subtle, reflective, mad for literature, painting, and scenes, human and natural. John relished the coincidence—I told him that August day—that
James died on February 28, 1916, twelve years to the day before John's
birth.

John was a lustier person than James, more directly frank, less indirect about his love of life and certainly of flesh. It was a surprise to people who saw only John's courtesy, thoughtfulness, and consideration for
others that he was so honest about his love of worldly pleasure. That beneath this love was a core of Protestant asceticism came out in strange
ways, even at the very end. Louis, his nurse, told us how he feared that his
beloved paintings would be stolen to punish him for not having been to
church for twenty years.

John had not been to church, but a church of sorts lived in him. There
were things one did and things one didn't do. When one did the things
one "didn't do," there was hell to pay. And John paid, although he sometimes went on doing them.

All John's friends relish the humor that he decanted from his own
imperfections. He was more than honest with himself; he was, I think,
unnecessarily punitive. For many years, he'd imposed the rigors of scholarship on himself, and he'd been, for those years, a first-rate scholar.
That he'd been worn down by those rigors and chosen easier ways to live

was something he never forgave himself. He kept praising, boosting, and helping those who kept doing what he'd stopped doing, and his friends will not forget either the constructive severity of his criticism or the generosity of his praise.

In a way, his self-discipline never stopped. Although he did not do much scholarship in the last years, what he did do was done with care, thoughtfulness, and stylistic beauty. His final essay on *Coriolanus* is one of the rare scholarly essays which one can call beautiful, indeed moving.

Most of John's life then was devoted to others, to Audrey [his only child], whose development into a wonderful daughter and mother was perhaps the single greatest pleasure of his last year, to his many friends— and who had so many as John?—and to the beautification of what surrounded him. To see him picking out the marble for the trim of his farm's new bathroom, to read the amazing descriptive bibliography he wrote for his great book collection (some of which he sold to a Japanese university), to observe the care and refinement with which he chose gifts for his friends and family, to receive the extraordinary notes of appreciation he wrote in his exquisite handwriting, these were to be around an artist of life.

John was a friend in many ways. There was next to nothing that you could not tell him. He would not condemn, and though he might criticize, he'd do it with sympathy and humor. He was himself so open about his own faults and misdeeds that you felt relieved of the pressure of your own. His honesty included such sympathy and humor that it's hard to imagine wiser consolation.

Which doesn't mean he was a pussycat. No, we've all—including his little granddaughter Erica—seen the gruff John, the curmudgeon who could be annoyed by stupidity, clumsiness, bad manners, ingratitude, or simple ineptitude. I myself never felt this lash, but I've seen waiters easing away from John's gruffness. Some students too must have felt it, although the same students and many more loved him as few professors are loved. He cared for them, supervised their work with exceptional diligence and generosity, kept up with them, helped them in professional and personal ways, and became their friend. He was the ideal member of the academic community, one who contradicted almost everything that is deplored about it, stuffiness, exclusiveness, pomposity, pretension.

He loved learning as he loved what it was about. He loved the world and what most beautifully expressed and enriched it. He felt that his life had been saved by the work of Eliot and James, Milton and Shakespeare.

From a boyhood of timidity and uncertainty, an adolescence of religious fervor, and a young manhood charged with love for beauty, people, and places, the years of teaching and scholarship, and then the attempts of his last years to overcome the brutality of his cancer by finding joy in books and birds, his farm, his trips, the seven hundred young oak trees he planted (knowing only Erica's children would see their full glory), his friends and relatives, Angela, Alec, Audrey, Chuck, Erica, Justine, his two wonderful, saintly nurses, Lucia and Louis, his apartment with the wonderful Tony Fry paintings and the other beautiful things he'd picked out and kept around him—in his last conscious days he debated buying a Walter Sickert drawing—John had and knew he had an exceptionally rich and fortunate life.

I can remember his last days without bitterness because of his bravery, decorum, and humor. I saw him break down only once. "No way out," he said. "There's no way out." Mostly, though, I remember our Sunday breakfasts and walks through Hyde Park, John assessing the vegetation and patching my ignorance with the names and behavior of trees, birds, rodents, and flowers. I think often of his happiness in Australia in the last unclouded weeks of his life. We met at the beautiful National Library in Canberra. After the talks, he took Alane and me and a half-dozen Australian scholars to lunch. (It was always a struggle to stop him from paying for everybody and everything.) He showed us his rooms in the university, overlooking a bird-filled lawn which each morning he contemplated as he drank his coffee. One afternoon we drove out to the Tidbinbilla Preserve, thrilling at the kangaroo and wallaby and, following Alane's intrepidity, petting a wombat. We were heading for a forest to search for a koala. John went off by himself to find birds in a swamp. When we met later, he glowed with triumph: he'd spotted several species he'd never seen before.

Weeks later, the glow went out. John's cancer was discovered, and he flew back to America for the decimating operation that so drastically altered the rest of his life. He lived the five canonical years and, on the whole, lived happily. There were plenty of laughs and bursts of good feeling; there was also, of course, grief, exhaustion, despair—John was as ready to die as anyone I've known well—and some coming to terms with the help of the words which had enriched his life and with which he'd enriched others. One better assessment of this most difficult part of life Audrey discovered marked in John's copy of "Little Gidding."

Since our concern was speech, and speech impelled us
To purify the dialect of the tribe
And urge the mind to aftersight and foresight,
Let me disclose the gifts reserved for age
To set a crown upon your lifetime's effort.
First, the cold friction of expiring sense
Without enchantment, offering no promise
But bitter tastelessness of shadow fruit
As body and soul begin to fall asunder.
Second, the conscious impotence of rage
At human folly, and the laceration
Of laughter at what ceases to amuse.
And last, the rending pain of re-enactment
Of all that you have done and been; the shame
Of motives late revealed, and the awareness
Of things ill done and done to others' harm
Which once you took for exercise of virtue.
Then fools' approval stings and honor stains.
From wrong to wrong the exasperated spirit
Proceeds, unless restored by that refining fire
Where you must move in measure, like a dancer.

On September 2, Louis Bushwa called to say that after comatose days John was awake and might relish a visit. David Malament, Alane, and I went over to the apartment. There John was, lying in bed but alert. Louis urged him to say something, and after a moment, eyes closed, he did. David heard enough to recognize some of John's favorite lines, the ones Captain Parolles speaks after he has been exposed as the wicked plotter and stripped of his captaincy in *All's Well That Ends Well*. He begs for his life, which is granted after he confesses his foolish wickedness. Then he says:

If my heart were great,
't would burst at this. Captain I'll be no more,
But I will eat and drink and sleep as soft
As captain shall. Simply the thing I am
Shall make me live.

John's self-deprecation and love of life apparently found expression even on his deathbed in Parolles's self-acceptance.

We who knew and loved him know that we were fortunate. That he is irreplaceable goes without saying, but my sense is, as I hope yours is, that the ache of loss is relieved by the memory of his person, his words, his smile, his ornery, wonderful being.

*Here is the wonderful poem Alane Rollings dedicated to John. It appears in
her book* The Struggle to Adore *(Story Line Press, 1994).*

## The Ones Who Do Things for Us

After surgery, Intensive Care:
No food; no sleep; no comfort but the morphine pump;
Tubes to live through; bandages to hold you.

We ask what you want; you can't reply; we read you:
At night, you want morning; mornings, night;
you're hoping you'll live to get better.

An uniformed prisoner, you think of how the hostages in Lebanon
Played "Twenty Questions" while expecting to be shot.
They counted rosary beads made from sleeping mats;
they asked for fighter bombers, taxis, wine;
they banged their heads; bled;
taught each other journalism, history, animal husbandry.
They didn't know we'd see these things
as transcendent acts.

For you, weeks of nothing to eat with substance or taste;
No visitors but us, fussing over you; nothing
in your teacup but your floating, futureless face; nowhere to live
but in your dispirited body with its scars, manners, glands, magnanimity,
eyes that see top secret qualities, hands that cheat at Solitaire.
You can't get wet, waltz, say "Terrific!," swing your arms, walk, talk, read.
They make a new tongue from the skin of your stomach,
something for your grief.

We want to be world class people, talking, embracing, improving,
singing on stages, charming, enduring, transformed by events, floating
twenty feet over the street. We need stand-ins to rise
to our painful occasions. We love, praise, pray for them.

Best not to get our own chances to show what we're made of.
You're reading Solzhenitzyn now, and *Newsweek*'s true
Hell-and-heaven stories. When we talk of you, you only speak,
haltingly, of progress. Who are you that you want what's coming to you?

One evening, Father Jenco was led by guards from his cell
to the roof, not to be shot but to look at the moon.
One day, the hostages were freed.
You also get released. You sit in your den with a cool, resigned
sort of yearning, ashamed to be better while some are worse.
Your gaze moves from skyline to treeline to people to skyline.
Music strokes your face; daylight on your shoulderblades
is almost palpable. Your handwriting is legible again.
You'll never write your memoirs, but we'll come like reporters,
Dragging our questions along, our wants and admiration,
Our need to create habitable rooms.
Tell us, what keeps you sitting up at nights
reading Emily Dickinson?
You aren't afraid to trust yourself to darkness anymore.

All the torture and despair are over, aren't they

*For John Wallace*

# Edward Levi

June 26, 1911–March 7, 2000

The obituaries and eulogies which followed Edward Levi's death in his Chicago apartment are heavy with virtue-words, integrity, honesty, truthfulness, commitment, reverence (for law, for the Constitution, for people's rights), intellectuality, reason, independence, responsibility, seriousness. The words are written by people themselves distinguished by seriousness and intelligence: Justice Scalia, Judges Posner and Bork, President Gerald Ford, college presidents Casper and Botstein, the publisher Katherine Graham, *Times* journalists Taubman and Lewis, Professor Bernard Meltzer, and the senior senator from Massachusetts. None come right out and say that Edward Levi was a "great man," although Bork's *Wall Street Journal* eulogy is headed "The Greatest Lawyer of His Time". That appellation is out of fashion in the serious world. It belongs to commercial advertising and the award nights of the entertainment industries. In the last century, you saw it frequently, until Stracheyian biographers and their wolfish descendants, investigative reporters, moved in to expose the eminent and unhorse the horsebacked. Still, as our times go, Edward Levi is being seen as a "great man."

I am neither journalist nor Stracheyian, and on my emotional thermostat it feels right to call the man I knew a great one, that is, a man whose intellect and character gave him power to move many others of intellect and character toward worthwhile goals and who did this for a long time. I knew him as a friend, a worrier, a pessimist, if not a depressive, a joker, a skeptic (not infrequently a cynic), a charmer uncertain of both his charm and his gifts, an almost-idolater of others', a man mad for learning and books, a man who, in his last year, mind almost completely gone, sat daily in his lakeside apartment turning the pages of books he could no longer understand (although, strangely, he had favorites, one of which was an issue of the *University of Chicago Law Review* dedicated to him and his work).

After he retired as a professor at the University of Chicago, where he'd spent almost all his life and whose law school dean, provost, and president he'd been, he ate frequently at the so-called Round Table of the University faculty club. Here he contributed to the arguments, the recollections, and the not-very-Shavian exchanges until we began to notice the increasingly vague garrulity, the forgetfulness, the substitution of words like "thing" for words and concepts he was trying to talk about. So terrible a turn in a man renowned as a scathingly forceful teacher, a socratic challenger of dogmas and familiar practice, a subtle, witty, and judicious leader, was heartrending.

Much about this man, past and present, began to seem heartrending. A couple of years before the decline was evident, the discussion at the table turned to happiness. Out of that cerulean blue—the color of his wide, oddly innocent eyes—Edward said, "I've never been happy." Retrospectively, one sees the internal disintegration generating the remark, but it is true that Edward came from and continued a tradition in which happiness did not rank as either a suitable end or a virtue; and he did enjoy saying unexpected things, trying them out for himself and others. Still, this remark seemed to lift the covers on a darkness I at least had not suspected. After all, I'd seen Edward in what certainly looked like happy moments. For instance, very few listeners or readers responded so deeply, so, yes, joyously to literature.

Seventy years ago, Edward had wanted to be a writer. He'd written stories and plays (some of which were read over the radio by the teenage Orson Welles). He loved good writing, and perhaps overvalued writers. That he himself had written so little may have been one source of the unhappiness or, at least, of the modesty which could close in on self-contempt. The *Times* obituary told the story he often told: that he'd been discouraged from doing graduate work in literature by a professor who told him that Anglo-Saxons wouldn't relish being taught their literature by Jews.

The son and grandson of rabbis, one of whom, Emil Hirsch, was what the *Times* called an "architect" of Reform Judaism, Edward lived through the transformation of Jews in America to American Jews. As the first Jewish dean of a major American law school and the first Jewish president of a major private university (which had once reserved its presidency for Baptists), he was himself part of that transformation. How important to him was his Jewishness? Hard to say. It was surely part of his consciousness, part of his waking time, but he was not, as far as I know, a believer. Jewishness was an element of the ethical standard the eulogists have talked about, a sense of living by the book (not necessarily the Book), a sense of the essential importance of honor, decency, equity, and justice, and, to a much lesser extent, institutional and social decorum

Edward, though, was a kidder, a mocker, even a clown; he loved to drink and either act or be a bit gaga. That is, he loved to go off record, off the book. At such moments, there was very little sacred, and these moments counted a great deal for him. Kate, his intelligent, charming, amusing wife, a war widow when he courted her during his first stint in Washington (as a deputy to Thurman Arnold in the Department of Justice) and who became the mother of his three accomplished sons, used to enjoy these moments but kept them from going too far.

They were a wonderful pair. For years, they gave dinner parties at their easygoing, easy-looking house on 50th Street in Hyde Park. They loved the mix of artists, politicians, philosophers, and bankers who were put at tables with University of Chicago professors encouraged to debate and challenge them. This was thought to be the best of Hyde Park society.

The parties were one way of Edward's breaking out of the brilliant provincialism of his upbringing and career. After the government had nearly sunk into the filth called "Watergate," he made his greatest break, leaving the university presidency to become Gerald Ford's attorney general.* In Washington, he and Kate were like children on vacation, Cinderellas at the ball. They loved their time with glamorous, powerful people of intellect who decided the fate of countries. (Their closest Washington friends were Justice and Mrs. Lewis Powell) Ford's loss to Carter in 1976 was a blow. Edward's idolatry extended to Ford. He talked about how wonderful he was at cabinet meetings, knowing each officer's business, agenda, and state of mind. "I know why you're grinning, Edward." (The sharpest critics turn to mush when they join presidential cabinets.) Edward was less idolatrous—and could be brilliantly comic—about his fellow cabinet officers, even those he admired, but I can remember Nelson Rockefeller, for one, going down for the count after a comical Levi uppercut.

The Department of Justice workdays were long and hard, so much so

* He was called to President Ford's attention by his fellow Illinoisan, Donald Rumsfeld.

that there wasn't time to take stock of all he was doing. (He did allow himself one note of jocular triumph after the FBI flushed out Patty Hearst: "Now if we can only dig up Hoffa.") Others have done and are doing it for him. Here is his solictor general, Robert Bork, writing about him the week of his death.

> Levi administered through discussions, often resembling seminars, as he undertook the physically arduous, politically delicate and intellectually demanding task of reform. He did so without the fanfare, recriminations, firings and moral posturing that would have made him popular with a press and public whose idea of "reform" consists of confrontations and pious utterances. He brought several institutions, not only the Justice Department, into conformity with legal and moral principles, and he did so without destroying their morale or effectiveness. He carried on the regular work of the department in much the same manner, as he made decisions about prosecutions, desegregation remedies, legislation and the complex interaction of the demands of the Constitution with the imperatives of national security. (*Wall Street Journal*, March 13, 2000)

After Ford's defeat, Edward brought his cabinet chair—an officer's privilege—back to the University of Chicago and resumed teaching. It wasn't easy. His scrupulousness became almost a pathology: lectures and grading were particularly difficult for him. Even his celebrated Socratic interrogations were blunted. He was beginning to wear down. He tried a term at Stanford; it only made him miss Chicago. He took on various honorific jobs (president of the American Academy of Arts and Sciences). He spoke at funerals. (In the last years, Kate wrote the eulogies he delivered.) He read, he traveled, he got a painful case of shingles or Guillain-Barré, his mind slid away. What had been noticed by relatively few in the early years, the sweetness of his nature, was now very noticeable. Admiration for him was mingled with affection, with love. In Chicago, he was a sort of alma pater. As he disintegrated further, those of us who cared for and loved him felt an almost Sophoclean pang at the way of the flesh, the breakdown of human grandeur. His death last week ended the story, reducing the years of disintegration to an almost inconsequential fraction of his remarkable life.

# Arthur Heiserman

1929–1975
Bond Chapel, The University of Chicago, December 12, 1975

No one I know tried to form his life as consciously as Arthur did. He was not a medievalist by accident, he was not a Catholic by inheritance but by choice, he did not become the complex man he was haphazardly. The decorum of his long walk with death was true to his life and in the tradition of the great man who was his patron saint and model, the man for all seasons, Thomas More.

Every now and then Arthur and I talked about death. Of course he'd thought about it a great deal, and those who loved him thought of it also. One notion we discussed goes back to the pre-Socratic philosophers, and, if we weren't mistaken, is not out of step with modern biology. The notion is that death is written into the contract of individuality itself. Colonial creatures have no real death because they have no separate existence. I think of this now because it occurs to me that Arthur's early death is somehow related to the very intensity and distinction of his individuality. If Arthur looked older than his years, it was because he was. He simply felt more, lived more in one hour than most of us do in twenty. He felt more about a tree, a stranger on a bus, a painting, a sentence, than most people feel about what they love the most. He enjoyed a greater variety of things than anyone I know; and he had an extraordinary capacity for expressing enjoyment. No one laughed better than Arthur. He was a great laugher. At some cartoon a six-year-old would think beneath him, Arthur roared as if the great comics of the world were behind it.

He was a fantastic audience. He could make you feel that your stupidities were fine insights, your ninth-rate jokes the delight of mankind. And then, no one was better with troubles. Since Arthur was exceptionally conscious about himself, he knew his own capacity for every sort of feeling and behavior, high and low, good and bad, the most absurd and the most sentimental. Because of the self-awareness and the ironic acceptance it brought with it, Arthur let his friends feel that their own idiocies, contortions, and disasters didn't exile them from humanity. If he didn't encourage their foolishness, he still made them—made us—feel not just understood but accompanied. That is the summit of friendship, of human sympathy.

I think Arthur understood his own exceptional force early—his mother was especially helpful there—and understood further that this force required some sort of balance, some form or forms which would not suppress but help him realize and express it. Literature, music, the church whose mass was just celebrated, and then medieval creativity were there for him. He told me what buildings such as this one meant to him when he came up here as a seventeen-year-old from Evansville, Indiana. To see the art of glassmaking transfigure the unbearable force of the sun into a sacred space of tranquility and exaltation was a deeply felt paradigm for him.

In the neo-medieval university, medieval study began to be more and more important for him. The way in which its cathedrals expressed that great desire for a universe which *loves* as well as *means,* the way in which the great poems of Chaucer and Dante fused sublimity with the most ordinary, ribald, profane, and pathetic human acts ignited his intelligence.

He not only became a lover and scholar of medieval solution, he tried to become a modern version of what lay behind it.

Many of us here know the two Arthurs, the Great Laughter and the Man of Decorum and Duty, the teacher and father who believed as deeply in institutions as in personality, in restraint as in passion. Like More, like Chaucer, like Dante, Arthur not only understood the human meaning of institutions, he served them, not just as teacher of many interests, but as tenacious, skillful, and often exhausted administrator. He was a constant worker. He studied, he taught, he wrote, and did not use knowledge as cloister or arsenal. Knowledge made him not just a medievalist but an alert, skeptical, yet almost naïvely passionate modernist. He was a marvelous teacher because he could expose the past in the bones of modernity. And he was a remarkable writer, because he could rejuvenate old texts as well as write brilliant ones of his own.

A word about his elegant if little-known fictions. Into these Arthur poured such intensity that he had to invent for it forms too complex for most to grasp. His disappointment that so few understood what he was doing led to his feeling that he had failed himself, that he hadn't realized his force and talent. I have almost never heard of a remarkable man who did not feel this way. No matter how outwardly triumphant, such internal disappointment becomes bitterness, although to others it appears as exemplary modesty.

In Arthur's extraordinary and clairvoyant intelligence lay a belief that the force in him, thwarted by not finding adequate expression for all of it, turned somehow into the internal enemy which finally defeated, or appeared to defeat, him. His final, and, perhaps, his most beautiful accomplishment is the way he defeated it. Arthur kept merry before fright, his dignity became more and more intimately personal, intimately—we might say—Arthurian; he persisted without self-pity or mockery, taught his classes, lovingly diverted and guided his children, even, heroically, worked against the terrible creeping weakness of his cancer to finish his book a few days before his death. It was the accomplishment of a marvelous spirit.

Arthur believed, no, he was sure, as he told a daughter this week, that there was a form of personal survival. The strength of his belief sweetens the difficult times for those who survive him. Some, like myself, less spiritually gifted than Arthur, can hold to another form of survival, one more personal even than his writing, almost as personal as the presence of his wonderful and wonderfully endowed children. For me, and perhaps for some of you, Arthur is simply a permanent part of thought. In those inner councils of sensibility and decision, Arthur is there, ironic, tender, cautionary, intrepid, wise and wild both. At this occasion, during which we say, "Goodbye," some of us can also say: "Here you are still, dear Arthur, and will always be."

## Imre Horner

### 1901–1988

The only person who knew Imre and didn't think he was remarkable was Imre. If he'd heard me say this, he'd say, "That person knew me best." I wonder.

I don't think Imre thought much about himself. Maria, who knew him best and knew his complexity, believed this also. Imre's expertise, knowledge, and devotion were directed to other people, to medicine, to the world, the arts. At the end, he did observe and analyze his own body, but this was a form of objectivity, not subjectivity. He knew what was happening to and in him.

In the last months of his life, Imre did make some attempt at assessing it. Some of the assessment was shadowed with regret. He was such an admirer of original, creative work that his self-assessment was excessively modest. He had done research at Columbia and had published papers, but he'd left the world of research and publication and become a physician. "My life," he said, "has been one of service." For Imre, this meant that he was not going to leave much behind him.

His patients and friends know otherwise. To have Imre's knowledge and probing intelligence pursuing one's trouble was a wonderful experience. It was so clear that he knew the sorts of things that went on in you that his spelling out the options in front of you, telling you that it might be this or that, was itself a form of medicine: you were included in the analytic process; you felt the process of therapy; and you were receiving a physician's education from a marvelous teacher.

*Physician.* From the Greek *phusis,* "nature."

Like all the great physicians, Imre was fascinated by natural process, the body's effort to maintain itself. A part of this maintenance involved the relationship of the patient's body to his personality, his character, the individual essence within the body. Many times I came to Imre for the sort of help that others request of psychiatrists. Imre would say, "You feel as you do in part because your blood pressure is low. And also because you have such-and-such a temperament." He'd give me some pills or recommend an activity, but the therapy had occurred. It was his understanding of me and my condition—to both of which I'd been blind. His physician's work was similar to my own, the analysis of character, although his included the biological source of disorder.

It's no accident that so many of Imre's patients became his friends. Imre understood them. They—we—felt the understanding and loved him for it.

Imre was not a sentimental man. He was ironic, witty, scornful of those he thought foolish or corrupt, but he was deeply affectionate. His care for you was just that—he *cared* for you.

Perhaps there was one sentimental component of his nature: Imre concentrated on the highest qualities, the nobler parts of his friends. The result was that you were not only physically better after time with him, you felt you were a better person than you were. When Imre pinned medals on you, you didn't bleed.

He also pinned medals on life itself. Imre was interested in, amused by, tender about all sorts of people, all sorts of creatures, and—influenced by Maria here—the vegetable world as well. His special devotion was for musicians, artists, and scientists. He himself had exceptional musical power, although he believed it was only—as he might have said—the power of discrimination, not creation. The depth of his pleasure in music makes me think that he might have been a fine musician. He liked all sorts of music, old and new. (Much more than people far younger, including me, he was *with it*.) He was also a responsive and subtle reader, and he loved painting and sculpture, photographs and drawings. His last decline began when he and Maria came in from Beverly Shores to see an exhibit of Italian drawings at the Art Institute. In the hospital he said, laughing—he was a great laugher—"Maybe it would have been better if we'd seen the exhibit." He meant that if Maria had not gotten him to the hospital, he would have probably died in the Art Institute, a proper place to die.

On the other hand, to die before it was necessary was wrong. He would have caused Maria and others too much pain if he'd died there. He wanted to live as long as he was mentally alert and in tolerable physical shape, able to participate in the world and to do what humans should do. The morning of the last full day of his life, he called Maria to come to the hospital early; there were some income tax matters he had to go over for her. She did not want him to think about such things, she could take care of them, but no, it was important for him to do everything he could while he still could. "Every hour counts," he said to her.

*Every hour counts.* One way or another, every waking hour of his eighty-six and a half years Imre made things count. The young nurse who attended him at the end said, weeping, how marvelous he was, how he'd helped and cheered her, made her see what a human being could be.

Nobility. Imre had nobility. And like so many real noblemen, he was not of noble birth but had formed himself. His people were Hungarian Jewish peasants. He had uncles who could barely read or write, who spoke only local dialects and never left their villages. His father had made his way up and become a high-level clerk but the strain was great and, depressed, he took his own life. Imre's gifts and energy brought him to Budapest, and then, for medical studies, to Berlin. He had wonderful memories of the place. (A professor who could not get used to women medical students began lectures by saying, "*Meine Herren von beide Geschlect.*" "Gentlemen of both sexes.")

That Imre's coming to America is part of the catastrophic century's worst catastrophe is the sort of historical irony which made history and politics so fascinating to him. They are the last of his passions I'll mention.

One thing he liked about his brief retirement was that it gave him more time to read the newspapers, newsletters, and periodicals which reported the comic and outrageous doings of politicians. Imre was an impassioned and responsible citizen who had strong views about almost every newsworthy event. This was a part of his living in the present, his love of life. It's what helped keep him young until the day of his death. His rosy, almost translucent flesh exhibited this amazing youthfulness.

What is a great man? Hard to say. Imre will not show up in books about great men. When all who knew him are gone, he will almost surely not be remembered. Yet for me, Imre was a great man. That is, Imre lived intensely as friend, colleague, citizen, husband, and physician; he raised one's sense of human decency. His exemplary life makes those who knew and loved him try to somehow make our own lives nobler and more significant.

## Misremembering Montale

I have to lose you. Not easy.
Everything moves me, email,
Screams, the salt breath bringing
Manhattan a dark spring.

(city of books, insomnia, rivers)

In the anger
of a nail on glass
I look for what

I owe you.

*The following was written for a celebration of Hugh Kenner's seventieth birthday in Athens, Georgia. I was unable to attend, and this little tribute was read by my student, Hugh's son, Rob.*

## Words about Hugh

I first saw the long, bespectacled man with the explaining, smoking hands in the autumn of 1956 or 1957. For years, though, he'd been a companion. Hadn't I roared at his obliteration of Ernest Jones's hagiography of Freud and of Robert Penn Warren's hasty epic, *Brother to Dragons?* Hadn't his lantern shown me minerals in the tough seams of Pound and Joyce? Half the age he—amazingly—is now, Hugh Kenner was already the indispensable guide to the Indispensable Guides. Some of them recognized it. Eliot, for one, who, reviewing Hugh's *Wyndham Lewis,* pointed out the ability of this hunter to take on the coloration of his prey. (A few years later, the hunter had made the reviewer's canny invisibility brilliantly visible.) What was surprising when the hunter showed up in the feral streets of Chicago was his geniality, his playfulness, his gentleness. Much has changed in these thirty-five years; not that. What has changed has to do with depth, range, complexity, mastery, grace. Early on, Hugh learned the cultural geography of this century and drew its first rough maps. Since, he has kept exploring, drawing ever finer, larger, more beautiful maps. It will be very difficult to travel twentieth-century intelligence without them. Hugh moved from drawing the landscape to explaining its geology, the forces which formed what forms us. More recently it became clear that the mapmaker himself was part of the map: the Kenner Islands, a delightful port of call in the Caribbean of mentality. The great exegete, the peerless paraclete, had put the comedians into his own comedies. The Joyce seen by Kenner is not all that different from the Bloom seen by Joyce. Of the sun, Galileo said that it "has all the planets . . . dependent on it for their orderly functions," yet it can "ripen a bunch of grapes as if it had nothing else in the world to do." I have been one of hundreds of grapes Hugh's generosity has ripened. One feels a special grace. Here's Hugh, he's writing a book, doing proofs on an-other, writing five reviews, four essays, preparing lectures, classes, working out geodesic equations, reading fourteen books, acknowledging nine-teen offprints, rewiring the lights, fixing the toilet, being a husband, a fa-ther to many children—yet the grape feels the intensity of a benevolent intelligence uniquely concentrated on the production of flavors it had no idea were in its dusky skin.

It is no small thing to be a component of the Kenner Winery. (And Chateau Hugh ages wonderfully. Have you tried the '67s, the '74s?)

It is not accidental that so fine an intelligence issues from so fine a na-ture. Has it to do with a special blend of deference and authority, of an intellect and sensibility at the service of a passionate curiosity, an almost furious need to make clear? In these thirty-five years I have seen Hugh at grand moments (receiving an honorary degree before ten-year-old Rob, forty years after ten-year-old Hugh watched his father receive one), easy ones (talking excitedly for four hours over glasses of whiskey and a mound of cigarette butts), and harsher ones endured with indomitability and grace (his own and Mary Anne's). We start with different politics, religions, ancestry, and training, Hugh and I, yet I am convinced that we could argue, defend, and intercede for each other's positions. This is due to the power of Hugh's comprehending sympathy. It is a beautiful part of life to read Hugh Kenner; it is a beautiful part of life to be his friend.

## For Ernest Sirluck

From 1956 until Ernest left for Toronto, I was his office-mate at the University of Chicago, an instructor, then an assistant professor. Ten or twelve years my senior, Ernest was an associate, then a full professor. He'd been an infantry officer who'd seen combat in the war. He was a leading seventeenth-century scholar engaged in his marvelous edition of volume 2 of the Yale *Milton*. He and his lovely wife Lesley lived in a substantial brick house on Woodlawn Avenue in Hyde Park. He wore conservative suits with matching ties, and, even in shirtsleeves, looked elegant, substantial, of a piece.

Ernest was a serious man. Even his joviality—and there was lots of it—was somehow serious. Literature was close to the center of this seriousness, and at the center of literature were Milton and Shakespeare. Milton's extraordinary intelligence, complexity, passion, learning, and revolutionary boldness spoke profoundly to and helped form, or at least deepen, Ernest's character. The gorgeousness of his prose and poetry, like Shakespeare's, an effulgence of grace and genius, spoke to another part of Ernest, his hunger for enchantment and sensuousness.

Among students and colleagues, Ernest was famous for strictness and high standards. His temper and temperament were inflammable, but almost always controlled. Still, there are men and women of accomplishment—I'll cite two men of letters, George Steiner, the critic, and George Starbuck, the poet—whose younger, frailer selves ran aground on Ernest's standards and who, following them, rebuilt themselves, gratefully.

Ernest brought to our English Department some of the swagger and intensity of a field officer who'd appraised himself and his men in battle. In the soft, unmilitary days between the Korean and Vietnam Wars, many were fearful and dismayed by such an appraiser. Mostly, though, there was gratitude and, in time, affection. From my desk I studied students trembling before Ernest's, but then I watched them absorb what I had also seen, Ernest's interest in their work and their beings. When later I heard of his brilliant reforms at the University of Toronto, it came to me that I had shared the office with a great educator.

At the time, though, Ernest was my senior colleague and friend, a guide, an encourager, a surprisingly gentle though firm critic, a strict, genuine, worthy appreciator of whatever little good work one did. I will never forget his enthusiasm over a call I received one afternoon, telling me that a publisher had accepted one of my books and contracted for another. "Now there'll be no question of tenure, Richard," he said with a smile that could not have been larger had he received such news about himself.

Occasionally, Ernest talked about important, moving moments in his life, his family, the provincial world of his home town, Winkler, Manitoba, of the anti-Semitism he'd experienced in Canada, his army life. I remember his telling me what I take the liberty of mentioning here, the terrible guilt he felt about canceling a date with his brother because of a tryst with a French girl. Shortly afterward, his brother was killed. We also talked about the war because I was writing a novel, one of whose characters was in the war, as I had not been. I owe Ernest many rich details about the war and London life during it.

I saw him only a few times after he left Chicago, briefly at an MLA meeting and once during an academic visit to Chicago. Four years ago [in 1992], I was in Toronto and called him. He came down to the hotel, and we spent the afternoon talking. Ernest's hair was now white, but his posture was erect, his clothes elegant, his diction precise, his affection both full and disciplined. He spoke as he always did, with the special frankness of people who have overcome civilized reticence to make clear what they feel, see, and believe. It was a wonderful afternoon, a renewal of affection for the honorable man whom you're so justly honoring tonight.

*Michael Anania delivered this brief tribute during a Chicago Art Institute day of tributes to Leon Forrest. Weeks before his death, Leon phoned to talk and thank me for it.*

## For Leon Forrest

Leon Forrest is two rare things, a wonderful writer and a wonderful man. The man, with whom I've talked too few times these last decades, is earthy, elegant, warm, humorous, spirited, modest, and self-assured, a classic and classy gentleman. The writer is more mysterious, though more clearly defined, a virtuoso of almost every literary technique, mode, and strategy, a mime, a painter, a dramatist, a rhetorician, a miniaturist and an—if the word exists—epicist, comic and tragic, regional and universal, ethnic and worldly, black and every color, a musician of dialect and of dialects, a genius of American prose and American life. Our literature, American and world culture, have been enriched by Leon Forrest's work. A few people—like those assembled at the Art Institute—are lucky enough to have been enriched by the man as well.

# VII

## ON MYSELF

*This miscellany is more conspicuously autobiographical than its predecessors. Even when it's dodging autobiography, explaining why its author doesn't want to write one, its "I" manages to get on stage. The reader can make of this what he wants. (I offer another explanation in the opening piece here.) The second piece is a monologue worked out of an interview for a book on University of Chicago writers by its editor, Molly McQuade (a former student of mine). The book,* An Unsentimental Education, *was a contribution to the centenary of the University of Chicago, where I've taught since 1955. My Chicago life is described elsewhere in this miscellany. For epigraph, I'm tempted to use what George S. Kaufman said to S. N. Behrman when he ran into him two days after attending his farewell party, but I fear it would be said of me if I keep postponing retirement from the University of Chicago: "Forgotten but not gone."*

*This piece was presented on January 10, 2001 (the twenty-second anniversary of my father's death) as one of a series of talks at the Franke Humanities Institute at the University of Chicago. A part of it appeared in the "Writers on Writing" series in the* New York Times *two and a half months later.*

## An Old Writer Looks at Himself

### 1.

I haven't wanted to write an autobiography, so when I recently took stock and noticed how much of my work these last years was flecked and sometimes saturated with autobiographical matter, I asked myself, "What's going on? Why all this calling attention to a self at least one part of which has never thought the whole particularly interesting? Or is that the point?"

Of course I know that many aging geezers find to our surprise and dismay that we're acting like—well, geezers. We're garrulous, our stories, many of them medical, wander, and, worst of all, we talk and write more and more about what we've been and done (or, more rarely, haven't been, haven't done). It's as if we're drawing our life around us like a blanket against the oncoming chill, a psychological equivalent of the theological bookkeeping supposedly done when the earthly package is delivered to heaven's gate for its ultimate disposition.*

For those of us who are writers, the autumnal accounting is often but another installment of a long, professional self-regard, one that differs from those of haberdashers and geologists or even historians and literary critics.

$\approx\!\!\approx$

---

* Sir Walter Scott's version of this (in his wonderful general preface, 1829, to the Waverly novels) is "old men may be permitted to speak long because they cannot in the course of nature have long time to speak."

Writers from Sappho and Hesiod, Catullus and Li Po, the Romantics and the Moderns on down to us have drawn on their lives and feelings for much of their best work. Some have been more embarrassed than I about it. Like Henry James, they've burned their papers and asked their friends to destroy their letters; like Eliot and Salinger, they've tried to forbid biographies, or again like Eliot, deprecate the work they regard as personal. (He called his greatest and most influential poem little more than "a lyrical grouse.") When supposedly cajoled into talking about their work, they find various, sometimes quite odd excuses for doing so. Thomas Mann wrote that he was writing about the making of *The Magic Mountain* because of "the healthy and sympathetic attitude of the American mind toward the personal, the anecdotal, and the intimately human."

In any event, the interfusions of life and art have been of great interest not just to tabloid columnists and readers but to serious biographers and critics. Perhaps such antibiographical criticism as that of Richards, Ransom, Tate, and Eliot and, more recently, Foucauldian deflations of the concept of the author flourish as counters to this stoking of the ego furnaces. Despite the intellectual status of the deflations, many intelligent and most unintelligent people remain persistently curious about the relationship of achievements, literary, political, cinematic, athletic, and even mathematical—see the spate of recent books about mathematicians—to the lives and psyches of the achievers.

## 2.

The curiosity is, I think, part of a common, if not universal, need to see the world in narrative terms. Story is so integral to human life that a non-biologist like myself wonders if there might be biochemical determiners for it. It is certainly not just the professional story-writer whose mind falls into narrative patterns. Indeed, the social role of the writer may well be the invention, refreshment, extension, and deepening of such patterns. Narrative forms are ubiquitous. Our waking and our sleeping lives are dominated by them; our private relationships form along them, and our public ones are constructed as serial stories whose protagonists are called celebrities. If these stories are sufficiently sensational, they can become national epics, or rather, since their makers are seldom homeric, epic materials waiting for their Homers, Shakespeares, and Whitmans, or, more recently, their cinematic and television geniuses. (See *Eyes on the Prize*, the marvelous television series on the civil rights movement.)

Of our own stories, we are, if not the Homers, at least the stewards and censors, and not a few nonwriters do what professional writers, often perilously, do, which is to not merely make experience into stories but to seek out experience which may make good ones. There's a startling intimation of this in book 8 of the *Odyssey* when King Alcinous tells the disguised Odysseus to stop weeping at the song the blind bard Demodocus has been singing about him and his fellow heroes. After all, says the king, the gods "measured the life thread of these men so that their fate might become a poem sung for unborn generations." Not even Mallarmé or Oscar Wilde claimed more for art than this.*

Although writing stories requires peace and security, the intrepidities of a Stephen Crane, an Ernest Hemingway, or a Norman Mailer—who enlisted in the infantry because he believed that ground combat would be grist for a novel—or, more recently, the daredeviling of a William Volkmann or Denis Johnson, risk losing not only peace and security but life itself. Still, many writers, not excluding this timid one, continue to risk at least common happiness (including the happiness of people they love) for what I won't degrade by calling "ambition" or "career" but for the closest thing we have to vocation, an almost superstitious commitment to the essentially accurate depiction of what we've felt, seen, thought, and believed. (As for the vocational call itself, it is, I'm pretty sure, a domestic rather than a long-distance one, and the caller is almost certainly the callee.)

3.

The kind of self-reflection in which I'm now indulging has been an important element of modern intelligence. Telling the story of the story, publishing the diaries and letters of and interviews with the story-tellers, and analyzing and psychoanalyzing them, all contribute to the ever-increasing complication of the self. Judging from the documents we have, I suspect that "ordinary people" today are more complicated— have more going on in them, including self-consciousness about it— than the sages and poets of earlier times. Complex as Hector and Hamlet are, they are simpler than many minor characters of George Eliot, Flaubert, Dostoievski , Proust and, say, Bellow and Cormac McCarthy.†

---

* A Jane Austen version of this but skirts its edges: "For what do we love but to make sport for our neighbors, and laugh at them in our turn" *(Pride and Prejudice).*

† This does not imply that the advance of complexity in self-consciousness and awareness of motivation means progressive intelligence. To say that any writers are "more intelli-

What's true for characters is true of their authors. Modern psychological analysis has played a role in this. Modern authors may, like Kafka, reject analysis out of fear that it will kill their desire to write, or may take to it believing that it removes obstacles to writing. Sometimes analysis is but a baffled counterpoint to the interfusion of the writer's life and work. One of Saul Bellow's frustrated therapists is reported (by Bellow's biographer, James Atlas) to have said that he "couldn't tell if his patient was really suffering" or "merely observing himself suffer." Another concluded that Bellow entered into situations "like a pin-setter," only in order to knock them down. Such set-ups and demolitions compose obvious narrative trajectories, which, according to Atlas, Bellow, consciously or unconsciously, imposed not only on his characters but on the lives of those who lived with him.

4.

I know that I myself have prolonged certain painful situations because writing about them became more important than eliminating the pain. Very recently, to my relief and happiness, I did force a change in what had been a very painful separation. Along with the consequent relief and happiness, I realized that the steam had gone out of the fiction I'd been writing about it. The happiness didn't lessen, but it was accompanied by an odd hollowness and anxiety. What was I going to do about the novel on which I'd been working for two years? In it, my protagonist, not a writer but a retired lawyer, deliberates—as I did—about clinging to pain. In a book of Emily Dickinson's given to him—and this is invention—by the loved one from whom he was separated, he finds his situation expressed in these remarkable lines:

> Rehearsal to Ourselves
> Of a Withdrawn Delight
> Affords a Bliss like Murder
> Omnipotent. Acute.

---

gent" or gifted than Shakespeare or Dante, or that, say, Frege and Wittgenstein are "more intelligent" than Plato and Aristotle, would be absurd. Indeed, if complexity of thought is measured by intellectual coherence, syntactic mastery, and richness of vocabulary, a case could be made that the intellectual power of the average person and his political leaders has declined.

We will not drop the Dirk
Because we love the Wound
The Dirk commemorate[s] Itself
Remind[s] us that We died.

A Bliss like Murder . . . Because we love the Wound. Astonishing insights, he thinks, and he wonders about the spectral Amherst spinster as well as about his own internal savagery.

How many like my protagonist and myself not only adjust to the resentment and hatred of those who, they think, have wronged them but flourish in it? Yet of this many, it is only the writer whose love of the wound involves a professional opportunity and makes dropping his dirk a difficult decision..

I can't remember who said something like, "Happiness is white and doesn't stain the page," but of course almost all stories are about such forms of unhappiness as disturbance, derangement, and disorder. These may be comic, may be imaginary, but they initiate storytelling.

In my case, two days after happiness whitened out my subject, or, as I said, took the steam out of it for me, I received a peculiar, indeed uniquely harsh letter from an old and intimate writer friend about something I'd published. Amid the puzzlement, anger, and dismay it aroused, I spotted a gleam of light: the possibility of translating this new schism into an equivalent of the painful one that had been whitened out. (A further complication: the letter-writer may well have been contemplating or even writing a work which needed to be fueled by one of his longtime themes, estrangement from those close to him.* I wrote him that I understood that.)

---

* Thinking more about this, I believe that the theme is more characteristic of his life than of his work. Although it shows up in his books, it is probably less important there than loyalty. My guess is that sensitivity to the way he's treated and the—usually generous and decent but sometimes insensitive—way he treats others is an even more important part of him than it is of most decent people. As for the disintegration of old friendships, that may be another sad consequence of human longevity. I note the recent collapse of the 60-year friendship between the photographers Cartier-Bresson and David Douglas Duncan following the latter's publication of a book of 80 candid shots of the former. That the greatest of candid shot-makers should be photophobic about shots of himself is similar to my—I guess I must say former—friend's sensitivity to the sort of published portraiture of which he himself has been a master. Another sign of the spread of this form of divorce appears in a recent poem of Donald Hall which begins "To grow old is to lose every-

Another coincidence: the day on which my subject whitened out was December 9, 2000, and the city in which it occurred was Washington, D.C. That morning, a friend had driven me to the street in front of Vice President Gore's house, where Bush / Cheney picketers were disconsolately waving their placards, disconsolately because the Florida Supreme Court had, the day before, ordered the vote recount in Miami-Dade and other counties which looked as if it would reverse what they regarded as the certain election of their candidates. Late that afternoon, as my personal situation was transformed, the U.S. Supreme Court ordered that the recount be stopped. The political reversal—a blow to me—fused with the happy personal reversal.* This confluence, this coincidence, was the sort of thing novelists not only look for but expect. In their work, coincidence will—should!—not seem haphazard but inevitable, the farcical or tragic manifestation of destiny.

## 5.

Most fiction writers feel free to exaggerate and otherwise alter actuality in the interest of narrative power, although some, like Turgeniev and Babel, have said that they don't or even can't invent anything, actuality being more than enough for their literary needs. Other writers are pulled so strongly by what instigated their stories that at times they can't change what another part of themselves, perhaps a cautionary one, wants to. You can see—in his notebooks—so domineering an inventor as Henry James trying in vain to shift the locale of a climactic moment of *The Ambassadors* from the place—Paris—where the initiating actuality occurred.

I too have sometimes felt and been incapable of altering the appearance, time, place, and character of an actuality, fearing that it contained indispensable elements for which I could not find fictional equivalents. Ulrich, the man without qualities in Musil's novel, says of scientists and truth, "It isn't at all true that the scientist pursues truth. It pursues him. It's something he suffers from. . . . He's a dipsomaniac whose drink is facts. And he doesn't give a damn . . . what comes of his discoveries." My rational self rejects such personifications. It rejects the idea of being cap-

---

thing" and which contains the lines "Another friend of decades estranges himself / in words that pollute thirty years" ("Affirmation," *The New Yorker*, May 21, 2001).

* My friend, the mathematician Persi Diaconis, has taught me a bit about the concept of coincidence, even slipping into my antimathematical head some persuasive quantifications. He's writing a book about the subject with his old teacher, Frederick Mosteller.

tured by abstractions, yet the feeling that I was incapable of altering details I had no apparent obligation to keep makes me aware that my credo must include some obeisance to the sort of thing Ulrich is talking about.

6.

A more complicated aspect of the interfusion of art and life has to do with the way art enters our awareness of what we feel and are. The familiar—if statistically questionable—literary examples of it are the suicides of young men following the publication of Goethe's *Werther* and of young married women following that of Flaubert's *Madame Bovary*. "It's like it was happening in a movie" is a common remark made by those for whom what's happening to or around them is unusual, but much usual experience is recognized and felt because those who experience it have first read about it. Don Quixote became himself by reading stories about knights and Emma Bovary herself by reading love stories. An oddity here is that at least most Western art works toward uniqueness and Western—what we call true—science works toward the elimination of uniqueness. What I'm suggesting, however, is that art makes our thoughts and feelings as much like that of others as DNA makes our bodies. Which doesn't mean that our deepest sense isn't that of being our unique selves.

7.

I want to say a few things about the taste and temperament which form whatever small uniqueness as a writer I have. "Taste" and "temperament" are words which cover complex phenomena. Much of what composes them—nature, nurture—may be difficult or impossible to trace and analyze; some of what may be, probably should be revealed only to intimates and therapists. I will try here to get at some of them indirectly.

First, a few days before first writing this, I attended a Court Theater performance of the Philip Glass-Rudolph Wurlitzer-JoAnne Akalaitis opera based on Kafka's story "In the Penal Colony," and found that, unlike some of my friends, I disliked it. The opera included what for me was a frantic and unreal Kafka character. Along with several synchronized, balletic movements, this made for the sort of exaggerated, overstylized staging that goes against my grain. One would think, then, that I would enjoy the rigor of Glass's music, but no, my taste, formed by the musical generosity of the great German and Italian composers, rejected it as miserliness.

Second, I was aware that in two weeks, there were to be a few performances of the only opera on which I'd collaborated. I'd been present at one rehearsal of its first performances a few years ago and tried to persuade the director and actors to perform it in a more down-to-earth, less farcical and exaggerated—that is, operatic—manner. Two years earlier, in Florence, I'd worked on the libretto with the brilliant composer John Eaton, and believe that I'd succeeded in persuading him that this first of his fourteen operas based on more or less contemporary material should be grounded in the realistic portrayal of post–World War II New York, the world of the novel *Golk,* which was the groundwork of the libretto. Now some of that portrayal was highly charged, almost fantastic; a semi-comic, though not satiric or unrealistic, view of television and postwar New York. When, for the libretto, I incorporated elements of a differently charged 1990s United States (instead of the novel's almost insanely snobbish senator being exposed on camera, a priapic, wheeler-dealer southern president was), I believed that it didn't stray that far from actuality.

My distaste for dramatic hyperbole does not, in my view, clash with a predilection for the absurd, the grotesque, the psychopathologies of everyday life.

Third, earlier that week, I'd had lunch with a friend whom I told about the personal difficulty which I've mentioned and recited the harsh opening sentence of the novel I was writing about it. That sentence—livid with hatred—revealed a part of me which I didn't much like to face and which was new to him. He reacted to it in a way which pleased the writer part of me but which confirmed the ugliness of what I neither exhibited to others nor much examined myself. I knew, though, that it was part of what fed some of the strongest sections of my work, and I trusted and trust it as I trust my dreams. The need to write and then publish such truths was at the heart of the painful separation they described. The irony is an unwelcome but familiar part of my life.

Fourth, the novel itself has much to do with Germany, my life there between 1950 and 1952, my several returns there, including one in 1999, when I saw a German woman about whom I'd written but whom I hadn't seen in almost half a century, my own German-Jewish ancestry, and my one attempt in Freiburg to find out about my great-grandparents. Viewing newsreel footage of postwar Germany had fused with two books which affected me a good deal, Victor Klemperer's 1933–45 diaries, published under the title *I Will Bear Witness to the End*, and John Felstiner's book on the poetry of Paul Celan. Then too, there was a visit to Felstiner's house during which he played a record of Celan reciting his poem "Todesfuge," as powerful a reading as I've ever heard. Finally—for this easily extendable list must end somewhere—I was absorbed by something Charles Rosen had written about Johann Sebastian Bach, especially this somewhat unwieldy sentence: "His separation from the world of public music outside his own small city turned Bach's concerns into a sphere at once more deeply personal and apparently more abstract."*

The Klemperer diary and Rosen's description of Bach's situation reinforce what I am trying to spell out as an artistic creed: Klemperer had saved his sanity and enlarged his mental and human power by scrupulously recording and commenting on his ever more excruciating life as a Jew in Nazi-dominated Dresden. Its account of the contradictory, ironic, almost insane but actual happenings made it for me a more believable and moving description than any of the thousand documentary and fictional works I'd read and seen about those astonishing German years. And it confirmed my regard for the work of sticking close to the actual.

As for Bach, I know that it's outrageously presumptuous to think of one's own situation or work in the same universe as that of the peerless musical genius, but it's long been a habit of mine to seek enlightenment and guidance from just such figures. "His separation from the world of public music outside his own small city turned Bach's concerns into a sphere at once more deeply personal and apparently more abstract." I've been praising the accurate registration of the world one feels around one, yet here I'm extolling Bach's separation from it. There is no contradiction for me. Reporting is not immersion. One lives in the world, but one's imaginative work requires the same sort of separation from it that Rosen claims was Bach's. If the world is felt intensely and described powerfully enough, it will be both uniquely personal and easily recognizable. Or, as Scott Fitzgerald famously put a similar relationship, "Begin with an individual and you end with a type. Begin with a type and you end with nothing."

* I don't think that this notion contradicts the evidence (offered and well analyzed in Christoph Wolff's recent book on Bach) that more than that of any other musician in Germany, Bach's intellectual curiosity led him to correspondence with advanced thinkers in many scientific and other intellectual fields.

8.

Too young to fight in World War II, I nonetheless experienced some of the excitement and tensions of a total war. In 1949, I went to live in a Europe where there were still bombed-out streets, shortages, resentments, and repellent opinions. Allied soldiers were everywhere; Germany was administered by the four occupying powers. The Cold War was in its ugly infancy. In 1950, I stood in a Berlin crowd when General Lucius Clay, standing beside Mayor Ernst Reuter, saluted the city's "defiance" of Soviet attempts to blockade it. In the four-year-old ruins of Berlin, I watched ragged old ladies in worn-out slippers filling little carts with rubble; hours later, in an East German concert hall, I heard a young Fischer-Dieskau, an aging Tiana Lemnitz, and a tottering Karl Boehm sing and play Mozart and Schubert. I watched a German audience able to laugh at the farce in Chaplin's *City Lights* but turn cold when it reached its transcendently moving conclusion. I worked two years in Frankfurt am Main teaching literally illiterate American soldiers fresh out of West Virginia coal mines and dried-up farms. I made German friends who, years earlier, might well have been at least indifferent to my disappearance or annihilation.

I believe that this limited but powerful experience inclined a nature perhaps naively open to become more watchful, more alert to the complexity of individuals and groups. It certainly reinforced my sense that actuality—however that was conceived and felt—was inexhaustibly, perhaps even mysteriously rich, and that if one departed from it, the departure had to be justified or it signaled a surrender to exhaustion, an abdication from the essential job.

As for my prose style, it had for as long as I can tell (from a few letters and papers written in my teens and even earlier) been a spare one, though not without a lyric streak or two. (This may not be much in evidence here.) The understatements of *Dubliners* and such Hemingway stories as "My Old Man" and "Hills Like White Elephants" gratified me and perhaps enriched it. Yet, for some years now, I've been convinced that the chief influence on it was my mother's almost pathological hatred of dirt and disorder.

My favorite author wrote very differently. This was Proust. The Proust I loved was a tragi-comedian of the real who demonstrated that every passion—love, jealousy, ambition—forms its own story and that the only passion which didn't disintegrate was that of the artist.

Later, Joyce would show me that style wasn't intrinsic to an author but the central way of defining his story matter. Tell the *Iliad* in the vocabulary, syntax, and rhythm of a sentimental novel, you get a totally different "epic." So the heroic proclamations at the end of *Portrait of the Artist as a Young Man* are undercut by the vocabulary and rhythms of—among others—Walter Pater. *Ulysses,* a parade of styles, is close to what Beckett said it was, a book about itself.

As I say, this Joycean sophistication came late and influenced only a few of my stories and books (*Shares* and *Pacific Tremors*). The other tutor of genius in my pantheon was the Tolstoy of the two great novels. Their largeness opened up the formal narrowness of the Jamesian story and novel which, passed on pedagogically by his amazing prefaces and by the books of his disciples, Percy Lubbock, Allen Tate, Cleanth Brooks, and Robert Penn Warren, dominated the writing classes at Iowa and the leading literary quarterlies of my apprentice years. The great novels, which James famously called "loose, baggy monsters," exhibited the power of long, interrelated stories enriched everywhere by psychological genius and magnificent reportorial power (even when the reportage was grounded as much in research as in observation). Nor did Tolstoy hesitate to attribute his own insights and feelings to any and every character, making only minor adjustments for age, class, gender and even—remembering his wonderful dogs and horses—species.

There have been countless other influences, human and literary, worldly and artistic. Recounting them would be the job of the autobiography I will not write. I've here tried to make a fairly straight, very limited statement about work which for more than fifty years has served me as amusement, purgation, self-taught seminar and, if I may risk the sort of word I dislike, transfiguration.

# Monologue

My parents had a big dictionary. Perhaps because they'd spent so much money on it, they felt it should be used. So I got in the habit of looking up words.

I would look up the word, then encounter it three or four times in the next days. I can remember looking the same word up so often that I began to doubt my ability to remember anything at all.

My father invented stories for us. My first memory is of sighting him through the slats of my crib as he told my sister and me stories.

He told us about a midget lady named Miss Demicapoulos, who had extraordinary adventures. He made up wonderful names, some of which I've used in my fiction. The stories were funny, tragic, enthralling.

He must have gotten a kick out of making them up, but he never wrote anything until he retired at seventy-eight, and I bought him a little notebook, suggesting that he write an autobiography. He did, and my sister and I had it printed. It's a brief, charming, heart-rending memoir about the family and his experiences as a dentist in New York.

At some point, one becomes this thing called a writer. It happened to me when I was twelve.

I had to write a story for class. Already I was reading a lot and had written sketches; my story was more or less pillaged from something I'd read. I had the gratification of laughter from the class and the approbation of the teacher. I'd never before had an audience of more than my father and mother.

As a boy, I went to summer camp and performed in plays. I was considered a pretty good actor. I enjoyed that, but it didn't bring the same sort of gratification writing did. The nicest thing about acting was the ensemble work. Part of that involves watching other people act.

Writing came from me, even when—as I've said—it was half-stolen. Then there's the pleasure of being by oneself, being able to think about anything, feeling that this is a justified part of life. Not being told, "You're daydreaming. Get with it."

Daydreaming is what you do.

Then of course you have to get it down. With luck, writing begets itself.

If I have a recognizable voice in fiction, it's a voice of parsimony, economy, omission—a certain obliquity and sharpness. I seldom get that in a first draft. The first draft is rather pompous, the syntax winding around as I'm trying to encompass the action.

I found a paper of mine that I'd written at seventeen at Chapel Hill. It was just two pages on Aristotle, and it was written in the same style I use now. I must have had a certain gift for concision. I've allied it to something I hated in my mother. After I'd read a Karen Horney book in 1947, I called it "anality." It was her obsession with cleanliness. I think that influenced my style.

What's easy for me—maybe it's connected to the old theatrical interest—is when I'm talking "for" other people. I can talk in different ways pretty easily. I enjoy it.

Then there's the question of breath. Isaac Babel said his sentences were short because he had asthma. Of course, Proust had asthma, too. Still, I think there's some relation between a person's physical being and his work.

I haven't analyzed it, but I know that after a certain time, I get tired, yet I know I'd be better off if I developed scenes more, let the characters bang each other around more than I do. I tend to edit sharply, narrowly, to keep the key signatures.

In the past ten years, my working method as a writer has been that of dictating to an assistant. His—or her—reaction is important. Does he laugh? Does he seem to tune out? The attentiveness is important. It means one person cares. At times, I've felt that nobody cared; sometimes I didn't care myself.

Writing doesn't get easier.

This year, I came out of a writing slump. I had been ready to throw in the towel. (I had begun to feel that way as well about some of my fellow writers. I thought they too should throw in the towel.) But I recovered from a hernia operation, went back to teaching, and started up again.

On the whole, the university has been a good place to be. I came here in 1955 after a year teaching at a small college for women in New London, Connecticut.

I had read about Chicago in a *Life* magazine article which called it "the greatest university that's ever been." (Henry Luce was a sort of PR man for Hutchins.) When I came here, I was impressed by it, and impressed with myself for being part of it. I was writing a novel, *Europe*, and stories at the time; I was writing a lot.

Norman Maclean was very helpful to me. He saw that I had mornings free to write; I taught in the afternoons.

Maclean was fascinating both for the power and the self-cancellation of power in him—for his authenticity and for his romantic elaboration of it. The clash between his complex feelings and his romantic, Hemingway-and-Western image puzzled him—baffled him.

Introspection worried him. He did not analyze his character, did not work out the clash between his nature and his romantic view of what a man should be. The sensitive "tough guy" is a tough role. There was much more to him than that. He believed in discipline but didn't know how to discipline or use his own feelings. His wonderful wife, Jessie, tightened that emotional knot; she was a purer "Westerner" than he.

An amazing thing happened after he was free of the theatrical tension of teaching. He'd been a part of a critical circle, the Chicago School, headed by R. S. Crane and Richard McKeon, the philosopher. What distinguished them was critical ferocity. I think Norman took a beating there. When he was free of that, too, he wrote down some family stories he had told for years, *A River Runs Through It*.

The great thing about the university is the remarkable people here in all fields. I've been lucky to know several hundred marvelous men and women who've been on the faculty. I've spent a lot of time listening to them, having all sorts of things explained.

The danger of teaching is that knowing things students don't yet know evokes their gratitude and amazement. You can get drunk on that. As a writer, you have to address an audience that can't be so easily amazed and delighted. You're not in a cozy apartment, but on the frontier.

It's been important for me to get out of the university from time to time. I wanted to get around the world, be at home everywhere. I've managed to see quite a bit. Maybe too much. I've loved the charged anonymity of travel.

One way in which I came to know Chicago involved a controversy surrounding the *Chicago Review* in about 1958 or 1959. I had been made chairman of its faculty committee.

The *Review* had an editor who was a friend of the San Francisco writers, Ginsberg, Burroughs, et al. He started publishing them, quite a coup. *Naked Lunch* appeared in it. Meanwhile, some of the kids on the magazine were telling me that other manuscripts were coming in and weren't being considered for publication, just rejected out of hand.

Such complaints were made before an obscenity controversy erupted. A columnist named Jack Mabley published a piece in the *Chicago Daily News* which said that the *Review* was publishing obscene material. (He, and the paper, were on an obscenity kick.) That in itself didn't create much of a stir, but as I was to learn from the university's president, Lawrence Kimpton, Mayor Daley was being pressured by certain prominent Catholics in the city about the matter.

Daley told Kimpton—he told me—"I've been trying to get the City Council to pass such and such an ordinance to save the university in Hyde Park." Hyde Park was in decay. If it continued, the university was endangered. Daley believed the university was essential to a great Chicago.

The ordinances had to do with squeezing the criminal and slum landlord element out. Cardinal Stritch had recently died, and there was a power fight in the church. Many of the people who were squeezed out of Hyde Park moved Back of the Yards. The priest there used the *Review*'s supposed obscenity to attack the university in his diocesan paper. Daley told Kimpton that the church was putting pressure on Catholic council members, whose votes he needed. Kimpton's initial reaction was, suppress the *Review;* cancel it. We committee members met with him in his office, and when he told us this, we said, "Are you kidding? Censor the *Chicago Review?* You'd degrade the university. You can't do it." Kimpton saw it immediately and drew back.

Meanwhile, a couple of the *Review* editors saw an opportunity in the situation. They wrote about it to John Ciardi at the *Saturday Review,* who wrote a column, most of it wrong. It became a great debate, some of which is recorded in many issues of the *Chicago Maroon.* My position was that everything accepted by the editors had to be printed by the *Review.* Instead, the editors took the pieces to start another magazine, *Big Table.* They staged a benefit to raise money for it. (I appeared at the benefit and read a story which *Big Table* printed.)

There are still people who think the *Chicago Review* was "suppressed." It's a myth, but a useful one to remind people that literature can easily become the casualty of other interests.

I learned a lot from the whole experience. It was amazing to me that a power fight in the church could reach the city council, and that in turn could affect the university. I also learned a bit about publicity and the distortions of claims along such sensational lines as "literary martyrdom." By chance, I was reading then a book called *The Montesi Affair* by Wayland Young. It was about what happened in Italy after someone misheard a conversation in a restaurant about the drowning of a girl named Montesi. The misunderstanding became a rumor which nearly overthrew the Italian government. The *Chicago Review* was my Montesi affair.

I had just started work on my Ph.D. at Iowa in 1952 when John Crowe Ransom wrote that he'd accepted a story of mine for the *Kenyon Review*. That wonderful moment when you're suddenly part of the makers of literature. I suppose the pleasure is connected to the pleasure I've had meeting Thomas Mann, Ezra Pound, and Samuel Beckett, the feeling that you're connected to those who've formed your mind and helped make your life comprehensible, moving, lighter, deeper.

I differentiate this acquaintance from friendships with such friends as Bellow and Roth. Their work has meant even more to me, but they are part of what Roth called "my life as a man." Actually Beckett, too, I regarded as a friend (though I saw him only eight or nine times). I spoke personally to him and I think he did to me. Yet when he spoke about Joyce, I felt the mental marble dissolve. When he praised Bellow's work and something of mine, I felt the literary earth shake, as if Sophocles or Chaucer had acknowledged me and my friends.

I try to tell my students, particularly my writing students, that they can be part of this linkage, that, in a way, through this minor connection in front of them, they're already part of it. It's important at the University of Chicago, where the Great Works loom monumentally, to free students from the paralysis of intimidation by them. I don't hesitate to compare the best student work with the work of masters. This is not meant to cheapen the marvelous, but to evoke it. The hope is to make students fall in love with sublimity and to show them it's not out of reach.

There's a lot of brilliance, even genius, around, but between flashes of genius and careers of accomplishment are pitfalls of life and character. To be an artist you need luck and tenacity, terrific tenacity. Maybe the obstacles to art exist to warn off those who can't bear the pain of creative exhaustion, misunderstanding, devaluation or devastatingly accurate evaluation, self-exposure, critical wounds, many other things. It's a long trip from the stories coming through the slats of a crib to those you have to get down on paper sixty-odd years later.

# Acknowledgments

Parts of this book were previously published, usually in quite different form, in *Callalloo, Los Angeles Times, Nation, New Republic, Poetry* ("To Go with an Old Necklace"), *Southwest Review,* and *TriQuarterly.* Some pieces appeared in books: *Certain Solitudes,* edited by Dana Goia and William Logan (Fayetteville: University of Arkansas Press, 1998); *A Community of Writers,* edited by Robert Dana (Iowa City: University of Iowa Press, 1999); *Great Chicago Stories,* edited by Tom Maday and Sam Landers (Chicago: Twopress, 1996); *The Struggle to Adore,* reprinted by permission of the author, Alane Rollings (Ashland, Ore.: Story Line Press, 1994); *There Is No End of Things in the Heart: A Celebration of Hugh Kenner in Honor of His 70th Birthday,* edited by Carroll Terrell (Orono, Me.: Northern Lights, 1993); *An Unsentimental Education,* edited by Molly McQuade (Chicago: University of Chicago Press, 1995); *Words to Live By,* edited by Karen and Lawrence Katz (Aurora, Ore.: Two Rivers Press); and my own book *One Person and Another* (Dallas: Baskerville, 1993).

For permission to reprint pieces that appeared in earlier forms in the following periodicals, I thank the editors or publishers: *Antioch Review* (vol. 53, no. 1, "Ralph Ellison"; vol. 53, no. 4, "Studs: WFMT, April 7, 1995"; vol. 58, no. 4, "With Auden"); *Chicago Tribune Book Week* (twenty-five pieces published at various times); *Literary Imagination: The Review of the Association of Literary Scholars and Critics* (vol. 3, no. 3, "My Ex, the Moral Philosopher"); *New Leader* (October 9–23, 1995, "Warriors of the Open, 1996"; *Republic of Letters* and *New York Times* ("Where the Chips Fall"); *Sewanee Review* (Winter 1998, "Remembering Pound").

I want here to acknowledge the brilliant editor of this book, David Brent, and want the acknowledgment to embrace the members of the remarkable Brent family, whose place in Chicago literature is worth contemplation and study. First is the family patriarch, Stuart, who ran the wonderful bookstore (last on Michigan Avenue) about which he has written so well in *The Seven Stairs*. Then there are the two wonderful editor sons, David, of the University of Chicago Press, and Jonathan, who has brought distinction these past ten years to the Yale University Press after doing the same for the Northwestern University Press. Adam Brent continues his father's work in his own Chicago bookstore, and their sister Amy runs a children's book club run through that store. What a civic blessing this family has been.

CPSIA information can be obtained
at www.ICGtesting.com
Printed in the USA
LVHW052353130219
607514LV00009B/169/P